LOUIS RIEL

LOUIS RIEL

LET JUSTICE BE DONE

DAVID DOYLE

RONSDALE PRESS

RONSDALE PRESS
3350 West 21st Avenue
Vancouver, B.C. Canada V6S 1G7
www.ronsdalepress.com

Typesetting: Julie Cochrane, in Granjon 11.5 pt on 15
Cover Design: Julie Cochrane
Cover Photo: Louis Riel, ca. 1879. Courtesy Glenbow Archives: NA-504-3.
Paper: 60 lb. Envirographic (FSC), 100% post-consumer waste, totally chlorine-free
  and acid-free.

Ronsdale Press wishes to thank the following for their support of its publishing program: the Canada Council for the Arts, the Government of Canada through the Canada Book Fund, the British Columbia Arts Council, and the Province of British Columbia through the British Columbia Book Publishing Tax Credit program.

Library and Archives Canada Cataloguing in Publication

Doyle, David G., 1947–, author
  Louis Riel: let justice be done / David Doyle.

Issued in print and electronic formats.
ISBN 978-1-55380-496-3 (softcover)
ISBN 978-1-55380-497-0 (ebook) / ISBN 978-1-55380-498-7 (pdf)

  1. Riel, Louis, 1844–1885 — Trials, litigation, etc. 2. Trials (Treason) — Canada, Western — History — 19th century. 3. Native peoples — Canada — Government relations. 4. Canada — Politics and government — 1878–1896. I. Title.

FC3215.D69 2017   971.05'4   C2016-907443-9   C2016-907444-7

At Ronsdale Press we are committed to protecting the environment. To this end we are working with Canopy and printers to phase out our use of paper produced from ancient forests. This book is one step towards that goal.

Printed in Canada by Island Blue, Victoria, B.C.

To the Friends of
Louis Riel Society

ACKNOWLEDGEMENTS

I am indebted to Paddy Doyle, the first of the Doyles on the Saskatchewan (1882). A homesteader-turned-guard at the time of Louis Riel's execution, Paddy and his stories have burned into family legend. Likewise, I thank Joseph Kinsey Howard, whose book *Strange Empire: Louis Riel and the Métis People* directed my generation of prairie youth to follow our prophet of the New World: Louis Riel. I also thank my late Saskatchewan high-school buddies and comrades, Donald Graham "the keeper of the light," Brian Rands and Eric Lee. Together, we young settlers, who were seeking justice for Louis Riel, marched, danced and sang, and distributed Riel's formerly lost 100-year-old Revolutionary Bill of Rights of the Saskatchewan, 1885, at the centenary of the North-West Resistance and beyond. Thanks also to Canadian historian Peter Newman for leading me to the "Crown Letters" and the misdemeanours of the Canadian government of John A. Macdonald in the trial and execution of Louis Riel.

I am also deeply indebted to the late oral historian of the Sweet Grass Cree, Alphonse Little Poplar, and his wife Irene Fine Day, for sharing their lives and their stories with a *môniya:s*, and the late James McCrorie, director of the Canadian Plains Research Institute, who honoured Alphonse and me with research fellowships. I would also like to acknowledge the late Tom Taylor and the Boundary Métis Community Association of the Métis Nation of British Columbia for honouring me with "honourary Métis" status, as well as the BC Métis Federation for their honouring and recognition of my work. I thank the Powell River Métis Society as well for their warmth and kindnesses extended to me, and for their presentation of my Métis sash. I express my deep gratitude to Métis historians and friends George and Terry Goulet. I am also proud to recognize the Friends of Louis Riel Society who remain committed to Riel's recognition as Canada's Indigenous Father of Confederation.

I would also like to thank Ann Irving whose early edits and advice guided my research. Also, essential to this work has been the guidance and direction I have received from Ron Hatch, editor and publisher of Ronsdale Press. Through Ron's guidance, I learned what it means to be a writer. Finally, I recognize my wife Maureen Mason and my daughter Freya (Doyle) Aikenhead, whose work and love remain my true inspiration.

INTRODUCTION

1

PART I

Regina v. Riel: The Trial

5

PART II

The Red River Uprising

43

PART III

Amnesty, Exile & Revelation

113

PART IV

The North-West Resistance:
Saskatchewan

143

Report of the Commissioner into
the Career of Louis Riel

199

Introduction

Fiat Justitia, Ruat Caelum
Let justice be done, though
the heavens may fall

In Canada's greatest and most controversial state trial, the Canadian Métis leader, Louis Riel, was convicted of the crime of high treason. Sentenced to hang, Riel prayerfully awaited his fate in the guardhouse at the North-West Mounted Police (NWMP) barracks in Regina, the little prairie capital of the then North-West Territories (Saskatchewan became a Canadian province in 1905). It was a time of great personal anguish and sorrow. Death circled Louis Riel, his family and his people. The failed resistance had left Riel's Métis nation defeated on the battlefield and reduced to unwanted exiles in their own land. Riel himself had not seen his wife Marguerite since handing himself over to General Middleton six months earlier. A month previous, Marguerite had given birth to a child who died in less than three hours. Marguerite, her happy prairie people devastated, her husband in jail, her baby dead, was beyond despondent. She would survive only a few short months after Riel's execution. The Riel children, Jean-Louis and Marie Angelique

Riel, were left orphans, lovingly cared for by the extended Riel family in St. Boniface.

While waiting for a final decision regarding his fate, Riel worked to clear up his affairs, both personal and social. He spent his time composing letters and appeals, seeking a solution for himself and his people. He sought personal salvation and social justice, even while keeping his dear mother, his sweet Marguerite, his precious son and daughter, and his little angel ever on his mind.

Riel's anguish is exemplified by the following "Dernière Mémoire," or "Riel's Song" as translated by Barbara Cass-Beggs, Saskatchewan's archivist of songs. Cass-Beggs collected this song from Joseph Gaspard Jeannotte, an old Métis living at Lebret in the Qu'Appelle Valley. Jeannotte said Riel had composed it while in jail. It appeared first in Cass-Begg's *Eight Songs of Saskatchewan* (Toronto, 1963).

> I send this letter to you,
> To tell my grief and pain,
> And as I lie imprisoned
> I long to see again
> You, my beloved mother,
> And all my comrades dear.
> I write these words in my heart's blood,
> No ink or pen is here.
> My friends in arms and children,
> Please weep and pray for me.
> I fought to keep our country
> So that we might be free.
> When you receive this letter
> Please weep for me and pray
> That I may die with bravery
> Upon that fearful day.

Charged with the heinous crime of high treason, tried in a colonial courtroom in the new capital of the North-West Territories, Regina "the Queen City," and effectively gagged by the magistrate and his own lawyers, Louis Riel had been unable to defend himself or his Métis people. Judicially bound, Riel was not allowed to give his testimony, cross-examine witnesses or ask or answer those questions so critical to his career and his good name. Most importantly he was not allowed to answer the charge of high treason. It was not until the last witness had been called and the trial concluded that Louis Riel was finally allowed to speak.

At this time, speaking in English, Louis Riel addressed the court. In a long and impassioned speech, he apologized for his lack of facility in the language and went on to speak of the plight, not only of himself but of his Métis people, the Indians and settlers. Frustrated with his inability to defend himself at his trial, Riel called out to Canada for justice. He requested a special tribunal or commission of inquiry be held by the proper authorities to review the various charges, slanders and lies that dogged him throughout his career. This tribunal would investigate whether he rebelled against legal authority in Manitoba in 1869–70; whether he murdered the Canadian Thomas Scott; whether he solicited bribes or pillaged the Hudson's Bay Company's Fort Garry; and whether he was a fugitive from justice when he was expelled from his seat in the Canadian Parliament in 1874. Finally, the tribunal would investigate whether Louis Riel was guilty of the crime of high treason in Saskatchewan.

There would, however, be no official inquiry into the career of Louis Riel. It was not to be. After Riel's conviction on August 1, 1885, his lawyers launched an appeal to the Court of Queen's Bench of Manitoba, the appellate court for the North-West Territories. Under the North-West Territories Act, amended in 1880, a person convicted of an offence punishable by death in the North-West Territories had a right of appeal. That court could confirm a conviction or it could order a new trial, but it had no jurisdiction to reverse a conviction. Chief Judge Wallbridge presided over the appellate court and heard Riel's lawyers argue for an appeal. Refusing Riel the right to present his appeal, Wallbridge determined that the acts attributed to Riel amounted to high treason. A final appeal to the Privy Council of England was bungled and again disallowed.

Prime Minister Macdonald then had a medical commission appointed to assess Riel's "present medical condition." Doctoring the commission's reports, ignoring the call for mercy coming from the jury, Macdonald ensured that Riel was declared sane, and the entire Canadian Cabinet concurred. The Macdonald government then worked to ensure the Imperial authorities did not intervene in support of commutation. In a letter to the governor general, Macdonald emphasized that this North-West outbreak was but "a mere domestic trouble."

On the morning of November 16, 1885, all appeals having failed, Louis Riel was taken to the North-West Mounted Police gallows where he was executed — hanged by the neck until dead.

For over 130 years the trial and execution of Louis Riel have been at the centre of controversy. Indeed, his execution has been the subject of Canada's "Great Debate." Prevented from having a fair trial, Louis Riel was never given an opportunity to defend himself. Now, considering the Canadian government's failure during its sesquicentennial to recognize Riel as Canada's Indigenous (Métis) Father of Confederation, and that we are approaching the 150th anniversary of Riel's ushering Manitoba into the Canadian Confederation, is it not well past time to hear Louis Riel's evidence? Was Louis Riel a patriot or traitor? Reconciliation calls out for an answer.

What follows is a work of creative nonfiction: an imaginative Inquiry into the career of Louis Riel that collapses historical time and provides Louis Riel a present-day opportunity to give the testimony he was denied at his trial. Using Riel's voice, this re-creation is based on evidence from the transcripts of Riel's trial as well as recent historical research into his career, all woven together to offer Riel the chance to have the Inquiry he was never allowed.

PART I

Regina v. Riel:
The Trial

COMMISSIONER: I now call to order this Inquiry into the career of Louis Riel. Mr. Riel, at your request this Inquiry will undertake an examination of your career. Please proceed to your opening statement.

RIEL: First, let me thank this Inquiry for your commitment to justice and fair play. It has long been my wish to have an opportunity to defend my career, as well as my person. Prior to testimony, I wish to speak to the support I have received, in particular from my adjutant general in Manitoba, Ambroise-Dydime Lépine, and our Métis "prince of the prairies," Gabriel Dumont. Never have I known such men of courage, wisdom and faith. I also acknowledge William Henry Jackson, our honorary Métis brother who was given the name Honoré Jaxon and who has stayed true to our cause.

Although I have been slandered as a "traitor to Canada," I have also been nobly defended over the years since my trial. I salute my Métis legal team, headed by Métis lawyer George R.D. Goulet, a twelfth-generation Canadian and direct descendant of Louis Hébert, Canada's first permanent colonial settler. Mr. Goulet has been ably supported by his wife Terry Goulet who collaborated in writing *The Trial of Louis Riel: Justice and Mercy Denied: A Critical, Legal and Political Analysis* (1999) as well as other books about the Métis. I also recognize Ronald J. Olesky, a Winnipeg lawyer, whose article "Louis Riel and the Crown Letters" in the publication *Canadian Lawyer* (February 1998) was brought to our attention by the distinguished Canadian historian Peter Newman. Olesky's research was critical in exposing the illegal and reprehensible activities of Canada's prime minister, his justice minister and other court officials in charge of my trial. James Lockyer, lawyer and a prominent social justice activist in Canada, the founding director of the Association in Defence of the Wrongfully Convicted, also offered his support, which is greatly appreciated. I would have this Inquiry note that what is in question here is not a "pardon," since a pardon presumes guilt, and I am not guilty of any crime, and especially the crime of "high treason." My goal is a complete exoneration and recognition of my work as a Canadian Father of Confederation.

I also wish to recognize that Canada is full of honourable citizens, Indigenous and settler, who have provided me with comfort and support. Amongst these I recognize the Honourable Prime Minister Wilfrid Laurier, former Governor General Adrienne Clarkson, former Prime Minister Joe Clark, and all of those Members of Parliament who have attempted to have my conviction of high treason revoked.

I have so many more people to thank, especially those who have maintained our Métis culture and ideals, those who remember and celebrate our Métis family and our way of life. Then there are those individuals who believe justice must be done. These include those elders, teachers and professors who have included "Louis Riel and the Métis" in our school and university curriculums. Although I do not always agree with their assessments, I must also recognize the writers who have chronicled my life and career. In this group I include A.C. Morice, William McCartney Davidson, George F.G. Stanley, Joseph Kinsey Howard, E.B. Osler, Mavor Moore, Jennifer Reid, Maggie Siggins, Chester Brown, Joseph Boyden, Bob Beal, Charles Hou, Rudy Wiebe and the authors of the many essays about the Métis and our world. Notably, I have not included those who for political or racial reasons have purposely slandered me and my career. Then there are the artists, cultural workers, poets and songsters whose drawings, music, poems, paintings and dance continue to tell our story. I thank them all and remind Canadians that together we can create a New World where all our children deserve the opportunity to live a bountiful life of meaning and love in this land we love, Canada.

COMMISSIONER: Mr. Riel, in light of the severity of the sentence passed upon you, and the subsequent accusations of improprieties and inappropriate behaviour during your trial, this Inquiry will start with your experiences after your defeat at Batoche in 1885. In the next phase of the hearing, we will move backward in time to examine the events in the Red River in 1869–70. Please begin your testimony.

RIEL: I thank the commissioner for your indulgence. I now respectfully submit my evidence to this Inquiry. As is now well known, on August 1, 1885, in Regina, North-West Territories, I was convicted of the crime of high treason. I was charged with six counts, the first three of which relate separately to my activities in the battles at Duck Lake, March 26, 1885, at Tourond's Coulee (Fish Creek) April 24, 1885, and at Batoche on the South Saskatchewan River, May 9–12, 1885. The other three treason charges, although of a similar nature, refer to my breaking of the allegiance owed by myself to the Sovereign of these lands, Her Majesty, Queen Victoria. Found guilty of high treason by a jury of six Anglo-Canadian "peers," I was sentenced to hang.

In regard to my so-called crimes of high treason, I wish this Inquiry to know first that I, Louis Riel, voluntarily surrendered to Major General Frederick Middleton on May 15, 1885, three days after our defeat by Canadian forces at the Battle of Batoche. It was my intention to explain and defend the actions of the Métis. It should be noted that I could easily have escaped to the United States with Métis Adjutant General Gabriel Dumont, Michel Dumas and others, but I could not leave my poor people scattered and starving, hiding along the banks of the South Saskatchewan River. As a citizen of the United States since 1883, moreover, had I escaped I would have been a free man as soon as I crossed the border. Upon giving themselves over to American authorities, Gabriel Dumont and company were briefly arrested, and then released on the order of President Chester A. Arthur.

For those who do not know, Adjutant General Gabriel Dumont led our Métis army in battle against the Canadians. A famous warrior of the northern plains, Gabriel fought his first battle at the age of fourteen at the Battle of the Grand Coteau along the Missouri River in today's North Dakota. This Métis victory was the last battle before peace was established between the Métis and the mighty Sioux nations. Settling down on the east bank of the South Saskatchewan River, Gabriel became a ferryman and ran a little store along the Carlton Trail south of the growing Métis community of Batoche. Here he became the civic leader of the ever-growing Métis population. Seeking land rights, schools, civic support and recognition of his people, he led the community petitioning for rights for nearly twenty years, until 1885, when he once again took up his role as military commander of our Métis forces.

At the final Battle of Batoche, Gabriel's strategic land defences were able to hold back Middleton's men successfully for three and a half days. His camouflaged and interconnected rifle pits were invisible to the attackers. In the end, on the fourth day, Middleton's men disobeyed orders and charged our rifle pits, killing many of our valiant defenders and overrunning the community. We were defeated.

Held in British Major General Middleton's compound, I had my initial interrogations with the general. My message to him was consistent: I am ready to face all charges against myself and all others who fought for our way of life, our lands and our customs. Through our discussions, I learned the general was a seasoned British colonial officer with a great deal of experience putting down local uprisings. Impressed by our defences, he had not seen such effective use of the natural topography in his service for Her Majesty in Australia, New Zealand, India, Burma, Gibraltar or Malta. I learned too that he had distinguished himself as a staff officer during the 1857–1858 Indian Mutiny and had twice been recommended for the Victoria Cross, although it was never awarded.

A little aside, if I may? For his service in our North-West war, Middleton was knighted by Queen Victoria. He also received the thanks of the Canadian Parliament and the sum of $20,000. Unfortunately for the general, in 1890, a select committee of the House of Commons dealing with claims arising from our war chastised him for the "unwarrantable and illegal" misappropriation of furs from a Métis non-combatant, Charles Bremner. Censured by the Canadian government, Middleton resigned as head of the Canadian militia and returned to England.

Returning now to my experience as a captive: when orders came that I was to be transported to Winnipeg for trial, I was placed in the custody of Brigade Major (Captain) George Young and taken on board the SS *Northcote*. On the way south, the *Northcote*, with scattered bullet holes all along her reinforced gunnels, limped along, with Captain Young concerned we would be attacked around every turn in the river. On our third day on the river, we arrived at a steamboat landing outside Swift Current station where I was transferred to a special Canadian Pacific Railway (CPR) train to take me to Winnipeg. En route, Captain Young received an urgent telegram from General Middleton. To my great surprise, on the orders of the minister of militia, I was no longer to be taken to Winnipeg but to the new capital of the North-West Territories, Regina. Here, I was placed in the custody of Inspector Deane of the North-West Mounted Police.

Incarcerated in a tiny cell, a 20-pound ball-and-chain fastened to my leg during my one hour of exercise per day, I was initially held in complete isolation, not permitted newspapers or anything beyond my scriptures. I was also initially disallowed pen, ink or writing paper, with my guards warned against fraternizing with the prisoner. For the first three weeks I suffered greatly, receiving no information about or from my family or regarding the situation of my poor people back at Batoche. It was a time of great anguish. I did not know if this new venue would be a temporary stop or if I was doomed to total isolation from the outside world. All I could do was pray.

When I sought answers to my isolation, Inspector Deane, a stickler for details, unfailingly refused to discuss issues beyond my immediate incarceration. I have since come to learn that my incarceration in Regina was but one component of an elaborate scheme on the part of my enemies, truly a Machiavellian plot directed by Canada's prime minister, my avowed enemy, Sir. John A. Macdonald.

COMMISSIONER: Mr. Riel, this Inquiry is tasked with inquiring into alleged political interference in your trial. Are you charging that there was malfeasance, wrongdoing, by elected officials, including the prime minister of Canada, and that these officials conspired to interfere in your trial?

RIEL: Yes, there was malfeasance and wrongdoing, carefully stage-managed by Prime Minister Macdonald, with his former law partner, Justice Minister Sir Alexander Campbell, in a supporting role. I have drawn

the conclusion that there was a cabal of Canadian politicians, legal officials and representatives of the Roman Catholic Church, all of whom
sought to influence my trial.

The first piece of evidence I wish to introduce relates to the reason for
my incarceration in Regina. As I will make clear, it is but a fragment of a
much larger collection of correspondence, some of which is still tucked
away in obscure fragments in the recesses of Ottawa. As mentioned earlier, while searching the Canadian Archives, Winnipeg lawyer Ronald
J. Olesky uncovered what has come to be known as the "Crown Letters." This correspondence, letters and telegrams, implicate Canada's
prime minister, justice minister and the chief justice of Manitoba in
criminally manipulating my trial, my sentence and my appeal.

From information gleaned from the work of Mr. Olesky, as well as
Métis lawyer George Goulet, we now know that Prime Minister Macdonald and Justice Minister Campbell initially assumed I would be tried
by the Court of Queen's Bench in Manitoba. Pondering what charge to
lay against me, Justice Minister Campbell reviewed the Canadian Stat-
utes passed by the first Macdonald government in 1868. He found that
the highest offence with which they could charge me was "treason
felony," a non-capital crime. This meant, if found guilty, my penalty
would be imprisonment, not execution. Or, I could get off altogether.
This option was unacceptable to Macdonald, who — I will declare
formally — was determined to see me hang. How it was to be done I
discovered later.

After three weeks in isolation, I finally received my first piece of good
news, or so I thought. Through the good graces of my former classmate
in Montreal, Romuald Fiset, a defence committee was established. Romuald Fiset, a Liberal Member of Parliament, was my companion back
in 1874, when I signed the parliamentary register and became an official
Member of Parliament. Knowing of my long association with Archbishop Alexandre-Antonin Taché, he naturally sought the archbishop's
assistance. The archbishop, however, would bring in "others" with
whom I was never acquainted and who in the end worked against me.

For those who do not know, Archbishop Taché has played a hugely
significant role in my life and career.

After the passing of my father, I took him for my "second father." He was responsible for my education, finding me a sponsor and sending me to a seminary, the Sulpician College in Montreal, supposedly to become the first Métis priest. Later, when I rejected this path to the priesthood to join the secular world, he never truly forgave me.

When I first learned who had been hired to defend me, I had high hopes. François-Xavier Lemieux Q.C., a thirty-five-year-old, up-and-coming lawyer and member of the Quebec legislature, was to be the lead counsel of my defence team. Lemieux was aided by James Greenshields Q.C. of Toronto and Charles Fitzpatrick Q.C. of Quebec City. For local advice, T.C. Johnstone, a Winnipeg lawyer, was recruited.

Allowed to write to my defence team, I informed them how pleased I was to have them working for me. Once again I stated unequivocally that I wanted my trial to turn on the merits of my actions. As would be customary henceforth, after I was finished writing, Inspector Deane reviewed my letter and collected the ink and paper. This was one of the cruelest punishments, as a poet without paper is like a bird without a song.

Fitzpatrick, Lemieux and Greenshields arrived in Regina on July 15, 1885. We held a meeting upon their arrival where I reiterated to these learned gentlemen my position: that I had given myself up willingly and that our defence should be based on the justice of our cause. I asked that they inquire about obtaining my papers seized by General Middleton and his staff after the fall of Batoche. These critical documents included my American naturalization papers and our petitions and letters. I asked for my witnesses, including Gabriel Dumont, William Jackson and others, to be given safe passage to testify at my trial. I also asked them to obtain clarification as to why my trial was now being held in Regina and not in Winnipeg as originally scheduled.

The meeting was seemingly cordial, with my attorneys apparently agreeing to my suggestions. Informing me that they would be appealing the jurisdiction of a magisterial court to try our case, I was encouraged, hopeful we would be able to expose the perfidy of John A. Macdonald's fifteen-year war against the Métis and myself. You cannot imagine how deeply hurt I was to discover later that upon leaving my cell, Fitzpatrick immediately telegraphed Archbishop Taché, letting him know they agreed "I was not of sound mind."

After this meeting, my defence team paid precious little attention to my wishes. As the trial proceeded, I found my suggestions more and more rejected, ignored, dismissed or misdirected. Without my approval, and in direct defiance of my authorization, they dispensed with any defence based on the merits of my actions. In court, they did not follow up on critical issues. Instead of attempting to subpoena my requested witnesses, or seek free passage for those witnesses in exile, or introduce my papers, they drew up their own list of "alienists" and priests to discredit me. I had a great deal of difficulty understanding their behaviour. Finally, it came out in court. I was not their client. They "had to go to the parties . . . who were really our clients in this case."

Who were these "parties?" What was the composition of this mysterious committee established in Quebec, not to defend me, but in fact to prove I was insane? It is a well-known fact that John A. Macdonald worked closely with Archbishop Taché, even calling him home from an ecumenical conference at the Vatican to deal with the first crisis in Manitoba some fifteen years earlier. To me, Fitzpatrick's telegram to Archbishop Taché after our first meeting leads to a most sinister interference by my bishop and forces within the Roman Catholic Church in the case.

Equally troubling, if not more so, my lead defence attorney, Charles Fitzpatrick, I was to later find, was also a junior partner in then Minister of Militia and Defence Adolphe Caron's Montreal law firm. It was this senior partner's directive that sent me to Regina, and not Winnipeg, in the first place. Fitzpatrick could have simply telegraphed his boss to find the answer to why my trial was relocated to Regina. He did not. I have since learned that my defence team followed up our conversations by meeting with "others" in Regina. Once again, who were these "others?" I still do not know. What I do know is that without informing me, before even meeting with me, my defence counsel embarked on a strategy which went completely contrary to my specific direction and wishes. They were not going to plead my case against the government. Their defence was to be "not guilty by reason of insanity" — of which I shall speak later.

Under the heavy guard of sixteen North-West Mounted Police, I was driven to the storefront-turned-courtroom in the heart of little Regina on July 20, 1885. My trial began at 11 a.m. before Stipendiary Magistrate Hugh Richardson of the Territorial Court of the North-West Territories. It came as a great surprise to find that this Magistrate Richardson was the former Lieutenant Colonel Richardson, an officer in the Canadian militia, who had previously served as chief clerk of the Department of Justice. A close friend of John A. Macdonald, Richardson was an appointed member of the Territorial Council and had served as legal adviser to Territorial Lieutenant-Governor Edgar Dewdney. Since 1877 he had served as a stipendiary magistrate in the territory, presiding part-time over a police court in Regina and Moose Jaw. Sitting beside Richardson was Justice of the Peace Henry Le Jeune, a Quebec barrister recently arrived from Ottawa. A jury of six, hand-picked by Richardson, also sat at the ready.

The counsels for the Crown were headed by two senior Ontario barristers, Christopher Robinson Q.C. and Britton Bath Osler Q.C. Both were long-time legal and personal associates of the prime minister. They were supported by Toronto lawyer Thomas Chase-Casgrain, with their local voice being Lieutenant Colonel Daniel Scott, the mayor of Regina. Coincidentally, Casgrain, like Fitzpatrick, was also a junior partner in Adolphe Caron's Montreal law firm. Right from the start they had me covered from both sides. I began to realize that I was in a helpless situation.

After opening proceedings in a stiflingly hot little courtroom, my attorneys launched a number of demurrers, appeals pleading for dismissal. It seemed to me that the first of these was particularly important. My lead counsel, Mr. Fitzpatrick, contended that a stipendiary magistrate, such as Mr. Richardson, did not have jurisdiction to try me, or anyone else, for high treason. His arguments then ranged from the jurisdiction of the North-West Territories Act (amended version, 1880) to the Magna Carta and its "right to a trial by a jury of twelve." In simplest terms, the North-West Territories Act, under which I was being tried, most certainly did not overrule the founding principles of the British Constitution. Trying me under the North-West Territories Act was *ultra vires*, or "beyond the powers" of the Act.

Following up on this point, Fitzpatrick then alluded to the real danger: "a government desirous of ridding itself of particular men in these Territories can, by a servile creature appointed as magistrate, with the absolute right to go out on the highway and streets and select his jury as he saw fit — might accomplish its end in this way." Surprisingly enough, throughout the demurrer, the Crown allowed my solicitor the floor, with little comment.

In fact, as I was to discover, the prosecution had already made sure that the legal arguments were in place to counter such arguments on my behalf. Upon my surrender back in May, Queen's Counsels Robinson and Osler had initially been approached by Justice Minister Campbell to provide a legal opinion on the validity of the North-West Territories holding a trial for high treason, a capital offence. Asked if having a lowly stipendiary magistrate try such a case would be "anomalous and inappropriate," they agreed that it would be and recommended against the strategy. They argued that as Canada has no statute of high treason, only treason felony, a non-capital offence, either a special commission would need to be created or a law passed empowering the government to have me tried for a capital crime anywhere in Canada. This opinion did not sit well with the prime minister.

As Ronald Olesky points out in another of the "Crown Letters," an advisory letter written to Justice Minister Campbell from Manitoba Chief Justice Lewis Wallbridge outlined the difficulties which might be found if I, or any of the thirty-six individuals charged with treason, should be brought to Manitoba for trial by the Manitoba Queen's Bench. Chief amongst these concerns was the fact that a jury in Winnipeg would be composed of twelve, of whom "the prisoner might insist that a moiety be half-breeds."

With Wallbridge's letter in hand, Justice Minister Campbell warned Macdonald that there would be a "miscarriage of justice" if I were tried in Manitoba. This "miscarriage," as John A. Macdonald knew only too well, would be that I would most likely not be found guilty in a Manitoba court. As a young lawyer, Macdonald had himself successfully defended a rebel charged with treason after the suppression of William Lyon Mackenzie's 1837–38 Upper Canada Rebellion. The prime minister was not willing to take a chance on my getting off or receiving a jail sentence in Manitoba. Calling Parliament to pass a special law, as suggested by Robinson and Osler, was also politically dangerous. The Liberal opposition would have a field day, calling the government to account for its mishandling of the whole North-West situation since the bungled purchase of Rupert's Land back in 1869. Nor did Macdonald have an appetite to call a special commission composed of such legal figures as the chief justices of Manitoba, Ontario and Quebec. What Macdonald needed was a statute and a venue that would ensure I was convicted and hanged for high treason.

Searching British law, the Department of Justice uncovered the British Statute of Treasons. Under this law passed back in 1351, those convicted of treason were hanged, disemboweled and ripped apart limb to limb, with their heads stuck on a pole outside the Tower of London. When Justice Minister Campbell suggested importing this antediluvian law into the North-West Territories "for judicial reasons," Macdonald agreed wholeheartedly.

There was still a major concern. As has been seen, the territorial court had no precedent for successfully trying, sentencing and executing a capital case. Seeking a means around any procedural or infrastructural problems, Magistrate Richardson provided a solution. A man by the name of Connor had been charged with murder. Found guilty in the Regina police court, Connor was sentenced by Richardson to hang — despite a recent amendment to the North-West Territories Act that strongly indicated that a grand jury indictment was required in such cases. Seeking to block such a ruling, after discussion with Lieutenant-Governor Edgar Dewdney, Magistrate Richardson requested a ruling by the Manitoba Court of Appeal, challenging his own jurisdiction.

The Connor case appeal was to be heard by Chief Justice Lewis Wallbridge in the Manitoba Court of Appeal in Winnipeg. Consulting lawyers Robinson and Osler were hired to act for the Crown in the Connor appeal. Upon a successful appeal, they were to proceed from Winnipeg to Regina to prosecute my case for the Crown. Needing time to get Mr. Osler to Winnipeg, Minister Campbell informed the prime minister that he had "privately" written to Justice Wallbridge requesting a delay in the appeal court proceedings until Mr. Osler was able to travel to Winnipeg and ensure the matter was "well argued." Upon arrival in Winnipeg, Mr. Osler went before the court of appeal and sought a ruling giving the territorial court the right to try a capital case and to hang Mr. Connor. His points were taken and the appeal was quickly approved. It was now cleared for me to be tried in Regina and found to be guilty by a territorial magistrate — all of the legal hurdles having been overcome by backroom manoeuvring.

Moreover, in his decision, Chief Justice Wallbridge referred to the British Raj in India, where cases of treason were routinely administered and tried by stipendiary magistrates. He also spoke of the development of British law in the North-West, claiming that prior to European occupation the land was *terra nullius* (empty land): "There can be no doubt that at the time of its occupation by English subjects the country now known as the North-West Territories would fall within the description of an uninhabited country."

When one looks at the larger implications of this legal opinion, one sees that it is a key principle of the European Doctrine of Discovery, in that *terra nullius* justifies the denial of rights and the expulsion or extermination of Indigenous populations from their ancient homelands. According to Wallbridge, applying this rationale to our North-West, the Indians and the Métis had no homeland. The government could treat us, not as citizens, but as little more than wanderers in an untamed wilderness.

COMMISSIONER: Mr. Riel, this Inquiry is pledged to review the proceedings of your trial. Please elaborate regarding your concerns in this regard.

RIEL: It has often been claimed that I received a "fair trial," impartially conducted under the prevailing rules of criminal procedure. Well, you can imagine my shock and indignation when, against my wishes and my plans to defend our cause based on its merits, it became obvious my lawyers were attempting to have me found "not guilty by reason of insanity." This tarnishing of my good name was not agreed upon. I vehemently rejected this defence. Furthermore it failed, and I was found guilty and sentenced to be hanged. This "insanity" defence was, however, highly successful in "muddying the waters" and thereby sidetracking fifteen years of utter negligence by the Dominion government in the North-West. Right from the start, my attorneys, Fitzpatrick, Lemieux and Greenshields, were merely actors upon a stage. In hindsight, their initial bluster, challenging the jurisdiction of Hugh Richardson as magistrate, was but a diversion.

In fact, my lawyers never really challenged the jurisdiction of Magistrate Richardson. As a non-elected, appointed member of the ruling North-West Territorial Council, he was in clear conflict with his role as an impartial judge, but this was never brought up. His bias in these roles should have invalidated his sitting my trial, especially as his prejudice against me was longstanding. As far back as 1880, while I was camped with the last of the buffalo-hunting Métis in Montana, Richardson warned the Canadian minister of the interior, at that time John A. Macdonald, to take prompt action in dealing with Métis land claims as the Métis were being "latterly subjected to the evil influences of the leading spirits of the Manitoba troubles. Influence has been circulating in Saskatchewan, doing no good."

Another serious issue was Richardson's jury of six, a total disregard of British justice, which demands that there be twelve jurors. Moreover, the North-West Territories Act allowed Richardson, as a magistrate, to personally draw up a preliminary list of thirty-six potential jurors. My lawyers were allowed to challenge six jurors, but it mattered little because the list was made up entirely of newly arrived, English-speaking Protestants, all dependent upon amateur translators for any testimony in the French language. By contrast, if the trial had been held in Manitoba or Quebec, the trial would have been conducted in the French language and up to twenty jurors could have been refused. No matter, my lawyers did not challenge the manner in which the jury was selected. Fitzpatrick's challenge to the territorial court's jurisdiction also went nowhere. John A. Macdonald had already seen to that with the "Connors Appeal." With Magistrate Richardson's ruling in his own favour, the Crown had what it needed. Conditions were in place to convict me of high treason.

COMMISSIONER: Mr. Riel, recognizing your concerns over the trial process, we ask that you please inform this Inquiry of the nature of the charges laid against you.

RIEL: As has already been made clear, after giving myself over to General Middleton on May 15, 1885, I was finally arraigned in Regina on July 26, charged with a lengthy indictment under the antiquated British 1351 Statute of Treasons:

> When a man do levy war against our Lord the King in his realm . . .
> giving them aid and comfort in the realm and elsewhere and thereof he
> proveably attainted of open deed by the people of their condition . . . this
> shall be one ground upon which the party accused of the offence and le-
> gally proved to have committed the offence, shall be held to be guilty of
> the crime of high treason.

Conveniently, for those opposed to me, my original indictment appears to be lost. Nevertheless, I recall clearly that the Crown crafted its case so as to prove I had incited a rebellion in the territory, solely for my own monetary gain. They had me starting an "Indian war" to get what I wanted and, in the process, I was accused of committing high treason against the Crown. All of this was framed as six counts of levying war against "Her Majesty in the Realm." Charged as a British citizen, I found that three of the charges referred to me as "being a subject of our Lady the Queen"; the other three referred to my "then living within the Dominion of Canada and under the protection of our Sovereign Lady the Queen."

None of these charges mentions, or recognizes, that I was a naturalized American citizen, or that I was a visitor and not resident in Canada. I indicated to my counsel how ludicrous these charges were. Both prior to making the journey into the Saskatchewan and during my stay, I demonstrated my intention to return to Montana. As to owing allegiance to Our Lady the Queen: there was a time when that was true. Patriating the province of Manitoba into the Canadian Confederation, I toasted the Good Lady's health. In the Red River in 1870, I raised a large body of men to defend British Canada from a Fenian invasion. I have also stood by Her Majesty's flag, stopping anyone who attempted to remove it. An admirer of the British parliamentary system, I have sought throughout my career to maintain our British rights as protected by the British Constitution and Her Majesty the Queen.

Alas, in our time of need, Her Majesty offered little protection to her subjects, both when Colonel Garnet Wolseley and 1,400 British regulars and Canadian volunteers invaded the Red River Settlements to indict me and put the community under martial law, and when General Middleton and thousands of Canadian troops invaded Métis lands, shelling and strafing our community before overrunning us. Today, I respect Her Majesty but owe her no allegiance.

The antiquated British 1351 Statute of Treasons is an evil document. As a practising Catholic, I took special offence to it as each of the charges against me stated that I was "moved and seduced by the instigation of the devil as a false traitor," and that I "wickedly, maliciously and traitorously did levy and make war against our said Lady the Queen . . . by force and arms to subvert and destroy the constitution and government of this realm. . . ." What more grotesque and hideous charge could there be? Now I am a disciple of the devil!

I came to Saskatchewan to serve my Métis brothers and sisters, to assist the Indians and the settlers. My work is to achieve their inalienable rights to land, life and liberty. This is not the devil's work. The devil is he who deprived the Indian of food and a livelihood. It is he who implements a policy of "feed one day — starve the next." Abrogating our Aboriginal rights, he defrauds the Métis through "scrips" and patents. He lets large corporations buy up our prairie and evict our priests. The settlers he leaves "high and dry," with no representation in Parliament, and no Canadian Pacific Railway to haul their produce. Long promised in the north, the railway was moved south, here to Regina, to Lieutenant-Governor Dewdney's new capital, "the Queen City of the Plains." No rail, no markets, just the North-West Mounted Police and the Hudson's Bay Company with its monopoly on goods and prices. That, to me, is the devil's work.

COMMISSIONER: Mr. Riel, you have expressed concern regarding access to your evidence, as well as challenges in regard to your lawyers during the preliminaries leading up to your trial. Please inform this Inquiry of the nature of these concerns.

RIEL: When Magistrate Richardson outlined the charges against me, he blatantly violated appropriate judicial proceedings. He failed to inform the court that, before I could be convicted, it required the jury to be satisfied that I am a "subject of Our Lady the Queen" — which, as a naturalized American citizen, I am not. It is my contention that both my counsel and the Crown purposefully ignored this, although I had specifically, and repeatedly, asked for my American naturalization papers seized by General Middleton at Batoche to be brought to the court. I wanted my documents to be used as evidence, yet they were never produced. Was this ignorance, negligence or worse — collusion?

When Magistrate Richardson asked for my plea, I pleaded "not guilty." My attorneys then entered a written general demurrer or objection to the information contained in the six charges of high treason. They were arguing that the charges were doubled, that the last three charges were identical to the first three charges, and therefore not to be allowed. The Crown countered, citing the ancient Doctrine of Natural Allegiance. They also unearthed the equally feudal Doctrine of Local Allegiance whereby allegiance is owed to a state while within its limits. Long abandoned in the United States, the concept of natural allegiance holds that a man continues to owe allegiance to his monarch eternally, an allegiance that can never be disclaimed, even if one pledges to another. This bit of historical parlance was good enough for Richardson. He ruled with the Crown, and again my counsel did not appeal. What the Crown was insinuating with this manoeuvre was that even if I was an American citizen, the very fact that I had once lived in Canada meant that I still owed allegiance to the Queen. They were clearly covering all their bases.

When I was asked to plead a second time, I again pleaded "not guilty."

COMMISSIONER: Mr. Riel, you have also expressed reservations concerning the complex legal proceeding that occurred leading up to and during your trial. Please elaborate on your concerns.

RIEL: Prior to my actual trial, my counsel made application for a deferment of proceedings to prepare our case. On Mr. Lemieux's suggestion, I submitted an affidavit to Magistrate Richardson requesting a month's adjournment to prepare my defence. I included a request for my papers taken from Batoche and asked that defence witnesses, including Gabriel Dumont, now a fugitive in the United States, be provided a special dispensation allowing immunity to attend my trial. I also requested Deputy Superintendent General of Indian Affairs L. Vankoughnet, and A.M. Burgess, deputy minister of the interior, as witnesses. The idea of a special dispensation for witnesses was rejected outright, as was the subpoenaing of the two deputy ministers. Richardson ruled it was contrary to the nation's best interests and security.

On the matter of my personal papers, and the various papers, petitions and documents that had been sent to Ottawa from the Saskatchewan, Crown prosecutor Robinson objected to their introduction, saying they were now considered the property of the government. My point is any document can be subpoenaed, provided it isn't protected by the Crown's confidentiality. These papers might not have been restored to me personally, but they certainly should have been called into court. I was the author of most of the papers, so no one else could claim privilege on them. This was really a death blow to my defence. As I have indicated, amongst the papers I sought was my Certificate of Naturalization, establishing my citizenship of the United States of America. I reiterate, I am not a British subject and should not have been tried as such.

Unbeknownst to me, in his affidavit, Lemieux did indeed submit a request for a month's recess, but it was not to work with me on my defence. He claimed to need that much time to arrange for three "alienists," specialists in insanity, to travel from eastern Canada and attend my trial as witnesses for the defence. Fitzpatrick's personal affidavit for adjournment had nothing to do with collecting documents for my defence either. He asked for an adjournment of just two weeks and, in a lengthy addendum to Magistrate Richardson, he made pointed reference to my past confinement in the Church-run asylums in Quebec in the 1870s. With the Crown opposing a month's recess, the Court agreed to give us eight days.

With little formal contact with my defence team over the eight days' adjournment, my trial recommenced on July 28, 1885. Crown Counsel Osler opened with a lengthy listing of events depicting me as the evil mastermind behind a Métis uprising and an Indian war on the South Saskatchewan. According to him, the Métis were merely my poor dupes. It was I who ordered my men to fire on the police; it was I who incited Poundmaker and the Cree. Everything I had done was for power and personal benefit. He asserted that I had broken with the priests and did not care whose lives I sacrificed. Wrapping up a litany of my so-called crimes, the Crown declared, "I think you will be satisfied before this case is over that it is not a matter brought about by any wrongs so much as a matter brought about by the personal ambition and vanity of the man on trial."

After an outline of the rest of my alleged crimes, the Crown started calling witnesses. Their first witness, Saskatoon doctor John Willoughby, told of my telling him that the only answer we received to our petitions was more police, and that we were going to strike a blow to gain our rights. In cross-examination, my lawyers fumbled about, going off on tangents and never getting him to admit the police were constantly provoking us into war. The next witness, General Middleton, testified he lost nine or ten men killed and forty wounded at Fish Creek, with six killed attacking Batoche and twelve or thirteen wounded. There was no mention of our losses or the barbaric treatment of some of our elders brutally murdered by Canadian forces. My counsel paid scant interest to the general's testimony and instead pushed him for indications I was insane. They met no success. As the day wore on, witnesses for the Crown continued to line up, each with a well-practised and almost identical version of events. Some were cross-examined by my counsel and some were not.

My counsel was getting nowhere, and it is little wonder. Although they nodded their heads, they refused to take any of my advice or even listen to me. They knew precious little as to what questions needed to be asked. Those questions that were asked were half-hearted in nature. They avoided direct questioning and focused their enquiries on such issues as my mood swings, my diet and my religious views. Listening to this, I realized that they were attempting something underhanded, something we had not discussed. As I have mentioned, they were laying the groundwork to claim I am insane.

The proverbial penny truly dropped when my counsel told the court "... no one of any nationality, of any creed ... can justify the rebellion. ...." In other words, they cared not for the issues that led up to the defence of our very lives. They ignored the issues behind our actions. They were ignoring my instructions and basing their defence on my "insanity." Greenshields even admitted that, in making this defence, "we are instructed by others than the prisoner."

Angered, I of course opposed this line of defence. During recesses I asked them to defer to my interests and to the cause they were defending. Without results. They were determined to go on, and I determined they would not.

COMMISSIONER: Mr. Riel, after an array of prosecution witnesses had been heard, you intervened in the proceedings of the court. Will you please explain to this Inquiry why you felt the need to intervene.

RIEL: Yes, I had come to the realization that I was not being served by my counsel and needed to defend myself. It was precisely at this moment that a new figure entered the court. My cousin, Charles Nolin, was called to the stand. My boyhood friend Charles has been a source of great pain to me over the years. Both in Manitoba in 1870 and again on the Saskatchewan in '85, he had first supported and then gone against our community's efforts to gain our democratic rights. Conspiring with the priests and taking Hudson's Bay Company contracts, he attempted to undermine our Métis movement, drawing men away with religious talk and promises of jobs.

With Charles working with Père André and the priests against our movement of self-defence, we had broken off relations completely in Batoche. On March 19, 1885, with reports of 500 police marching on Batoche, I had Charles Nolin arrested. He was court-martialled by the Métis Council as a traitor. Although condemned, his sentence was revoked and he was released from custody. A few days later he managed to escape, seeking sanctuary in Prince Albert. Now, here he was attempting to put the noose around my neck.

Cousin Charles's testimony was venomous, making all sorts of crazy claims against me. Time after time, Nolin was asked leading and improper questions by the prosecution. He responded, stating his opinion on a number of key subjects and telling the court his version of what was in my private papers — the same papers denied me and my defence. Cousin Charles had me writing a book, in buffalo blood. Although no such book was entered in evidence, he claimed it was my plan for destroying Canada, England, Rome and the Pope. Also, according to him, I had attempted to blackmail the Canadian government, and had raised my price for deserting the Métis from $35,000 to $100,000. I was, according to him, extorting this money to start a newspaper in the United States. He claimed that my long-term plan was to "raise the nationalities." Indians and foreign armies would sweep into the Saskatchewan, and I would take possession of the North-West to become Pope. These were lies and deceit by a coward and cheat.

Nevertheless, here was a chance to get to the heart of our resistance against Canadian colonialism and genocide. But, alas, in cross-examination, Lemieux dropped the matter and began to ask Nolin about obscure incidents in our relationship, fishing for signs of my supposed mental derangement. Nolin was only too glad to oblige, characterizing me as a religious megalomaniac who received psychic messages and inspirations through every part of my body. He related how even the mention of the word "police" puts me in an uncontrollable rage. He even criticized and mocked my efforts to avoid bloodshed at the Battle of Duck Lake, when I carried a cross instead of a gun.

Knowing that Nolin had recently been in jail in Prince Albert, Lemieux asked Nolin if he had "been put at liberty since he came to Regina to give his evidence in this case?" He answered, *"Oui, monsieur."* At this point, it looked to me as though my counsel was beginning to open up a central question: Why was Charles Nolin on the stand? What was his motivation to destroy me, to paint me as a megalomaniac? Unfortunately, Lemieux did not take up these fundamental questions. My counsel had no idea what questions to ask. They did not know Nolin's history. They did not know that he had been an early advocate, calling for me to come to the Saskatchewan from Montana to support the constitutional struggles of the Métis. They had no clue that he had been the most vocal, calling for direct action to further our cause. Yet, when I called for an economic boycott of Hudson's Bay Company and government contracts, as a major contractor, he had balked and sought to subvert our actions, throwing his support to Père André. Later, when we were attacked by Middleton, he had bolted from Batoche, deserting his own blood and people. Seeking to gain "refuge," Charles Nolin had made the "yellow run" to Prince Albert. Instead of being given sanctuary, he had been thrown in jail, not as a rebel but in order to secure him as a witness against me. After his testimony, unlike the bulk of our men, charges were never brought against him.

This was all too much. Rising to my feet, I interrupted the cross-examination. I asked Magistrate Richardson if there was any legal procedure that would allow me to speak. I told him I wished to question this witness before he left the box. Immediately, Fitzpatrick, my own counsel, rose and vehemently objected to my saying anything in court without defence counsel's permission or approval. He told the magistrate that I must be made to understand that anything done in the case must be done through them. I must not be allowed to interfere.

Clearly annoyed and bothered by my request, Richardson responded, pointing out that I had the right to counsel but also the right to defend myself. I then interjected, asserting that this case is extraordinary: that while the Crown prosecutors, with the great talents they have at their service, are trying to show I am guilty — as it is their duty — my counsellors have been trying to induce Nolin to say that I am insane.

Fitzpatrick then again requested Richardson to forbid me from interrupting. With my defence having allowed Nolin to raise the question of my supposed insanity, I was now told that I must leave the case in the capable hands of my advisers, and that I would have an opportunity to speak — at the proper time — which was not specified, but would be after both Crown and defence proceedings had been completed.

Angered, I persisted. I told Richardson the witness was stepping down. I was missing my opportunity. Again, he told me that if there were any questions I wanted put to Nolin then I should tell my counsel and they would say whether they should be put. I said, "I have on cross-examination 200 questions."' This was too much for Richardson, and with his court in discord, the magistrate called a brief adjournment.

After the adjournment and having conferred amongst themselves but not with me, Fitzpatrick and Lemieux told the court that I was obstructing the proper management of my own case, and that if I was allowed to ask questions, they would not continue to act as my counsel. Magistrate Richardson then asked me if I was defended by counsel. I replied, "But partly, my cause is partially in their hands, I want their services, but I want my cause defended the best which circumstances allow." I asked the magistrate if I could thank them for their services and then fire them.

Adamant, Richardson said, "No." If I were to take control of my defence and attempt to fire my counsel, he would assign a court-ordered defence by which I would be bound. My choice was to accept the lawyers I had or be defended by Richardson's appointed lawyers. That was no choice at all. He finished, lecturing me that at this stage in the proceedings he could not refuse to recognize Fitzpatrick, Lemieux and the others as having the charge and the responsibility for my defence. Like a jackrabbit, Lemieux jumped up: "We accept the responsibility."

I felt terribly torn. While I wished to retain them, I could not abandon my dignity. I had to defend myself against the accusation of high treason or consent to the animal life of an asylum. I told the court that I did not care about my life if I was not allowed to carry with it the moral existence of an intellectual being. Richardson replied that I must leave it in their hands. I attempted to tell him this was ridiculous. My counsel were from Quebec. They had to put questions to men with whom they are not acquainted, on circumstances of which they know nothing. They cannot follow the threads of the questions. They lose more than three-quarters of the opportunities of making good answers. That was it. Thereafter, I was not allowed to speak, let alone defend myself, and my lawyers were now free to attempt to prove I was a madman.

COMMISSIONER: Mr. Riel, please inform this Inquiry of the nature of your relationship with the next witness, the Roman Catholic priest Father André.

RIEL: With Charles Nolin's testimony now over, and my counsel providing me with absolutely no support whatsoever, they now called the head of the Missionary Oblates of Mary Immaculate, Father (Père) Alexis André, in my defence. Not having been informed that my old foe was to be called, I was somewhat surprised and confused at Father André's being called as a witness for the defence. It is also somewhat ironic that since my trial and conviction André has been asked to attend to my spiritual rehabilitation.

Having ministered to the scattered Métis and Indian populations of the West since the 1860s, Père André knows our people well. It was under Père's guidance that the Métis on the South Saskatchewan River formed their own government in December of 1873. Gabriel Dumont was elected president, along with eight counsellors. It was this council that established the historic Métis Laws of St. Laurent as a governing code. Based on the laws of the buffalo hunt, these rules ensured there would be collective interests on the land and its resources. Like that classic English document, the Magna Carta, these Métis laws represent a moral compass and point the way to common law. The distinction between the English sense of law and that of the Métis code is that the latter leads to a collective way of life, whereas the English moved toward the rights of the individual. Needless to say, the Métis laws were not what the Canadians wanted to be happening in the West.

As in Manitoba, since the 1820s, the Hudson's Bay Company ruled the prairie economy in a near monopoly. Lawrence Clarke, chief factor of the Saskatchewan District of the Hudson's Bay Company, regarded himself as the most important man in the district, with responsibilities extending well beyond the fur trade. In 1875, he provided crucial assistance to the North-West Mounted Police (NWMP) during their first winter on the North Saskatchewan. When informed that Gabriel Dumont was enforcing his prairie law on a group of Métis hunters whom Clarke had sent ahead of the yearly buffalo hunt to gather hides and meat for the HBC, Clarke sent an urgent letter warning the Canadian government that, as in Manitoba, the Métis were once again declaring sovereignty over the North-West. As a result of Clarke's letter, Commissioner French of the North-West Mounted Police was ordered to take action against this upstart Métis government. Accompanied by fifty police and Major General Smyth, the officer commanding the Canadian militia, French and his police marched north to confront and put an end to Gabriel's "little government." In one of the North-West Mounted Police's first official acts, Gabriel Dumont and the Métis councillors were escorted to Fort Carlton and called before the magistrates, one of whom was Clarke. Threatened with arrest, and told to disband their government, they did so at Père André's insistence.

At this time, with the Canadian government preparing conditions for the Great Plains Treaties, federal resources were directed to clearing the plains, not settling them with half-breed communities. Thereafter, with the federal government's basic refusal to recognize the Saskatchewan Métis as an organized community, began the long line of petitions, requests and pleas for recognition and rights. Speaking for the Métis in 1881, André presented a petition to Lieutenant-Governor David Laird and the Council of the North-West Territories, where Lawrence Clarke was the first man to be elected to a legislative post for the new District of Lorne, calling for the registration of Métis land claims. Two years later André once again presented another petition calling for registration of river frontage farms rather than quarter-section acreages.

Upon my arrival in Saskatchewan, I paid a visit to St. Laurent, the village north of Batoche, and sought Père André's blessing. We had a pleasant visit, and I attended Mass with him numerous times. Relations cooled, however, as I worked amongst the Métis population, seeking clarification of their status and concerns. Père had long been the arbiter at the centre of Métis matters on the Saskatchewan. Now as I carried out an enumeration of those who had not received their lands as set out in the Manitoba Act of 1870, he grew possessive, concerned about my influence over his congregation. Over time, our relations turned acrimonious, especially over issues of religion.

Conservative by nature, Père had no patience when I brought up issues such as modernizing the liturgy. He was incensed when I criticized Pope Leo's last letter on "the submission that is incumbent on writers as regards religious affairs and the action of the Church in relation to Catholic society." After that, he attempted to herd me back to

Montana with threats and bribes. Then, with the police threatening to arrest Gabriel and me, he sided with the police. When we established the Provisional Government he opposed me with heart and soul and withdrew his priests, refusing the sacraments to those who had taken up arms.

Despite our differences, when asked at my trial about the claims of the half-breeds prior to my arrival, André told the truth. He informed the court that he was involved in the agitations and had sent, with others, a number of petitions demanding rights such as land patents, river frontage lots, abolition of taxes on wood, and rights for those who did not have scrip in Manitoba. When asked if they received an answer to these petitions, André said that once they had received an answer, but it was evasive, saying only that the issues would be taken into consideration. Then Lemieux asked a most puzzling question. He wanted to know if there was an answer sent to Charles Nolin.

This was most peculiar, for Lemieux was referring to the grand petition that Will Jackson and I sent to the government in December 1884. It was we who sent the petition, but Lieutenant-Governor Dewdney had sent his answer to Père André who passed it on to Charles Nolin, stating Ottawa would establish a commission to investigate the claims of the half-breeds, and would direct an enumeration of those who had not participated in a land grant in Manitoba. I was very curious: what did the old priest know? André's answer was evasive. Lemieux then asked, "After these petitions and resolutions had been adopted at the public meetings and sent to the government, was there a change in the state of things that existed then?" André paused and then answered: "The silence of the government produced great dissatisfaction in the minds of the people." Lemieux probed further, "Today, are the people in a better position than they were before, in regard to the rights they claim?" André answered, "They have not yet received the patents for their land on the South Saskatchewan."

For the first time in my trial, the questioning was bearing fruit. It was now clear that the government had not responded to our requests. I anxiously waited for Lemieux to dig deeper, to get to the root of the problem: the lack of action by the government on land title. But just at that moment, Mr. Osler stood up. Objecting to "this class of questions," he expressed his concern that if this line of questioning persisted, the question of justifying the policies of the government would come up. Claiming "his learned friends" were seeking to justify armed rebellion, he argued that a counter-claim against the government was not an option in a trial for high treason. "Such complaints as the Métis had did not excuse an armed uprising and therefore were not relevant to the issue of guilt in a trial for high treason."

Mr. Lemieux replied that he was not justifying rebellion but wanted to get further facts, to explain the circumstances under which I came into the county. Over Osler's objection, Lemieux put the question to André: "Will you say if the state of things today is the same as in 1882, '83 and '84 . . . if justice has been done with regard to the claims and just rights of the people?" Osler objected again. Lemieux was asking for an opinion; it was a leading question and irrelevant to the issue. Before Richardson could make a ruling, Lemieux asked André: "Do you know if at any time the Dominion government agreed or acceded to the demands made by the half-breeds and clergy relative to the claims and rights that you have spoken?"

There it was, the question everything turned on. Finally it had been asked: "Had justice been done?" On his feet again, Osler opposed this question, unless it was confined to a date prior to the time I entered the country. Richardson agreed and asked Lemieux to limit his question to the period prior to my arrival in Saskatchewan. Lemieux responded that he would ask the question generally. Then, in what was probably his boldest move throughout my trial, he asked André: "Will you state if, since the arrival of the prisoner in the country and up to the time of the rebellion, the government has made any favourable answer to the demands and claims of the half-breeds?"

I waited in anticipation. Père knew what the government had done and what they had not done. Then, almost unbelievably, instead of indicting the government that had ignored nearly twenty years of his petitions, he began to recite the changes the government had promised in Dewdney's message to Nolin. He told the court that, regarding the alteration of the survey of lots on the river, there was an answer from the government saying they would grant it. He also spoke about the government acceding to certain demands in regard to those who did not have any scrip in Manitoba. It was as if he were reading from a script, for this was not the Père I knew. He understood well enough what neglect and mismanagement had done to the North-West. When asked what questions remained to be settled, André answered, "The question of patents." Then again he jumped back on his talking points and told the court that patents too had been settled "in a certain way."

John A. Macdonald himself could not have done a better job as André went on to say the Dominion government was looking into other issues as well, such as wood and timber rights. Championing Macdonald's deceptions and concessions, André made it clear that our resistance had been a meaningless and futile exercise as the government was meeting the demands of the Métis. He made it crystal clear that he thought I should have gone back to Montana when I had a chance. Now I was getting what I deserved for breaking with the priests and taking up the armed self-defence of our community. What André left out was the fact that although the government established a land commission, it was a mockery. After all these years of inaction, with General Middleton and a Canadian expeditionary army steaming westward on the CPR, Macdonald's government magically "gave" the Métis 160 acres and preemption for 160 more. It would, of course, be of little consequence as Middleton was on his way and many of the farms were destroyed in the war. With the men in jail at planting time, little in the way of crops could be sown. The lands lay fallow. In the end, as had happened in Manitoba, those scrip lands that were distributed were often sold to provide the necessities of life. With his testimony, Père André effectively tightened the rope around my neck, indicating I had been the author of our own misfortune as all was being put to rights.

Once again addressing André, defence counsel Lemieux switched his questioning from the government issues leading to our resistance to asking André about me personally. Where and when had he seen or met me? He specifically asked if André and I spoke of religion and politics. André answered, "Unfortunately, yes, that we had spoken on these subjects many times," and André found that "I was no longer the same man" when discussing these issues. There were two men in me: I had lost all control and I "had become a fool!"

After André left the stand, my counsel ignored all my requests and suggestions and presented only five witnesses. Their defence took less than one full day. Closing their case, they then called two "expert" medical witnesses: Dr. François Roy, the superintendent of the Beauport Lunatic Asylum near Montreal, and Dr. Daniel Clark, superintendent of the Toronto Lunatic Asylum. Roy, who had been my jailor and tormentor, declared I suffered from "megalomania" and was clearly of an unsound mind. Dr. Clark, who had but briefly interviewed me, told the jury that he considered that I had been insane since 1865 — at the age of twenty-one.

In rebuttal, the Crown called a number of witnesses. General Middleton was the first, and I am sure his testimony surprised them because he spoke of my "acute intellect . . . able to hold his own upon any argument or topic we happened to touch on." The second witness was Captain Young, and he also spoke favourably of my state of mind, saying that in our discussions he "found a mind more clever than [his] own." Ironically, the Crown rebuttal, with major witnesses recognizing my sanity, was one of the only satisfactions I received throughout the whole trial.

On a personal note, by the afternoon of the fourth day, although buoyed by these two witnesses to my sanity, I felt as though I was in a bear trap. None of my own witnesses had been called, nor had any of my documents been brought forth. I was even disallowed my United States naturalization papers. How could this be? Charged as I was with treason, disloyalty to Her Majesty, Queen Victoria, my American naturalization papers were conclusive evidence of my American citizenship. They absolve me, an American citizen, of any sovereign responsibility to Her Majesty. I could not have committed treason as I am an American.

In despair, I waited for my lead defence attorney, Mr. Fitzpatrick, to give his peroration. At the beginning of his two-hour summary speech, full of lofty and pompous language, it looked as though he was recognizing the government's duplicity. Fitzpatrick stated that although no one could justify the rebellion, "criminal folly and neglect would have gone unpunished had there been no resistance." A future Liberal politician, Fitzpatrick also asserted that the Government of Canada "had wholly failed in its duty toward these North-West Territories."

He then proceeded to backtrack, recognizing that he himself was not sure if I am insane, but asking rhetorically if it was consistent with sanity to pick a fight with the British Empire. According to him, even that $35,000 so-called "bribe" had had a lunatic aspect. Nolin had testified that I hoped to use the money to establish a newspaper in the United States to rally foreign help to take the North-West for the Métis. Surely, this too was madness. Wrapping up, he pleaded: "I know that you shall not weave the cord that shall hang him and hang him high in the face of all the world, a poor confirmed lunatic — a victim, gentlemen, of oppression or the victim of fanaticism. I rest my case."

COMMISSIONER: Mr. Riel, this "insanity" defence was put in place against your wishes. Were you able to inform the court of the nature and merits of your actions?

RIEL: It was extremely difficult. There are set procedures for criminal trials and, in effect, Magistrate Richardson had his own rules. He waited until both the Crown and defence had fully exhausted their rosters of witnesses before informing me that I was now entitled to make a closing statement. Turning to the jury, he emphasized that my statement to the court was not to be considered as evidence. No questions were to be asked. Just the same, springing from his chair, my lawyer, Lemieux, once again, declared that whatever the prisoner had to say was not sanctioned by the defence counsel. The defence team was "not responsible for any declaration I make."

Lifting my iron ball to my lap and apologizing for my English, I humbly and formally addressed Magistrate Richardson, Justice Le Jeune, the jury, my lawyers, those of the Crown, as well as those ladies and gentlemen present. I told them that today, although a man, I am as helpless before this court in the Dominion of Canada and in this world as I was helpless on the knees of my mother the day of my birth. The North-West, I said, is also my mother. It is my mother country and although my mother country is sick and confined in a certain way, I am sure that my mother country will not kill me any more than my mother did forty years ago when I came into the world, because a mother is always a mother. Even if I have my faults, if she can see I am true to myself, she will be full of love for me.

I went on to explain that I have a life's mission in the service of my nation and that negotiating Manitoba's entry into Confederation and the passing into law of the Manitoba Act brought me great joy. My dream was to bring two nations, one large and one small, to bargain as equals. I told the court that since my time at the Red River, I had been caught up in a fifteen-year war with John A. Macdonald. I then listed the grievances of the various sectors in the North-West, telling the court that when I came to the Saskatchewan, the Indians were starving on their reserves, the Métis were eating rotten Hudson's Bay Company pork and watching as federal surveyors staked out adjacent lands in rectangular lots. The settlers, mostly Canadians from Ontario, were also denied their democratic rights with no representative in the Canadian Parliament. The Territorial Council, too, was but a sham council controlled by the despotism of Lieutenant-Governor Dewdney and the Hudson's Bay Company factor Lawrence Clarke, a key instigator of the recent war.

I also used this opportunity to explain to those assembled my ideas about land ownership. I pointed out that God cannot create a tribe without locating it, and that the North-West belongs to the Indians and the Métis, those who have lived upon it and raised their families, generation upon generation: "We are not birds. We have to walk on the ground. Our land is ours, but there is room for a diverse society in the Great North-West. We have a splendid great territory and we welcome the settlers: the Irish, the Bavarians, the Swiss, all nations, to our territory. We will share equitably upon recognition of our title to our lands."

I told the court how, through the grace of God, I am the founder of Manitoba, and with the help of others, I obtained a constitution guaranteeing rights for all in Manitoba and the North-West Territories. Is this the work of a madman? As to religion, what is my belief? What is my insanity about? My vision is a New World without the old division between Catholics and Protestants, French and English, Indigenous and settler. Boldly, I told the court that I truly believe I am a prophet, and my Métis nation is my mission. My goal has been to leave Rome and the Old World aside. I see white, half-breed and Indian children walking hand in hand towards a new bright future.

Speaking to Magistrate Richardson, I told him that in my view his jury of six, appointed by him, was deficient, their number no guarantee of liberty. Addressing the Crown's prosecutors, I reiterated that Sir John's Conservative governments showed an absolute lack of responsibility. Petition after petition had been ignored. Parliament and Cabinet did not provide representation for the peoples of the North-West. Instead of responding to our petitions with representation, they attacked us. Our agitation was constitutional and would have been recognized as such had we not been attacked.

COMMISSIONER: Mr. Riel, you have been convicted for leading a rebellion, yet you speak of constitutional agitation and resistance. Were you able to explain the nature of this constitutional agitation to the court?

RIEL: My life has been devoted to constitutional agitation for such reforms in Métis land tenure as are necessary to make the union with Canada tolerable and fair. I wanted to call the jury's attention to the following set of facts:

> First, that the House of Commons, Senate and Ministers of the Dominion who make laws for this land and govern it, have no representation whatever from the people of the North-West.

> Second, that the North-West Council generated by the Federal Government has the great defect of its parent.

> Third, that the number of members elected for the Council by the people make it only a sham representative legislature and no representative government at all.

I told the court that British civilization and its constitution have defined the government imposed on the North-West as "irresponsible government" in so much as it ignores the needs and requests of her prairie peoples. This plainly means that there is no responsibility, and by all the science which has been shown here yesterday, you are compelled to admit that if there is no responsibility, it is insane.

Turning to the jury, I told them that if you accept the defence plea of insanity you should still acquit me completely since I have been quarrelling with an insane and irresponsible government. But, if you decide I am sane, you should also acquit me on the basis that, having reason and a sound mind, I acted reasonably and in self-defence. It was the irresponsible and insane government that acted wrongly. And, I told them, if you pronounce in favour of the Crown, which contends that I am responsible, acquit me all the same. You are perfectly justified in declaring that, having my reason and sound mind, I have acted reasonably and in self-defence while the government, my accuser, being irresponsible and consequently insane, cannot but have acted wrong. If there was high treason, it was on the government's part, not mine. What more could I say? With no resources, but my belief in God, I completed my defence as best I could.

The court had little time to reflect on my words. Immediately after I relinquished the floor, Magistrate Richardson called on Crown Counsel Robinson to make his final address to the jury. Straightaway, Robinson addressed Fitzpatrick's "insanity" defence. Disputing my team's so-called medical evidence, he countered, pointing out that it was for the law to determine legally excusable insanity and not the good doctors who travelled so far to declare me "insane." Theirs was but an opinion. He then rehashed details of my blameworthiness. Citing the testimony of Charles Nolin and the others, Fitzpatrick emphasized that it was I who was guilty of masterminding the rebellion, and that I am of sound mind and deserve to be found guilty of the highest crime of civilized nations: high treason.

With the defence and prosecution having given their closing statements, Magistrate Richardson next addressed his jury. In a long, rambling address, well beyond the bounds of impartiality, I was accused of organizing "an insurrection accompanied by force to accomplish an object of a general nature." The jury's task was to completely satisfy themselves "that I am not answerable by reason of unsoundness of mind." Putting his emphasis on my culpability, he then reread significant portions of the evidence presented until the court was recessed for the evening.

On the fateful morning of August 1, 1885, Magistrate Richardson continued his address to the jury. It was all quite extraordinary. A Shakespearean at heart, Richardson continued to lavishly define the nature of the charge, all the while reminding the jury of its duty to decide if I was implicated in the acts charged against me and, if so, whether I was accountable for them. He dismissed out of hand the argument against the jurisdiction of his court in a case of high treason, and he stressed that the defence had needed to prove my insanity beyond all question of doubt. Concluding in a flourish, he told the jury that it was their responsibility to consider society at large and the people who live in this country. "You have to ask yourself: can such things be permitted?"

COMMISSIONER: Mr. Riel, you have expressed concern over the legality of Magistrate Richardson's instructions to the jury. Please elaborate.

RIEL: My present-day legal champion, Métis lawyer George Goulet, points out that Richardson's instructions were far from impartial. He failed to explain to the jury that the Crown has the burden of proving, beyond a reasonable doubt, every essential element of an alleged offence. If the Crown fails to prove an essential element, charges must be dismissed. With nary an interruption from the Crown or defence, Richardson neatly dealt with all six charges against me as though they were one charge only. He did not deal with each charge separately, as necessary. He, my defence counsel and the Crown prosecution avoided any mention of the fact that I am not a British subject as claimed in the first three charges. This alone would have thrown out those charges. There is more: I was accused under the 1351 Statute of Treasons of all of these acts "within the Realm." But there was no discussion, or challenge, regarding the fact that Canada and the colonies are not part of the "Realm." The Realm at the time of my trial refers to the waters around Great Britain. I was not in the Realm. Nor was their discussion of the irrelevance of my allegiance to Queen Victoria. I was an American citizen invited to the Saskatchewan as a guest. The reality is that, with all of their legal finagling, this ancient statute was not applicable in the North-West Territories. Nor was it applicable to me. The state had not proven that I countenanced rebellion or refused to fulfill my legal responsibility to Her Majesty, Queen Victoria.

COMMISSIONER: Mr. Riel, please speak to the verdict in your trial.

RIEL: As the jury left to deliberate, I felt a pang of sadness and went down on my knees and prayed for them. They were honest working men, farmers. I prayed they find me sane. They left the courtroom at two o'clock in the afternoon and returned at quarter past three. Once they were back in the jury box, the clerk of the court asked the jury foreman: "How say you, is the prisoner guilty or not guilty?"

Looking over, I saw that the foreman of the jury had tears in his eyes. Fumbling over his words, he pronounced me "Guilty." Then he said, "I have been asked by my brother jurors to recommend the prisoner to the mercy of the Crown." Magistrate Richardson made a note, then advised the foreman that their recommendation would be forwarded to the proper authorities. Crown Counsel Robinson next asked Richardson and the silent justice Le Jeune if they were ready to pass sentence. Turning to me, Richardson asked if I had anything further to say.

Looking around that courthouse, I could not but think I was alone. I had, however, held onto my good name. In pronouncing me guilty, they had at least found me to be sane. Addressing the jury that had so kindly asked for mercy, I prepared to thank them. Richardson abruptly stopped me. He informed me that although still seated, having performed their duty, the jury was discharged.

Now, addressing the court, I told the assembled that my only consolation is, if executed, it will not be as an insane man. With this "guilty" verdict I ceased to be "a fool." I then told them that having been misrepresented in a lowly territorial courtroom, with both my own defence and the Crown against me, it would have been easy for me to be incendiary with my protest. After all, I could have excoriated a jury composed of only six members, their selection, the one who selected them, and the competency of the court. I told them that they needed to know that the troubles in Saskatchewan stem from the difficulties in the Red River back in the years 1869–70. I told them of the injustices done to my Métis people by the Canadian government of John A. Macdonald, and my determination to remedy those injustices. I also told them that after having been attacked by Crozier of the North-West Mounted Police at Duck Lake, our resistance was necessary. It was the logical conclusion to the government's fifteen-year war against my people.

With my final words to the courthouse and the world, I called out for justice. I requested a commission of inquiry or special tribunal to review my life's work, once and for all. I wished my career tried, not just the last part of it — my time in Saskatchewan. I asked that those questions that have haunted me over the past fifteen years be addressed: Did I rebel, murder, and pillage in Manitoba, as my detractors have claimed? As a Member of Parliament, was I a fugitive of justice? Was I guilty of taking bribes and inciting rebellion and Indian wars in Saskatchewan? I called for justice and a ruling: Is Louis Riel guilty of high-treason as accused? Is Louis Riel a traitor to Canada, or is Louis Riel a true patriot? Am I Canada's Indigenous (Métis) Father of Confederation?

COMMISSIONER: Mr. Riel, it is with the deepest respect that we now ask that you please inform this Inquiry of the sentence you received, and your thoughts upon receiving that sentence.

RIEL: It was surreal. Magistrate Richardson told me to stand. He then let me know that my counsel had "defended me with as great ability as they could have" and that the jury had been exceedingly patient, putting up with my antics and courtroom outbursts. Banging his gavel, he then told me that I, Louis Riel, have been found "guilty of a crime the most pernicious and greatest that man can commit." He said I had opened the floodgates of rapine and bloodshed, aroused the Indians, and brought ruin on many families. Scolding me like a schoolmaster, he said, "There was no excuse whatsoever" for my actions. Then, banging his gavel three more times, he told me to prepare for my end: "Louis

Riel, you are to be taken to the Regina jail until September 18, and on that day taken to your place of execution and there be hanged by the neck till you are dead. May God have mercy on your soul." At that moment, I felt the weight of the world upon my shoulders and asked my God for strength as I was being led out of the courthouse and back to my cell.

COMMISSIONER: Thank you, Mr. Riel. This first session of the Riel Inquiry is in recess.

Upon reconvening we will receive Mr. Riel's testimony regarding the Red River Insurrection of 1869–70.

PART II

The Red River
Uprising

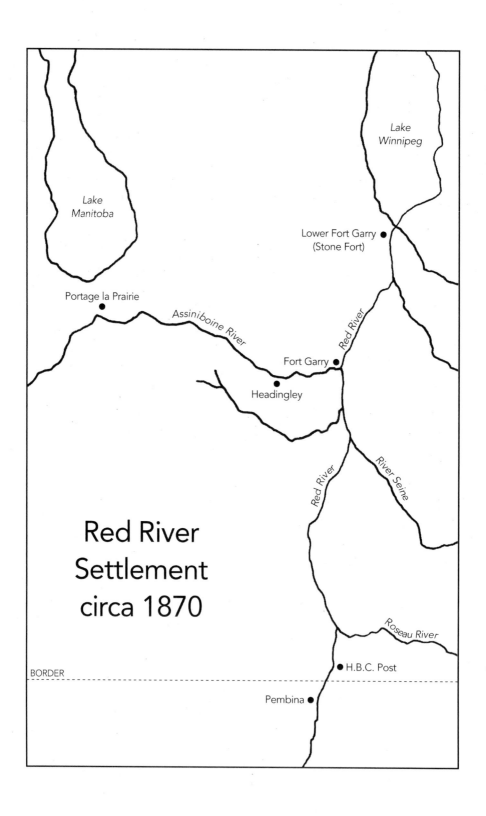

Lake Winnipeg

Lake Manitoba

Lower Fort Garry (Stone Fort) ●

Portage la Prairie ●

Assiniboine River

Red River

Fort Garry ●

● Headingley

Red River

River Seine

Red River Settlement circa 1870

Roseau River

BORDER

● H.B.C. Post

Pembina ●

COMMISSIONER: The second session of the Inquiry into the career of Louis Riel is now underway. Mr. Riel, we have already examined your trial for the insurrection at Batoche in 1885, but there have also been a number of earlier parliamentary and senate hearings concerning the insurrection in Red River in 1869–70. In that case you were also accused of treason, commencing with your refusal of permission to Mr. William McDougall, a British subject under orders of the Canadian government, to enter British territory as the lieutenant-governor of the Assiniboia Territory. You were further accused of driving him away by force of arms: disallowing the Queen's representative access to the Realm, hence treason. In short, Mr. Riel, you were accused of fomenting a rebellion, trampling underfoot all law and order and preventing British subjects from entering or passing through British territory. You have been accused of acts of treason, robbery and murder. How say you to these charges?

RIEL: Before going into the details of the accusations against me, I want to deal with the root causes of our resistance to Canadian colonial policy, leading to the Manitoba insurrection of 1869–70. We Métis of Red River and, for that matter, the whole North-West, have always been a strongly independent people. Settling on the plains during the era of the fur trade, living with the many Indigenous peoples, working for and with the French, and then the Canadian traders of the North West Company (Nor'Westers), our life was good. All the while, our hunters followed the buffalo and trapped for furs while our women raised strong, healthy children on our riverfront lots. By the late 1700s, based on the customs and traditions of both our parents' peoples — the Indians and the French — we had our own prairie civilization. God looked after us, and we praised him for our good life.

After the British-American War of 1812, we Métis of the Great North-West were caught up in the territorial and economic aggression of the fur trade wars between the North West Company and the Hudson's Bay Company. It is well known that by the early years of the 19th century our homeland was playing an important role in the provisioning networks of the North West Company. Eager to obtain Métis pemmican, the nutritious mix of dried buffalo meat, fat and berries, the Nor'Westers put up a provision post at Pembina, in today's Dakota Territory, as far back as the 1790s. With the 1809 establishment of Fort Gibraltar at the forks of the Red and Assiniboine Rivers, today's Winnipeg, the North West Company held the gateway to the West. This key location provided a huge advantage over their Hudson's Bay Company competition. All of this did not sit well with the Hudson's Bay Company, with its Royal monopoly over all trade and commerce in the so-called Rupert's Land, and there was a battle royal between the two companies.

At about this time, the fifth Earl of Selkirk, a Scottish nobleman with philanthropic tendencies, purchased a major interest in the Hudson's Bay Company, later acquiring 116,000 square miles of land in the Company's Assiniboia Territory. Here, on our Red River homelands surrounding "the forks," he attempted to establish a colony of mainly impoverished Scottish crofters. Through the first winter of 1812, Selkirk's settlers, with little in the way of provisions or shelter, survived through the generosity of the Métis. Thereafter, the establishment of a settlement on our lands, and the attempted imposition of a Hudson's Bay Company governor, created conditions of increasing tension. In January 1814, with food still in short supply, Miles Macdonell, Selkirk's governor, issued a proclamation forbidding the export of provisions from the colony, especially pemmican. With Macdonell's edict directly cutting into the North West Company's trade, the Nor'Westers retaliated, and in the summer of 1815 they sacked the Hudson's Bay Company's Brandon House. In return, the Hudson's Bay Company destroyed Fort Gibraltar. The Nor'Westers then burnt the crops and homes of Selkirk's settlers, sending them north to the lands at the south end of Lake Winnipeg.

In 1816, Selkirk brought in reinforcements and a new governor, with plans to repopulate his wrecked colony. Amongst the settlers were retired Swiss military men who acted as Selkirk's police, restricting our buffalo hunts and production of pemmican. With pemmican the life-blood of the fur-trade and our livelihood, we now actively fought this expansion. Under the leadership of Cuthbert Grant, captain general of all the Métis, we defended our national territory, and our economy. A battle ensued at a point known as La Grenouillère (Seven Oaks). Transporting North West Company supplies and pelts, Cuthbert Grant was confronted by Hudson's Bay Company Governor Semple and a number of his men. When Semple sent for his cannon, gunfire erupted and Semple and many of his men were killed.

That decisive battle became a rallying point for our people. Defending our sovereignty, we now saw ourselves as a nation able to defend itself: a prairie nation with a common territory, customs, languages and economic interests. Commemorating our independence, Pierre Falcon, the Métis balladeer, composed and sang "Chanson de la Grenouillère," known in English as "The Ballad of Seven Oaks." It remains our Métis national anthem.

With the amalgamation of the North West Company and the Hudson's Bay Company in 1821, we Métis and our English-speaking cousins, parochially known as the "half-breeds," became the very backbone of the Hudson's Bay Company's fur empire. In 1836 Governor-in-Chief George Simpson moved the Hudson's Bay Company headquarters to our colony on Red River. Thereafter, the community grew rapidly while a governor and council, appointed by the governor and committee in London, oversaw us. Its factors (managers) employed us and finally, as I will prove, its board of governors sold us like cattle to the Canadians.

With the coming of Hudson's Bay Company governance, our North-West peoples went to work for the Company as labourers, where they suffered the slings and arrows of racial discrimination, and knew from whence it came. The English concept of racial differences breeds discrimination, and it was used to subjugate and defraud us. Charges of "stupid" or "dirty drunks" or "lazy breeds" have been used wherever and whenever we complained over wages or working conditions. It is of note that the racial card was played when the Company was challenged, such as when James Sinclair led the boat brigades on strike. However, if material assistance was needed, we are then the wisest, kindest, strongest people in the universe. When Anglos and Scots castigate us, they need to remember that we have long been successfully settled on this land, bringing up our children to be skilled in the ways and means of our prairie life. They may not all read and write, but they are productive members of the community.

COMMISSIONER: Mr. Riel, at your trial you made numerous references to your close connections to your Métis nation and your family, as well as the Métis homeland. Please provide this Inquiry with the background of your family history in the North-West.

RIEL: I am most honoured to tell you of myself and my people. I was born on October 22, 1844, on the east bank of the Red River, close to St. Boniface, in the Assiniboia Territory, then under the rule of the Hudson's Bay Company. My ancestry dates back seven generations. My forefather Jean-Baptiste Riel, *dit l'Irlande*, left Normandy in 1660, lived in Ireland for forty-four years and arrived in New France in 1704. Our family followed the fur trade over the generations and my father, Louis Riel Sr., the son of Jean-Baptiste Riel and Marguerite Boucher, was born at Ile-à-la Crosse in the Saskatchewan in 1817. My grandmother was a Franco-Chipewyan Métisse. My beautiful mother, Julie Lagimodière, was the daughter of Jean-Baptiste Lagimodière, a French Canadian who made his living as a *coureur de bois*, and Marie-Anne Gaboury, the first white woman to settle in the Canadian West.

Raised in a deeply religious home, I was brought up in an atmosphere of Godliness, dignity and understanding, with a great respect for my father's achievements in the name of his people, and a great faith in my mother and her devotion to God's miraculous ways. In 1858, Bishop Taché sent me to Montreal with the aim of training me for the priesthood. He also sent my classmates, Daniel McDougall and Louis Schmidt, to Quebec to be educated. Daniel was sent to Nicolet; my dear friend Louis, who would be the first secretary of our provisional government, was sent to St. Hyacinth. I was sent to the Sulpician Collège de Montréal where I received a classical education: Latin, Greek, French,

English, philosophy and the sciences, as well as religious studies. As a lad I gained my love of poetry and have found great peace in its composition. To my eternal sorrow, my father died in St. Boniface in 1864, while I was away at college. It was upon my dear father's death that Bishop Taché became my "second father," hence his anger at my decision to forgo the priesthood and leave school.

My father had been a hunter and a trapper before establishing his grist mill on the little Seine River, near St. Boniface in our old Red River Settlement. A member of Le Comité national des Métis de la rivière Rouge (the Métis National Committee), father was a leader in the struggle against the arbitrary political and economic powers of the Hudson's Bay Company. The Company monopolized prices and continually sought to repress independent fur traders operating on what they considered their company's territory. This was our homeland.

Father's goal was to break open the fur trade monopoly of the Hudson's Bay Company. It all came to a head when the Métis free-trader Guillaume Sayer was found guilty of illicit possession of furs in 1849. Father, at the head of three hundred armed men, had his people surround the Company's court, all the while shouting, "*Le commerce est libre! Le commerce est libre!*" (Free trade! Free trade!). With his courthouse surrounded, the judge wisely found an error in the proceedings and Sayer was declared not guilty and released without penalty. Thereafter, the Company's courts were no longer able to restrict the right to free trade. Consequently, we Métis gained the right to sell our furs and pemmican to the highest bidder rather than only at the Company's store.

Father also insisted that the Company's Council of Assiniboia have Métis representation, and that the courts of Red River employ the French language. In 1850, he and Le Comité national des Métis de la rivière Rouge demanded the removal of the Hudson's Bay Company official Adam Thom, the "Recorder of Rupert's Land," for his arbitrary, racially tinged judgements and his refusal to use the French language, which he knew, and the duties of his office required. In a special meeting of the Council of Assiniboia, HBC Governor George Simpson removed Thom from active duty and, for the first time, agreed to Métis representation on the Council of Assiniboia. Opening up a new chapter in our Métis history, my father's accomplishments were historic. I treasure his memory and his life. Truly he was a Métis son of God.

In 1864–65 I removed myself from my priestly studies in search of a job. My father had died and I had been a ward of the Church since age twelve. I needed my independence. That year was an electrifying year as Quebec was the centre of great excitement and controversy. It was the time of the Canadian Confederation debates and I found employment in the Montreal law firm of Toussaint-Antoine-Rodolphe Laflamme. I spent the next whirlwind year as a law clerk under the flamboyant Rodolphe Laflamme. An ardent French-Canadian nationalist, deeply opposed to Confederation, Laflamme and his associates had a profound distrust of the Quebec hierarchy of the Roman Catholic Church, and an even deeper distrust of the Canada West politician and co-premier of the United Province of Canada, John A. Macdonald, an Orangeman and an alcoholic.

Fascinated with politics, I became acquainted through my Laflamme association with the personalities, procedures and machinations involved in the proposed Canadian Confederation. I readily admit that I did not agree with Laflamme's assessment of Confederation as a compact between Anglo-Canada and the senior officials of the Roman Catholic Church. From personal experience over the intervening years, however, my assessment of this relationship has changed significantly. Laflamme's position was that the strong support for the Confederation scheme by the Catholic Church set the tone. It tended to drown out critical analysis of Confederation's terms. It was all orchestrated by the architect of Canadian Confederation, John A. Macdonald.

It is at this point in my declaration that I must recognize the qualities of the man who became my adversary, John A. Macdonald. It is impossible to speak about Canadian Confederation without speaking of him. Truly, he is the first Father of Confederation. Quite rightly, Macdonald is recognized as the man whose determination and courage confederated four of Britain's North American colonies: Canada West and Canada East (which were to become Ontario and Quebec) and New Brunswick and Nova Scotia. The Confederation of Canada on July 1, 1867, was a momentous achievement by Macdonald, who was also created Knight Commander of the Bath, becoming Sir John A. Macdonald.

It is to be noted as well that Macdonald was already thinking in the long term: to purchase the North-West Territories from the Hudson's Bay Company; to bring the other maritime colonies into his Confederation; and to entice the Pacific colony, British Columbia, with his plan for a transcontinental railway within ten years. Sometime later, in 1881, Macdonald was proud to say that when his scheme is carried out, "the steamer landing at Halifax will discharge its freight and emigrants upon a British railway, which will go through Quebec, and through Ontario to the Far West, on British territory, under the British flag, under Canadian laws."

In order to achieve this new Canada, Macdonald also established the conditions to accelerate the disenfranchisement of the Indigenous inhabitants of British North America — from coast to coast. Consolidating the patchwork of colonial legislation passed since the old province of Canada approved the assimilationist Gradual Civilization Act in 1857, Prime Minister Macdonald had his new Canadian Parliament pass the Gradual Enfranchisement Act of 1869 which was later transformed into the now notorious Indian Act of 1876. This act, a culmination of all of the past laws, disenfranchising and subjugating the Indigenous nations, declared that Indians could not be in lawful possession of any land without a permit from the minister.

This interference in the affairs of the Indigenous nations and their right to their hereditary lands was contrary to the Royal Proclamation of 1763 recognizing Indigenous rights in British North America, and the subsequent treaties made between Britain and the Indigenous nations — treaties that were often made in order to gain Indigenous military support during the inter-colonial wars with the French and the Americans. It is my position that it is fundamental for Canada to fully recognize Indigenous ownership of traditional lands based both on hereditary and legal right, as these rights predate the Canadian Confederation and had been guaranteed by the British monarchy and legal system.

Moreover, when I use the term "Indigenous," I also include my Métis people, as is the common practice today. Yet, none of this crucial matter of entitlement to the land was a concern to the pragmatic Macdonald and the eager Canadian colonialists. With the passage of the Indian Act, which has since been updated and revised with ever more draconian measures, the Indian nations and peoples lost their independence and became "wards" of the fledgling Canadian state.

Having observed the first stage of the Confederation of Canada, I decided that I had completed my eastern education, and I began my journey home, spending some time in Chicago with the poet and journalist Louis Frechette. Here I learned of life in the new post-Civil War American hub of immigration and industry. Chicago was the microcosm of the new capital-intensive industrial America, home to vast fortunes as well as working class and racial struggles. Most interesting to me, the National Convention of the Republican Party of the United States was held in Chicago in 1868. After being the Union commander in the Civil War, General Ulysses S. Grant was nominated for President. After the cataclysm of the Civil War, Grant won the election that followed. He captured the dreams of the American people with his acceptance speech: "Let us have peace."

I certainly hoped so, but going on to St. Paul, back amongst my extended Métis family, I learned first-hand how their lives had changed since I was last here as a boy saying goodbye to my father. Peace would not happen in the North-West. Their old way of life — trapping, trading and transporting, the life of my father — was coming to an end. They also had stories of the horrors that had occurred some years earlier when the American Indian Wars had crossed the Mississippi. In what has come to be known as the "Minnesota Uprising" of 1862, the Santee Sioux, who had been abused and tricked onto an inadequate reservation with little or no food, rose in anger. Minnesota Governor Alexander Ramsey, a famous old "Injun fighter" and land expropriator, called on federal forces to intervene. As the Civil War was raging at the time, the governor enlisted his close ally and associate, former governor Brigadier General Henry H. Sibley, another hardened annexationist, to drive out or kill all Sioux in Minnesota. When President Lincoln had sent troops to quell the violence, the federal army, assisted by Sibley's Minnesota volunteers, defeated the Sioux at the Battle of Wood Lake. The remaining warriors were forced to surrender. Their subsequent trials were a fraud and gave no attention to the injustices the Indians had suffered on the reservations. Despite pleas for mercy, in the largest mass hanging in American history, thirty-eight Dakota Sioux, including some Métis warriors, were hanged at one drop.

These horrors had had a devastating effect on all Indigenous peoples in the American West. For the Métis, the old transportation route, that is to say, the Red River cart trail, was severed, causing a loss of income and blocking transportation to Pembina and beyond. Across the United States, wars big and small raged as Ulysses S. Grant had his U.S. cavalry expanding its chain of forts farther and farther west in preparation for the construction of the Northern Pacific and other railways.

With an ever-increasing American population moving westward, our Métis people, who had been the backbone of the old fur economy, were becoming redundant. Steamers and rail transportation were expanding rapidly. The American Métis were no longer needed, or treated with respect. Where a vibrant multi-ethnic, multilingual civilization had existed for decades, racism now ruled. For me, it was time to go home; my education was complete.

COMMISSIONER: Mr. Riel, you asked this Inquiry to review your career in what was to become Manitoba. Did you lead a rebellion in the Red River in 1869–70?

RIEL: I did not lead a rebellion in the Red River in 1869–70. This question goes to the very heart of my career, my being. I appreciate the opportunity to finally prove that I was not a "rebel" against Canada, but fully justified in leading my people in a democratic insurrection, as we had no sovereign government to which we owed allegiance, and we had every right to establish one of our own.

I arrived home to my Red River Settlement of St. Boniface on July 26, 1868. I was twenty-four years old, classically educated, somewhat conversant in the law, and ready to support my widowed mother and my younger brothers and sisters. It took no time at all to see that, as elsewhere, life in our Red River Settlement was no longer as it had been. The American Civil War and the Sioux War, which drove refugee Sioux, including the great Chief White Cloud (Mahaska) to the

"Grandmother's Land," had been the cataclysmic events of the last decade. Although geographically isolated, we Métis and the other residents of Red River were not immune to the influences of the outside world.

The new era in our North-West really began in 1856 when British financial interests and Britain's Canadian colony of the Province of Canada began manoeuvring against the Hudson's Bay Company's Charter bestowed by Charles II upon his cousin Rupert back in 1670. In 1857 the British government appointed a "select committee to consider the state of British Possessions in North America presently under the administration of the Hudson's Bay Company." The findings of the select committee were favourable to the ceding of certain portions of the Hudson's Bay Company's territories, in particular, the two most fertile areas, the Red River and Saskatchewan Valleys, to the Canadians. In 1858 the combined Canada West and Canada East (Cartier-Macdonald) government dispatched a delegation to London to press for federation of the Canadian colonies, including the North-West. With British financial interests concurring, Canadian Confederation was inevitable. Most unfortunately, the inhabitants of the North-West were not consulted on any of this.

We, the Métis, had worked out a functioning relationship with the Hudson's Bay Company dating back to 1821, when the amalgamation of the old North West Company and the Hudson's Bay Company took place. As I have explained, this relationship was not always smooth, as was the case when, in 1848–49, my father forced the Company to concede a limited political role and certain property rights to our people. Thereafter, we accepted the Company's Council of Assiniboia as the legislative body of the land and the Company's quarterly General Court as our judiciary. As long as the Company did not interfere with our basic interests, we never seriously challenged their right to administer the affairs of state or act as our chief supplier of trade goods. The Company had functionaries looking after the making and upkeep of roads, they collected customs duties and looked after the mails. It was, you could say, endowed with practically all the machinery necessary to the good administration of a civilized community.

A major change occurred in our area in 1863, although once again the inhabitants of the North-West had no indication of the change. A cartel of largely British financial interests, aptly named the International Finance Society (IFS), purchased the stock of the Hudson's Bay Company. The IFS set the value of the stock at £2,000,000 (pounds sterling). This sum represented the trading assets as well as the real estate holdings of the Hudson's Bay Company in the Great North-West. They purchased the Company "lock, stock and barrel," as the phrase goes. Unlike the old staid Company, they had grand plans for the future. Initially, they planned to carry on the operation of the fur trade, but they also planned the colonization of the fertile areas and the establishment of major communication links with the Pacific, including a telegraph and, although not officially stated, a rail system. This was definitely the end of the old regime.

The purchase of our homelands by this financial syndicate occurred at the height of the American Civil War, a time of high anxiety in both Britain and in Britain's North American colonies. It was at this time as well, while I was still a student in Montreal that, with the support of the financial establishment and the British colonial office, the Canadian vice-premier of the British Province of Canada, John A. Macdonald, publicly proposed the confederation of the Canadian colonies. This idea was immensely popular in London, Ottawa and Toronto, but not so in Montreal or Quebec. Militarily, it provided a broader population base for defence. Economically, this plan provided the individual colonies with broader "British," in other words non-American, markets through internal trade. Politically, it provided a stronger administrative unit.

And last, but not least, it provided an entity large enough to construct a key piece of infrastructure: a British North American transcontinental railroad that would allow access to the huge, alluring prairie lands to the west! With the American war in the background, Macdonald skillfully moulded a coalition and successfully lobbied colonial leaders towards a new British confederation in North America. Setting forth the legal ground rules for the new country of "Canada," the British North America Act of 1867 passed the British House of Commons, providing the new federation composed of the new provinces of Ontario, Quebec,

New Brunswick and Nova Scotia, with two main levels of government — provincial and federal.

Most importantly for the peoples of Rupert's Land, who had not been invited to or attended the Confederation conferences, under Section 146 of the British North America Act, Rupert's Land and the North-West Territory were to be admitted to the Canadian Confederation "under terms to be arranged." John A. Macdonald's plan was to replace the Hudson's Bay Company's government in the North-West Territories with a Canadian colonial government. Almost immediately he began negotiations with the colonial office and the new owners of the Hudson's Bay Company for possession of Rupert's Land. These negotiations were held under a cloak of secrecy. In April 1868, William McDougall and George-Étienne Cartier, ministers of the new Canadian government, went to London to complete the negotiations and transfer of the North-West to Canada.

The new owner of the Hudson's Bay Company, the International Finance Society, was in an excellent position. The "sale" of the North-West Territories to Canada, financed by London, would compensate them for their charter lands and remove the burden and expense of governing the Red River Settlement. Shrewd negotiations would also allow them to retain and develop extensive commercial and real estate rights across the West. After some initial haggling, the Company agreed to dispose of its rights and privileges for a "token" cash payment and "other privileges." The Privy Council in London and the directors of the Hudson's Bay Company, also in London, quickly ratified the terms of the agreement between the Hudson's Bay Company and Canada:

> The Canadian Government shall pay to the Company the sum of £300,000 when Rupert's Land is transferred to the Dominion of Canada.
>
> The Hudson's Bay Company to retain one-twentieth of the land in the fertile belt [the southern territories], with an additional 50,000 acres in the vicinity of the Company's trading posts; The Company to retain all the posts or stations now actually possessed or occupied by them . . . and may within twelve months after the acceptance of the said surrender select a block of land adjoining each of their posts or stations. . . .

The Company may, at any time within fifty years after such acceptance of the said surrender, claim in any township or district within the fertile belt in which land is set out for settlements, grants of land not exceeding one twentieth part of the land so set out. For the purpose of the last Article, the fertile belt is to be bounded as follows:

On the south by the United States boundary; on the west by the Rocky Mountains; on the north by the Northern Branch of the Saskatchewan River; on the east by Lake Winnipeg, the Lake of the Woods and the waters connecting them.

The Hudson's Bay Company to retain the right to carry on its trade without hindrance or "exceptional" taxation.

This agreement, known as the "Deed of Surrender," was signed November 19, 1869, and was initially to go into effect October 1, 1869, but altered to December 1, 1869 owing to a delay in making the necessary financial arrangements. It would be altered again in what would be the most crucial period for our survival as a free people.

Secret negotiations! It was outrageous! Even the old "wintering partners," the chief traders, men who over the past two hundred years had made the Hudson's Bay Company one of the richest commercial enterprises in the world, knew nothing of the sale. These "factors," men who had been the "Lords and Masters of the North-West," were now treated no better than the lowest company servant. Neither they, nor we, the actual inhabitants of the land, were informed of the negotiations until after the sale was completed.

Upon the completion of the sale of the North-West, the Canadian Parliament adopted an "Act for the Temporary Government of Rupert's Land." This Act called for a government by a lieutenant-governor and council with the power to make provision for the administration of justice, and generally to make, ordain and establish all such laws, institutions and ordinances as may be necessary for peace, order and good government. The Honourable William McDougall was to be dispatched to rule the North-West Territory as lieutenant-governor. He was to assume his new responsibilities as of December 1, 1869.

Our concern was not so much with the concept of joining in a British North American union, as with being bought and sold like cattle, especially by and to the Canadians. This legislation denied the democratic rights of citizenship to the actual residents of the land. It did not guarantee property rights or the use of traditional rights and customs already established in the territory. It smacked of Canadian colonialism. In my opinion, it is a crucial point in international law to recognize that once the Hudson's Bay Company withdrew from administrative control of Rupert's Land, the Indian and Métis nations had right of succession — in other words, the right to repossess their hereditary homelands. They and other long-term residents also had the right to self-determination, the right to choose a form of governance acceptable to themselves. The agreement between the Hudson's Bay Company and the Canadian government was to dispose of land rights claimed by a trading monopoly and an administrative regime that were not recognized as binding by the people already living there.

It is my contention that this sale was "illegal." Although, under its charter, the Hudson's Bay Company claimed ownership of all lands known as Rupert's Land, this was not the case; in fact, they exercised only the right of stewardship. The Hudson's Bay Company, which had been the de facto administrator of the land, had in fact no moral right to enter into negotiations with the Canadian government. Contrary to the Eurocentric 1493 Papal Bull of Discovery, the so-called Doctrine of Discovery, the Company's claim to ownership was never valid. The native peoples possessed the land before the coming of the Hudson's Bay Company, and they possessed it after the coming of the Hudson's Bay Company. We Métis, through "mother right," shared the natural right of ownership as heirs to our native land.

The recognition by this Inquiry of the sovereignty and right of self-government possessed by the Amerindian peoples since before the age of European discovery and colonial expansion is a critical component to the eventual healing of the Canadian nation. My fundamental position is that European occupation of the New World, based upon the assumption that the original inhabitants were incapable of ownership of the land, is a racist conception used to justify the occupation and theft of the land. We, Indians and Métis, are indigenous to this land and as such possess the right to self-government and self-determination.

COMMISSIONER: Mr. Riel, with Canada passing the bill allowing for the temporary government of Rupert's Land and the imposition of a Canadian lieutenant-governor, you have also expressed concern regarding the actions and behaviour of a group of Ontario immigrants known as the "Canadian Party." Please provide this Inquiry with a review of your concerns.

RIEL: The experience of our community with a number of Ontario-based Canadian settlers had not been good. By the late 1860s, this new group had increased in number to about six hundred. Protestant immigrants from Upper Canada, they were known locally as the "Canadian Party." They entered the North-West strongly opposed to the Hudson's Bay Company and its monopoly. Unlike the original peoples, however, they were strongly in favour of the annexation of Red River and the North-West to Canada. Also, unlike the producing peoples of the North-West, they, as pointed out by the Right Reverend A.G. Morice, OMI, suffered from "that great mischief-maker," that "many headed hydra and mental disease, prejudice." In fact their ideological mentor, the so-called "Canadian poet" Charles Mair, was publicly horsewhipped by a prominent Métis woman for his slanderous, racist comments about Métis women. As pointed out by Rev. Morice, this group had come to the North-West with one purpose in mind: "Their avowed object was to do away with that patriarchal state and annex the country to the newly formed confederation."

The leader of the Canadian Party was Dr. Christian Schultz, who arrived in the Red River in 1861. Initially, he advertised himself as a physician and surgeon, although no indication that he actually graduated or ever held a license to practise medicine has yet to be found. An Ontario Orangeman, Schultz was a founder and grand master of the Northern Light Masonic Lodge. He also ran a trading post on the outskirts of the community. For a time he was also the editor of the vitriolic little Canadian newspaper, *Nor'Wester*, where he declared: "It was from Ontario this movement to add Red River to the Dominion commenced. It is to Ontario the territory belongs."

Prior to the Hudson's Bay Company's transfer of its charter lands to Canada, Dr. Schultz and his companions were most interested in the complete destruction and repudiation of Company rule. In February 1867, Schultz was fined £300 for illegal trade, a fine he refused to pay. In January 1868, the sheriff, with a posse, went to Schultz's trading post to seize his goods. Schultz and the Canadians resisted, and both sheriff and posse were ejected. Later, Schultz was arrested and jailed in the Hudson's Bay Company lock-up at Upper Fort Garry.

Interrupting my testimony, I feel it is important that I ensure the Inquiry is cognizant of the fact that there are two forts called "Fort Garry" in the area now known as Winnipeg. At present, we are referring to Schultz being held at Upper Fort Garry, colloquially known as "Fort Garry," located at the forks of the Red and Assiniboine Rivers. This fort is not to be confused with Lower Fort Garry, known as the "Stone Fort," located some distance north on the banks of the Red River.

In a daring evening assault on Fort Garry, tearing down the jail walls and battering in the lock-up door, Schultz's friends released him. After this episode, the Hudson's Bay Company was completely unable to preserve law and order. Schultz's jailbreaking went unpunished, and thereafter he considered himself not only above the law — but to be the law himself.

Those years, the late 1860s, were a period of drought and depression on the Great Plains. The massive northern herd of buffalo was greatly diminished due to the lack of fodder, and grasshoppers and other pests destroyed our crops two years in a row. Famine was near. To relieve the shortages, the Hudson's Bay Company gave £8,000 credit at its stores, the U.S. government sent $4,000 cash, Quebec sent $3,000 and the Ontario government promised $5,000. This Ontario money was never delivered. Instead of cash, at the very time that Canada and the Hudson's Bay Company were completing the sale of the North-West, the Canadian government used the money to send in two survey crews and a road-building crew to begin construction of the "Dawson Road" to be constructed between the Red River Settlement and the Lake of the

Woods in Ontario. This road was to be Canada's contribution to the desperately needed relief program.

Early in 1869, our shock over the sale of the North-West to Canada turned to anger with the entry into our community of the Canadian survey crews. Led by Lieutenant Colonel John Stoughton Dennis and Captain C.A. Boulton, two Canadian military men, these crews immediately drew our suspicion. Dennis was already well known as the Canadian officer who led his militia troops in the "Fort Erie Disaster," a botched operation against the Irish-American Fenian invasion of Ontario in 1866. In that instance, Dennis had been accused of leading his men into a trap and deserting them under fire. When the Canadian road crew descended upon our community, we were shocked. They were a wild bunch, an unruly mob that spent most of their time drinking and brawling amongst themselves. In one dispute, one of their members, Thomas Scott, attempted to drown his supervisor, John Snow. This road project was supposed to provide jobs for local people and circulate cash in the Red River colony. However, the local people who found work clearing brush and doing the hard labour received their pay in "chits," which could be exchanged only at Schultz's store.

With the news of Canada purchasing the North-West and this new Canadian presence in the community, I accompanied a Métis delegation that met with the governor of the colony, William Mactavish of the Hudson's Bay Company. We pointed out that, although loyal to the British Crown, we were protesting the imposition of a Canadian government without consultation. I reminded the governor that the Canadians did not have the right to send surveyors or road crews into our community, since no official connection existed at present between our community and the new Canadian Confederation. Governor Mactavish assured our delegation that he would inform his superiors of our sentiments, but that there was nothing he could do to stop the Canadian surveys or road construction.

With further Canadian intrusions and disturbances, the Métis population grew angrier at the Canadians' presence. Well aware of our sentiments, Colonel Dennis reported back to the Canadian government that "a considerable degree of irritation exists among the native population, in view of surveys and settlements being made without the Indian title having been extinguished . . . the uneasy feeling which exists in the half-breeds . . . with regard to what they conceive to be premature action taken by the government."

After a series of meetings in our community, with the call going out to rekindle the Métis National Movement, Dennis again wrote to Ottawa: "You will, no doubt, have become aware that the half-breeds lately in a public meeting called the Company here to account in the matter of the money paid for the transfer to Canada. . . . Whatever may have been the views of the government as to the character of the title to be conveyed by the deed of transfer . . . I am satisfied that the government will, in the first place, have to undertake and effect the extinction of the Indian title. This question must be regarded as of the very greatest importance."

The situation deteriorated rapidly with the *Nor'Wester* telling its readership that when Canada assumed sovereignty "the tenure of land is precisely the same with the new-comer as it is with the Hudson's Bay Company, you hold as much as you occupy. . . . The wise and prudent . . . will be prepared to receive and benefit by them whilst the indolent and careless, like the native tribes of the country, will fall back before the march of a superior intelligence." Much to our anger, the Canadian Party then proceeded to carry out this policy.

James Stewart, a Canadian, staked a claim in a block of land directly adjacent to Fort Garry, while members of the road-building crew claimed land at Sainte Anne des Chênes. John Snow, the superintendent of the road crew, along with Christian Schultz then claimed traditional Métis pasturing lands at Oak Point. This transaction was taken to the Company court and Snow was fined for bribing Indians with liquor to sign over this land.

As our citizens became more and more concerned with the outlandish behaviour of the Canadians, I attended meetings being held in the community. As one who had lived in the "outside," I was asked to assist in these matters, much as my father had in 1848–49. Whereas my father had played a key role in breaking the oppression of the fur-trade monopoly and opening up a position for the Métis on the Hudson's Bay

Company's Council of Assiniboia, I slowly began to realize that my role would be to lead our people in the struggle for nationhood and justice — against an even more aggressive foe than the Hudson's Bay Company. Our new foe was the hybrid coming out of the Canadian Confederation: "Anglo-Canadian colonialism."

COMMISSIONER: Mr. Riel, please provide this Inquiry with your mandate to resist, under arms, the imposition of a Canadian lieutenant-governor.

RIEL: Yes, certainly. I would like now to introduce the "great pretender," Mr. William McDougall, minister of public works in the Canadian Cabinet in 1869. Under instructions from Prime Minister Macdonald, McDougall was in charge of the Dawson Road project, and much more. I would like to enter into evidence the instructions from Macdonald to William McDougall:

> I now request you to proceed without delay to Fort Garry, Red River, for the purpose, as explained to you, of selecting the most suitable localities for the survey of townships for immediate settlement. The American system of survey is that which appears best suited to the country, except as to the area of the section. The first emigrants, and the most desirable, will probably go from Canada, and it will therefore be advisable to offer them lots of a size to which they have become accustomed. This will require you to make the section 800 acres instead of 640, as on the American plan.

Macdonald was ignoring completely that our Métis farms were already established. Composed of long, narrow lots, each with river frontage, extending back a mile and then on to common hay meadows, our riverfront farms follow the traditions of our ancestors and the seigneurial properties of Quebec. With his directive to McDougall, calling on him to send twenty surveyors into the Red River colony, Macdonald planned to impose the American survey system (only with sections of 800 acres and not 640), overtop of our farms, although he later admitted: "We had no authority until the transfer to make surveys at all."

Beginning in the rural areas, the survey crews moved ever closer to the Métis communities until they began trespassing onto our hay meadows. With these intrusions, we decided to stop the survey from cutting across properties already in existence. On October 11, 1869, I and a group of eighteen men stopped a crew of surveyors on the property of André Nault. Putting my foot on the survey chain, I told the surveyor, Captain Webb, "You go no further!" When he protested, I told him the Canadian government had no right to survey our lands, and that they were to get off this land immediately. That night, Captain Dennis reported to Ottawa that "Captain Webb was stopped in his surveying operations by a party of men . . . having projected the base-line mentioned easterly from the meridian to within about three miles of the Red River [St. Vital]."

Regarding this incident, for which I have been criticized, it is my desire that this Inquiry recognize that Louis Riel, André Nault and the Métis National Committee were defending their basic rights when they stopped the illegal Canadian survey on the farm of Mr. Nault and that these surveys amounted to criminal trespass in violation of the civil and common rights of the inhabitants indigenous to this land.

Shortly after our protest, the "Honourable" William McDougall was dispatched on the journey of his lifetime. I would like to put into evidence McDougall's commission from Prime Minister Macdonald:

> We do hereby constitute and appoint you on, from and after the day to be named by us [December 1, 1869] to take possession of the North-West Territories as the Canadian lieutenant-governor of Rupert's Land.

Let it be noted by this Inquiry that, until the date of transfer, William McDougall had no official rights in our Red River colony except as a private citizen.

With no Canadian route through and across the Canadian Shield of western Ontario, Lieutenant-Governor designate William McDougall was forced to travel by rail through the eastern United States to St. Paul, Minnesota. Here he hired carters and drivers in preparation for his trip to the British North-West. Through the "moccasin telegraph," the carters, mostly Métis, reported that McDougall's "ready-made government" was armed with over three hundred rifles and crates of ammunition.

In light of this news, on October 16, 1869, we, the concerned citizens and Métis patriots, officially reconvened Le Comité national des Métis de la rivière Rouge. John Bruce was elected president and I was requested to act as secretary. As of old, the Comité met, taking up the defence of our people and organizing opposition to the seizure of our homelands. Our first order of business was to prevent the establishment of McDougall's Canadian government. On October 20, 1869, with the news of McDougall's imminent arrival at Pembina on the American side of the international border, the Comité sent a member of our executive, Ambroise Lépine, armed with a warning to McDougall from the Comité. We advised him not to enter our country without special permission. I enter that notice for your attention:

Wm. McDougall Esq.

Sir: The National Committee of the Métis of Red River orders Mr. William McDougall not to enter the Territory of the Northwest without special permission of this Committee.

By order of the President, John Bruce

After this, following the age-old custom of the buffalo hunt, Ambroise Lépine and a brigade of armed men on horseback, a Métis cavalry, erected barricades where the trail from Pembina crossed the La Salle River and also at St. Norbert. With these bold moves, we took control of our destiny, effectively blocking McDougall's access to our Red River community. The outraged McDougall and his entourage, including a number of wives, were forced to "hole-up" in the shanties of Pembina.

The Canadian Party in Red River was also outraged. On October 25, 1869, Hudson's Bay Company Governor Mactavish convened a meeting of his Council of Assiniboia. John Bruce and I were summoned before the council. After the minutes of the last meeting were read and approved, Judge Black stated that an official address had been prepared for the purpose of being presented to the Honourable William McDougall on his arrival in the settlement. He said that the address was prepared with the conviction that the feelings of welcome and loyalty therein expressed were concurred in by the settlement generally, or at least were so far shared by the great majority of people as to preclude all idea of open demonstration of dissent. Judge Black was now very much concerned that, unhappily, such was not the case and that a large party amongst the French population appeared to be animated by a very different spirit. He went on to say that according to information lately received by the council, we, the Métis, had organized ourselves into armed bodies for the purpose of intercepting McDougall on the road with the openly avowed intention of preventing his entry into the settlement.

When asked to reply, I stated that we were perfectly satisfied with the present government and wanted no other. I further stated that we objected to any government coming from Canada without our being consulted in the matter, and that we would never admit any governor unless delegates were previously sent with whom we might negotiate as to terms and conditions under which we would acknowledge him. I assured the council that we were acting for the good of the whole settlement and in defence of our own liberty, and that we would continue on this course until a satisfactory outcome was accomplished.

It is my wish that this Inquiry recognize that, because Governor Mactavish of the Hudson's Bay Company, the nominal ruler of the colony, refused repeatedly to prosecute elements interested in the destabilization and seizure of our community by a foreign power, and that as the Council of Assiniboia was unwilling to protect our rights, that we, the Métis, indigenous to this land, formally constituted ourselves as a representative agency of the inhabitants. This was a body tribal (the Métis National Committee) which was justified in resisting foreign authorities with no legal right of entrance or of jurisdiction. May it be further recognized that the actions of the Métis National Committee were fully justified as the Hudson's Bay Company had abrogated its authority, its agencies had become moribund, and the people were without any form of government. This account of the situation is highly significant, as it represents one of the key tenets of civilization: it is a justifiable procedure for a people without a government to form a government of their own.

COMMISSIONER: Mr. Riel, please inform this Inquiry of your intentions upon blocking Lieutenant-Governor designate McDougall and his party at the border with the United States and defying the wishes of the Canadian government and the Council of Assiniboia.

RIEL: This is one of many accusations my enemies have hurled at me over the years, especially after we created the Provisional Government. It bears on our opposition to a handover of the HBC administrative apparatus to our foes. Our position was clear: Mr. McDougall would not be allowed into the country until there were negotiations as to terms and conditions under which we would acknowledge him, not as our governor, but as a representative of the Canadian government prepared to negotiate with the Red River population.

Early on the morning of October 30, 1869, two of McDougall's Canadian military men were captured attempting to avoid our barricades. Halted, they were escorted back across the American border. From their threats and bombast, we realized an incursion was imminent. The Comité issued a call for the mobilization of the manpower of the Métis. Some five hundred men immediately reported for duty.

We understood only too well that the threat to our national sovereignty was not only external. In the English-speaking settlements, where the Canadian Party had influence, meetings were being held to oppose our position. After one of these meetings it was announced that the Dominion should assume the responsibility of establishing among us what it, and it alone, had decided upon. We noted with satisfaction that the sentiment of the English-speaking population was not wholly pro-Canadian. Amongst the long-term residents a different attitude prevailed:

> We have not been consulted in any way as a people in entering into the Dominion. The character of the new Government has been settled in Canada without our being consulted. We are prepared to accept it

respectfully, to obey its laws and to become good subjects: but when you present to us the issue of a conflict with the French party, with whom we have hitherto lived in friendship . . . we feel disinclined to enter upon it.

On November 1, 1869, Lieutenant-Governor designate William McDougall and his entourage crossed the international border, with McDougall's soldiers taking up a very threatening attitude and openly talking of seizing the seat of government, Fort Garry, at the confluence of the Red and Assiniboine Rivers. To prevent such an event, Ambroise Lépine and our Métis cavalry surrounded Mr. McDougall and his troops. Herded like buffalo into a run, they were blocked from advancing any farther and removed back to the U.S. side of the border without incident.

Our knowledge of Mr. McDougall's scheme to seize Fort Garry, which we were concerned might still be carried out, suggested to us the need for further preventive action on our part. As a result, the Comité decided that as Fort Garry was the seat of government, it was necessary for us to occupy it. On the afternoon of November 2, 1869, I led approximately 120 men through the open gates of the fort where we proceeded to billet ourselves within the fortified enclosure. When asked by Dr. Cowan, the officer in charge, the purpose of our entering the fort, I told him we had come to guard the fort against impending danger. Then I went to see old Governor Mactavish, who was ill in bed. He first complained to me of our actions, but then confided that it was a logical move. He added that he had no doubt that if I had not done it, someone else would have.

We did not seize the seat of power lightly. The inability of Mactavish and the old Council of Assiniboia to act decisively was crucial in the decision. As governor, Mactavish had attempted to govern the colony in a fair and honest fashion. He had made, and would continue to make, the necessary protests against those acts which he considered to be "undue," but from the time of Christian Schultz's jailbreaks, his administration was largely impotent, incapable of enforcing the law. Mactavish remained a loyal British governor, but he did not have the energy or resources to prevent the depredations of the Canadians prior to the sale to Canada, nor to stringently organize against our opposition to these actions. I feel that there are two explanations for this. He was not a well man, but also, as a wintering partner, he had himself been treated in a high-handed manner by both the London Board of the Hudson's Bay Company and the Canadian government.

I feel it is important for this Inquiry to understand that in my position, as the nominal head of the Métis National Committee, I was fully justified in the seizure of Fort Garry to prevent bloodshed and the seizure of the seat of government by a foreign power. We endeavoured to keep Mr. McDougall at a distance in order that his party, which was so hostile to our interests, might not under the circumstances take possession of the government of our native country. All of this was at a time when the Hudson's Bay Company was unable to hold the seat of power and had sold its right to govern.

As events unfolded, it became clear to us that practically all the long-term people of the settlement, whites and half-breeds, as well as the Métis and the French Canadians who lived amongst us, even the Hudson's Bay people, were more or less against this transfer to Canada — as it was being proposed. We also knew that the Anglo-Canadian party was circulating rumours that we Métis wished to rule our fellow inhabitants. I met this lie head on. With the full approval of the Comité we offered the English-speaking minority equality with the French-speaking Métis in all negotiations. We worked to reunite with our fellows, to ensure all were represented in any negotiations with the Canadian government. In this regard, we issued a call for a series of meetings to be held in the Red River Settlement:

> The President and Representatives of the French-speaking population of Rupert's Land in Council — the invaders of our rights being now expelled — already aware of your sympathy, do extend the hand of friendship to you our friendly fellow-inhabitants, and in doing so invite you to send twelve representatives, in order to found one body with the above Council of the French-speaking population, now consisting of twelve members, to consider the present political state of the country and to adopt such measures as may be deemed best for the future welfare of the same. A meeting of the above Council will be held in the Court

House at Fort Garry, on Tuesday, November 16, at which the representatives will attend.

By order of the President,
Louis Riel, Secretary,
Winnipeg, November 6th, 1869

With our call for a council, McDougall, now thwarted from taking control of the colony, wrote a series of letters to Governor Mactavish of the Hudson's Bay Company. His letter of November 2, 1869, the day our committee appropriated Upper Fort Garry, informed Mactavish of his ejection from Assiniboia and asked for advice. His November 4 letter called upon Mactavish to issue a proclamation against the insurgents. His letter of November 7 protested strongly against the Company's lack of opposition to the seizure of Fort Garry and announced that he would stay on the U.S. side of the border until official word of the transfer arrived. On November 9, Mactavish replied, stating:

> Measures . . . of a positively coercive nature have not been resorted to, for the simple reason that we have had no reliable force to ensure their safety and success. . . . We have been insistent in our efforts to impress upon the leaders . . . a just sense of the illegality and danger of the course upon which they have entered. . . . To the Council [of Assiniboia] and myself it appears that your early return to Canada is advisable.

At this time, with the hope of legitimizing the Canadian government with the prestige of the Governor of the Council of Assiniboia, the Canadian Party petitioned Mactavish to proclaim McDougall's rule. I remind this Inquiry that it was this same Canadian Party that had refused to obey the laws of the council in the past. Nothing came of the Canadian Party's petition, and on November 16, 1869, the first historic community meeting of the citizens of the Red River Settlement (Assiniboia) was held. Delegates were elected, twelve English-speaking, twelve French-speaking, to what became known as the Convention of Twenty-four. Meeting in the courthouse outside Fort Garry's walls, two days of work established the first historic List of Rights for Rupert's Land, which I would like to enter into the record in its entirety:

Louis Riel, age twenty-three, when he was working as a law
clerk in the office of Rodolphe Laflamme in Montreal, 1868.

Louis Riel, at age twenty-four, established the Provisional Government of Assiniboia in 1869. The following year he created the terms for the entrance of Manitoba into the Canadian Confederation.

PHOTO: 1869, GLENBOW ARCHIVES S-222-25.

Canadian Prime Minister Sir John A. Macdonald (ca. 1880s) sent
Canadian troops to block the democratic movements of Louis Riel and
the Métis in Manitoba in 1870 and Saskatchewan in 1885.

Lieutenant-Governor designate William McDougall unlawfully
declared Canadian sovereignty over the North-West Territories (Dec. 1, 1869)
and was repulsed by the Métis when he attempted, with arms, to take
control of the North-West. PHOTO: GLENBOW ARCHIVES NA-659-63.

Ambroise-Dydime Lépine, Adjutant General in the Provisional Government of Assiniboia in the late 1860s, was falsely tried for the murder of Thomas Scott and sentenced to be hanged. Although his sentence was commuted by the Governor General, his lifetime political rights were revoked.

After convening the Convention of Twenty-four and the Convention of Forty, Louis Riel with the councillors of the Provisional Government of Assiniboia (ca. 1869) was able to defend the community and bargain with Canada, nation to nation, to establish the Manitoba Act of 1870. PHOTO: GLENBOW ARCHIVES NA-1039-1.

Edgar Dewdney, Conservative politician, Indian Commissioner and
Lieutenant-Governor of the North-West Territories, was responsible for
the implementation of John A. Macdonald's disastrous colonial
policies for the native peoples in the North-West.

Naturalized as an American citizen, Louis Riel, age thirty-nine, was teaching school at St. Peter's Mission on the Sun River in Montana when he was called by his Métis people to assist with their petitions on the Saskatchewan.

LIST OF RIGHTS FOR RUPERT'S LAND
(CONVENTION OF 24) 1869

The right to elect a legislature which could override a veto by the Executive

The right to approve or reject, through the Territory's representatives, any Dominion legislation which directly affected the Territory

The right to elect sheriffs, magistrates and other local officials

A free homestead law

Land grants for schools, roads and public building

Guaranteed railroad connection with the nearest existing line

Payment of the Territory's governmental expenses for the first four years from the Dominion treasury

Recruitment of any military force to be stationed in the Territory from among people already living there

Treaties with the Indians to preserve peace

Use of the French and English languages in the legislature, in all public documents, and by judges of Superior Court

Respect for all privileges, usages and customs which had existed before the transfer of sovereignty

Full and fair representation in the Parliament of the Dominion of Canada

That all privileges, customs and usages existing at the time of the transfer be respected

I remain proud of our Convention of Twenty-four and List of Rights. While protecting the interests of virtually all elements of our unusually heterogeneous community, they laid the foundation and are the precursors to our claim to the rights of self-government, while also offering a feasible program for union with the Dominion. Moderate in tone, the reasonable demands of our List of Rights garnered our movement a good deal of support and recognition in the English-speaking districts. Key to our progress was equal English- and French-speaking representation. We now had a united position from which to bargain as equals with Canada. Although there were still many challenges to face within the settlement, except for the annexationist Canadians, we were allied around our List of Rights.

COMMISSIONER: Mr. Riel, please elaborate on the challenges you faced to create and maintain the Convention of Twenty-four.

RIEL: We suffered a minor setback on November 18, 1869, when Governor Mactavish, in an attempt to legitimize the waning HBC government, capitulated to Canadian Party pressure. He was persuaded to sign a proclamation in which he declared our actions illegal. Meant to counter our List of Rights, this proclamation opposed the measures we had taken in preventing McDougall from entering the country. It denounced our actions in billeting ourselves in Fort Garry and claimed we Métis had no right to "resist arrangements for the transfer of the government of this country . . . made under the sanction of the Imperial Parliament."

This proclamation by our former governor, with no ability to enforce his order, had little effect on our French-speaking delegates who were fully united in their determination to prevent the establishment of a foreign power without consultation. Amongst the English-speaking delegates there were setbacks and waverers. On November 22, 1869, one of the Convention, Mr. Bunn, proposed the defunct HBC Council of Assiniboia allow Mr. McDougall into the community and that we then negotiate for the acceptance of our List of Rights. I was quick to point out that although Bunn might be suspicious of the men that the Comité kept under arms, surely he was not unaware of the fact that the Council of Assiniboia is without power and that McDougall has at his disposal three hundred rifles.

It was shortly after that, on November 24, 1869, when I proposed a four-point declaration proclaiming our right to form a provisional government and enter into such negotiations with the Canadian government as may be favourable for the good government and prosperity of our people. Where I had unanimous approval by the French-speaking delegates, and generous support amongst English-speaking delegates, it passed. Amongst the English delegates, however, there were those who regarded this proposal as beyond the scope of their authority and felt obliged to consult their constituents before taking such a radical step.

With our English-speaking delegates back in their communities, Andrew G.B. Bannatyne, a well-respected independent trader and long-time member of the Council of Assiniboia, called an alternative meeting of electors, hoping to resurrect the Council of Assiniboia. He was too late as William McDougall's subsequent actions would put an end to Company rule.

COMMISSIONER: Mr. Riel, having been prevented from accessing the British North-West, the Canadian Lieutenant-Governor designate William McDougall was not unaware of your activities. What was his response to your successes in preventing his establishment of a Canadian government and your calling for the establishment of a provisional government?

RIEL: Isolated in Pembina, Dakota Territory, Mr. William McDougall was thoroughly thwarted. His attempt to enter our colony before his official powers had come into effect had been rebuffed. Expelled from our homelands, he and his retinue now had little choice but to wait for December 1, 1869, the official date for transfer of Hudson's Bay Company ownership and governance to Canada.

Awaiting receipt of his "Imperial order of transfer" to Canadian jurisdiction, McDougall kept in touch with affairs in the Red River Settlement through Charles Mair of Canada First and numerous other Canadians. He was assured that the "loyal" Canadians would rally to his new government once a Royal Proclamation had been issued, and that they would dispose of the "insurgents" in quick order.

In Ottawa, however, there was concern that McDougall's impulsiveness would lead him to exceed his authority. Ottawa knew of our earlier actions in rebuffing McDougall at the international border and did not want a repeat of the fiasco. Already on November 19, 1869, Cabinet

Minister Joseph Howe had dispatched a letter warning McDougall that "as things stand, you can claim or assert no authority in the Hudson's Bay Territory, until the Queen's proclamation, annexing the country to Canada reaches you through this office." Due to the logistics and distances involved, McDougall would not receive this letter until December 6, 1869. Likewise, in a private letter written shortly after, but not received by McDougall until the second week of December, Prime Minister Macdonald warned McDougall that "a proclamation such as you suggest . . . would be very well if it were sure to be obeyed. If however, it were disobeyed your weakness and inability to enforce the authority of the Dominion would be painfully exhibited, not only to the people of Red River, but to the people and government of the United States." Macdonald's message concluded that his Canadian government was refusing to complete the transfer at this time (December 1, 1869) and that "we have thrown the responsibility on the Imperial government."

So it was, on November 26, 1869, Prime Minister Macdonald cabled the colonial secretary in London, informing him: "Canada cannot accept North-West until peaceful possession can be given." Although taken aback over Canada's decision to delay the transfer, the colonial office decided that a "moderate delay" was necessary to prevent bloodshed and allow for a peaceable transition. No new date was set. Please note that even as John A. Macdonald passed the responsibility of administration of affairs in the North-West to the Imperial government until "peaceful possession can be given," the wily old Scot prudently instructed the Canadian agent in London to refrain from paying the £300,000 Canada owed to the Hudson's Bay Company for the transfer.

Still, with no official confirmation regarding the surrender of the Hudson's Bay Company government and acceptance of sovereignty by the Crown, on November 29, 1869, William McDougall sent notice to his prime minister that he had prepared his "Proclamation" annexing the North-West Territories to Canada. Two nights later, still without authority but blinded by ambition or stupidity, the Honourable William McDougall, accompanied by his followers, represented by Mr. Richards, Mr. Provencher and four others, crossed the snow-covered international border and rode through a raging blizzard to the door of the Hudson's Bay Company's border post. There "Lieutenant-Governor" McDougall solemnly posted and read the following document to Keewatin — the north wind:

PROCLAMATION TO THE PEOPLE OF THE NORTH-WEST

Victoria, by the Grace of God, of the United Kingdom, of Great Britain and Ireland, Defender of the Faith. . . . To all whom it may concern, greeting. . . . We have seen fit by our Royal Letters Patent . . . to appoint the Honourable William McDougall of the City of Ottawa in the Province of Ontario in Our Dominion of Canada . . . to be at Our pleasure the Lieutenant-Governor of the North-West Territories . . . and we do hereby authorize and empower and require and command him in due manner to do and execute in all things . . . according to the several provisions and instructions granted or appointed him by virtue of Our said Inquiry . . . of all which Our loving subjects . . . are hereby required to take notice and govern themselves accordingly.

(Under the Royal Seal) Victoria, Queen of England, etc.

This Proclamation, a bold-faced appropriation of the Queen's name and authority, changed everything. McDougall had done what his prime minister most feared. He had illegally claimed Canadian jurisdiction, and in so doing, formally disbanded the former Hudson's Bay Company government.

COMMISSIONER: Mr. Riel, how is it that once William McDougall issued his Proclamation, under the name of the Queen, your government had a legal claim to governance?

RIEL: Both Howe and Macdonald had warned McDougall against issuing such a proclamation. Macdonald knew that it would destroy the authority of the Hudson's Bay Company in the North-West, and if McDougall were to take such a step, and was rebuffed, there would be no legal government. Anarchy would follow and as stated by Sir John, "no matter how anarchy is produced, it is quite open, by the law of nations, for the inhabitants to form a government ex necessitate for the protection of life and property." By crossing the international boundary and declaring Canadian authority, where none existed, McDougall exercised an illegal assumption of Canadian jurisdiction as no transfer of title had taken place. In this process, he also officially decommissioned the authority of the Hudson's Bay Company to rule in the North-West.

As for McDougall's so-called Proclamation, even in the pro-Canadian districts it was seen as unlikely to have been genuinely issued with the Queen's authority. It aroused even more suspicion with McDougall's next outrageous action: fomenting a civil war. I would like to put into evidence the following account of what occurred when the self-proclaimed lieutenant-governor of the North-West Territories, William McDougall, declared war on the people of the North-West.

When I use the word "war," I am not using the term in a metaphoric sense. On December 1, 1869, from his hovel in Pembina, the now self-appointed lieutenant-governor, William McDougall, recognized the erstwhile surveyor John Stoughton Dennis as his "Lieutenant and Conservator of the Peace." Dennis was instructed to establish his headquarters at the Hudson's Bay Company's Lower Fort Garry, the old Stone Fort. His commission was to raise and equip a force to disperse the rebels, and ". . . to fire upon any stronghold in their possession; to purchase or confiscate supplies; cattle, horses or vehicles, and to attack any private home in which Louis Riel may be found." Enlisting some four hundred recruits, fifty of whom were mercenary Chippewa and Salteaux Indians, he had his men marshalled and awaiting his orders to storm Upper Fort Garry.

Something was very wrong and everybody in the communities knew it. In the past, the lower Stone Fort had been used to house British troops. Now Canadians along with Indian mercenaries were organizing there, drilling for war against their French-speaking neighbours. With this flurry of military activity, large numbers of those English-speaking citizens who had previously been sympathetic to the Canadians were now backing off. They could not support a government whose first act was to prepare to launch civil war. As secretary of the Convention of Twenty-four, I continued to attempt negotiations and maintain peace in the face of Canadian Party provocations.

I told the Convention that I did not trust McDougall and that I did not like the arbitrary tone that ran through this Proclamation that he claimed had been issued by our Queen. I told the delegates that we are not slaves to be bought and sold, but a free people who have a right to negotiate terms of union with the free people of Canada. I then told them that if they think I am wrong, to return quietly to their farms: "But watch what we do. We will labour and obtain a guarantee of our rights and yours." My goal, of course, was the implementation of our right to form a provisional government as passed at our November 24, 1869, session of the Convention of Twenty-four.

Then on December 7, 1869, the war moved into our community with Dr. Schultz and forty-five Canadians converting his large home-warehouse into an armed fortress. In the heart of the new town of Winnipeg, filled with armed men and a large quantity of armaments and supplies destined for the surveyors and road crews, this armed camp was a serious provocation against the peace of the land. We now had Schultz in the heart of the community, McDougall with his ready-made government with three hundred rifles on the border, Dennis with four hundred men in the Stone Fort, as well as an unknown number of armed men out on the prairies with the other "surveyor," Colonel Boulton.

Recognizing the necessity of acting decisively, we dealt with the immediate threat of Schultz and his men in short order. Ambroise Lépine and I had two cannon brought out from Fort Garry and aimed at the door of "Fort Schultz." All inside were told to surrender within fifteen minutes. Their position was untenable. Giving up their arms, which we later found included over four hundred rounds of ammunition, they surrendered. Further, they had booby-trapped the house before surrendering, placing gun powder in the chimneys, which could have caused a carnage had it not been discovered. I had them marched off to the reinforced jail in Fort Garry where they were told that before they would be released we demanded they sign the surrender terms to keep the peace and not bear arms against their fellow countrymen. Most signed, but a hard-core group led by Christian Schultz did not. Fortunately, our decisive action broke the back of McDougall's army. Most of the men at the Stone Fort now deserted. Dennis ducked out in disguise as an Indian woman. With Lépine's cavalry blocking the border and guarding the community, the Canadian Party was in disarray and McDougall's dreams of power and glory were dashed to smithereens.

McDougall had done what his prime minister most feared. His coup had collapsed and the old Hudson's Bay Company government was incapable of governing. On the next day, December 8, 1869, the Convention was convened, and I told the delegates that from this day on, the people of Rupert's Land and the North-West became free and exempt from all allegiance to the previous Hudson's Bay Company government. I pointed out that this government, which we had always respected, had abandoned us by transferring to a foreign power the sacred authority confided to it. With no Canadian or Hudson's Bay Company government in place, our provisional government, as approved back on November 24, 1869, issued the following Declaration:

THE DECLARATION OF THE
PEOPLE OF THE NORTH-WEST

We hold ourselves in readiness to enter into such negotiations with the Canadian Government as may be favorable for the good government and prosperity of this people. The resistance had been solely against establishment of Canadian authority "under the announced form."

It is admitted by all men as a fundamental principle that the public authority commands the obedience and respect of its subjects. It is also admitted that a people, when it has no Government, is free to adopt one form of Government in preference to another, to give or to refuse allegiance to that which is proposed.

In accordance with these principles, the people of Rupert's Land had respected the authority of the Hudson's Bay Company even if it had been "far from answering the wants of the people." But "contrary to the law of nations" the Company had transferred to Canada "all the rights which it had or pretended to have in this territory, by transactions with which the people were considered unworthy to be made acquainted."

1st. We the Representatives of the people in Council assembled at Upper Fort Garry on the 24th day of November, 1869, after having invoked the God of nations, relying on these fundamental moral principles, solemnly declare in the name of our constituents and in our own names, before God and man, that from the day on which the Government we had always respected abandoned us, by transferring to a strange power the sacred authority confided to it, the people of Rupert's Land and the North-West became free and exempt from all allegiance to the said Government.

2nd. That we refuse to recognize the authority of Canada, which pretends to have a right to coerce us and impose upon us a despotic form of government, still more contrary to our rights and interests as British subjects than was that Government to which we had subjected ourselves through necessity up to a recent date.

3rd. That by sending an expedition on the 1st of November ult., charged to drive back Mr. William McDougall and his companions coming in the name of Canada to rule us with the rod of despotism without a previous notification to that effect we have but acted conformably to the sacred right which commands every citizen to offer energetic opposition to prevent his country being enslaved.

4th. That we continue and shall continue to oppose with all our strength the establishing of the Canadian authority in our country under the announced form. And in case of persistence on the part of the Canadian Government to enforce its obnoxious policy upon us by force of arms, we protest beforehand against such an unjust and unlawful course, and we declare the said Canadian Government responsible before God and men for the innumerable evils which may be caused by so unwarrantable a course. Be it known, therefore, to the world in general and to the Canadian Government in particular, that as we have always heretofore successfully defended our country in frequent wars with the neighboring tribes of Indians, who are now on friendly relations with us, we are firmly resolved in future not less than in the past, to repel all invasions from whatsoever quarter they may come. And furthermore, we do declare and proclaim in the name of the people of Rupert's Land and the North-West, that we have on the said 24th day of November, 1869, above mentioned, established a Provisional Government, and hold it to be the only and lawful authority now in existence in Rupert's Land and the North-West, and that we are ready to enter into such negotiations with the Canadian Government, as may be favorable for the good government and prosperity of this people. In support of this declaration, relying on the protection of Divine Providence, we mutually pledge ourselves, on oath, our lives, our fortunes, and our sacred honor to each other.

John Bruce, President   Louis Riel, Secretary

McDougall's failure to assume power through civil war, and the attrition and collapse of the Hudson's Bay Company's government, had left a vacuum where no official government existed. On December 8, our own representative provisional government of Assiniboia now assumed that jurisdiction.

With our decisive actions, and the establishment of the Provisional Government, the "great pretender" Mr. William McDougall had suffered a severe blow to his ambitions. Not only did we foil his attempted coup, he had disgraced himself with what was now universally seen as a fraudulent proclamation — a Royal forgery. The glorious career of William McDougall was reduced to naught on Christmas Day, December 25, 1869. With every indication that the English-speaking population of Red River were not rallying to his cause, and he himself stuck in the frozen shanties of a little American border village, his "ready-made" Canadian government rebelled against this lunacy and declared their intention to return to Canada. His reign as lieutenant-governor was over — before it ever started.

William McDougall had attempted to seize control of the Red River Settlement by all means possible. He tried fraud and forgery, he tried trickery and deception, and he tried civil and Indian war. All to no avail. With his bag of tricks empty, and his tail between his legs, McDougall and his entourage left Pembina for Ottawa on December 26, 1869. I am told that upon McDougall's return to the capital, he received a less-than-popular welcome. In fact, the whole of the Canadian Cabinet was furious with his performance. Macdonald exploded, demanding of McDougall: what the hell did he think he was doing? McDougall had created a state of anarchy, he had disregarded his mandate, he had disregarded his orders and he had incited a civil war under his fraudulent Proclamation and assumption of sovereignty. The case against McDougall was too embarrassing. The House was forced to repudiate him for using the Queen's name without her authority and organizing an armed force without warrant or instructions. William McDougall was defeated in the federal election of 1872 and went on to sit in the Ontario legislature as an independent-Liberal for some years. He should have been prosecuted as a war criminal.

COMMISSIONER: Mr. Riel, you have asked that this Inquiry review the accusation that you are guilty of pillaging the Hudson's Bay Company's Fort Garry. What say you?

RIEL: Our "People's Government" raised the hastily made flag of the Provisional Government of Assiniboia at (Upper) Fort Garry on December 10, 1869. With our Métis cavalry in attendance, a white flag, with the lilies of France and the shamrock of Ireland arranged around a buffalo on the plains, was raised to the sky. The first act of our new government took place immediately as I administered a solemn oath to our band of patriots. All those participating guaranteed to put the protection of the community before their own interests. Those entrusted with the welfare of the community swore to carry out their assigned tasks and to forsake liquor while on public duty.

The Provisional Government moved to maintain peace and order, the streets were patrolled by Métis guards and, most enjoyably, a period of calm and security prevailed. To ensure this situation continued we even stopped the sale of hard liquors in the taverns during the Christmas season. The only disruptive elements in our community were the prisoners in Fort Garry, and they remained locked up until they had sworn on the Bible not to bear arms against the Provisional Government.

We quickly learned that the business of government is complex and that this government, like all governments, had expenses. Under these circumstances, on December 22, 1869, I asked Governor Mactavish for a loan of £2,000. The loan, I suggested, was to be refunded by Canada at the end of the troubles. Mactavish refused, and I was forced to have the Company safe opened against his wishes. I removed £1,090 from the safe, leaving a receipt in the name of the Provisional Government. None of this money was used for personal gain but for the legitimate expense of protecting the community and ensuring that peace prevailed.

Would this Inquiry please note that when Bishop Taché received Papal permission to leave the Ecumenical Council in Rome in December of 1869 to return to Canada at the request of John A. Macdonald, the prime minister not only promised to repay the expenditures incurred by the Hudson's Bay Company but to provide amnesty to the "insurgents" — if the Company's government was restored: "Should the question arise as to the consumption of any stores or goods belonging to the Hudson's Bay Company by the insurgents, you are authorized to inform the leaders that if the Company's government is restored, not only will there be a general amnesty granted: but in case the Company should claim the payment for such stores, that the Canadian government will stand between the insurgents and all harm."

It is my contention that although the Company government was never restored, the intent was clear, and the Provisional Government, acting as the responsible government, had every right to expect the Canadian government to live up to the spirit of the letter. As I will substantiate, the Canadian government did not do so. In my mind, the monetary claim remains unsettled, as does a full and free amnesty for all members of the Provisional Government.

I am forced to clear my name on both of these questions. I ask this Inquiry to definitively clarify the question of the Hudson's Bay money as I am not a thief, nor did my associates or I commit pillage. Troops had to be paid and fed. This was not plunder but a necessary expense of government. I would further point out that the Canadian government, in 1884, admitted liability to make good the losses of the Hudson's Bay Company consequent to the events of 1869–70. This so-called "compensatory" money was paid, and once again, I might add, the Company made a handsome profit.

Regarding accusations I stole monies that did not belong to me, I enter a final submission coming from a most unlikely source: Mr. Edward Blake, leader of the Liberal government in Ontario. Although this man put a $5,000 reward on my head, he is quoted as saying, "I know that when Riel was in power in 1869–70, when he had at his disposition all the resources of the Hudson's Bay Company, his own family was in misery in his own house, and he would never consent that any part of what he called public property be sent to his people, even to prevent them from dying from hunger, and this same provisional government was obliged to send secretly a sack of flour or something of that nature to his mother."

COMMISSIONER: Mr. Riel, as the president of the Provisional Government of Assiniboia you sought to maintain peace in the community as well as to conduct negotiations with Canada. Please inform this Inquiry of your experience with the Canadian delegates who came to Red River.

RIEL: On December 27, 1869, I became president of the Provisional Government of the Red River and the North-West Territories. I was twenty-five years of age at the time. The Convention of Twenty-four had been successful, uniting both English-speaking and French-speaking delegates in one functioning convention. Our common goal was to lay out the claims of our communities, which were to be taken to Ottawa as our terms in negotiating a "treaty" with Canada. My dream was to unify the various English- and French-speaking communities around a central program, and the opportunity was now coming ever nearer. It was at this time, however, that there were a series of jailbreaks. In the first one, the Canadian paymaster, Charles Mair, and the troublesome road worker, Thomas Scott, were amongst twelve men who escaped. In the second breakout, the ringleader, Dr. Christian Schultz, with the assistance of his wife, escaped from the furnished room in which he was being held under guard. We found out later that Schultz was hidden in the parish of St. Andrews by the Reverend George Young, the father of Captain Young, my captor fifteen years later on the SS *Northcote*.

With McDougall gone and the Canadian escapees on the loose, we eagerly waited for Canadian commissioners to arrive from Ottawa. In short order, a number of Canadian notables did make their way to the Red River. In fact, the diplomatic entourages were literally bumping into each other. Canadian Cabinet Minister Joseph Howe had paid a hurried private visit in the fall, and after that I can state that they all came to pry into, spy on or subvert the Provisional Government.

Amongst those who came to the Red River at this time were Father Jean-Baptiste Thibault, who had formerly been the vicar-general of the diocese of St. Boniface and the parish priest of St. François-Xavier. Thibault was accompanied by Charles de Salaberry, a Canadian military man and scion of the Quebec aristocracy. Both men had come to represent the Canadian government but had no authority to guarantee any measures in the future or grant any of our demands. They were, I'm afraid, no more than interlopers. Confiscating Thibault's papers, I had him put in the Episcopal Palace. After he agreed to be disarmed and put under an informal guard, Charles de Salaberry was allowed to enter the country. The next to arrive was Dr. Tupper, the former premier of Nova Scotia who led the maritime colony into Confederation, and himself into Macdonald's Cabinet. Tupper too had no authority. Allowed in, he was treated respectfully, and dismissed as useless. Up to this point, our experience with the Canadian delegates who came to Red River was frustration, for although they came at the behest of Canada, and came with the best of intentions, they were without power, mere meddlers. We needed commissioners with the power to negotiate with us in the name of the Government of Canada.

COMMISSIONER: Mr. Riel, please refer to your experience with the next Canadian commissioner to arrive in the North-West, Mr. Donald Smith of the Hudson's Bay Company.

RIEL: Diplomacy is based upon a set of rules and very few assumptions. It needs to be honoured by both sides. Unfortunately, my experience had been that a whole parade of Canadian diplomats were sent with no power to negotiate. Or, as would occur next, they possessed power but would use it in their own self-interests and not those of our community. The prime example was the highest-ranking official of the Hudson's Bay Company in North America, Governor-in-Chief Mr. Donald A. Smith.

Donald Alexander Smith, who has since been elevated to First Baron Strathcona and Mount Royal GCMG GCVO PC DL FRS, is a Highland

Scot, whose family had long roots in the Canadian fur trade. As a young man, Smith immigrated to British North America, where he worked with the Hudson's Bay Company on the St. Lawrence River. After a scandal, involving the young wife of Hudson's Bay Company Governor-in-Chief George Simpson, Smith was sent north, exiled to trade on the frozen craggy shores of the Labrador coast. Over the years, as fur-trade profits grew, Smith diversified, establishing a salmon fishery, exporting seal oil and exploring for mineral wealth across Labrador.

After nearly thirty years, "Labrador Smith," now a wealthy man, was summoned to HBC headquarters in London. Here he met an old "Canada hand," HBC Governor Sir Edmund Walker Head, a member of the British Privy Council, who had been governor general of British North America from 1854 to 1861. As the Queen's representative in her North American colonies, Walker Head wielded enormous control over the economic and political future of the fledgling colonies. All the while, he was running the largest economic enterprise on the North American continent, the Hudson's Bay Company. I found it less than surprising to learn that Walker Head had also acted as a mentor to the rising Conservative politician of the era, John A. Macdonald.

With his Canadian duties completed, Walker Head had returned to London as the leading figure in the HBC hierarchy, the twenty-first governor of the great company. Sizing up Donald Smith, he saw the man he had been looking for. Taking Smith under his wing, Head prepared the Labrador trader for his part in the rapid changes that the financiers of London planned for both Canada and the Hudson's Bay Company. Key to the information Head passed to Smith was the United Kingdom's imminent approval of the Confederation of the North American colonies into the Dominion of Canada, and the orchestration, already underway, for the surrender of the Hudson's Bay Company charter of land to the Canadians.

Upon his return to North America, Donald Smith re-established contact with his cousin, George Stephen, one of Montreal's leading financiers and entrepreneurs. Stephen, who had been made president of the Bank of Montreal, had acquired a good deal of experience and won a large measure of success financing railway enterprises in the United

States. Together, the two Highlanders looked to expand their enterprises in the North-West while completely reorganizing the old Company. When rumours of the imminent demise of the Hudson's Bay Company swept the markets of London, share prices dropped, and Smith and Stephen quietly bought up masses of shares, seizing control of the Company, just as Selkirk had done fifty years earlier.

As we know, Walker Head's prediction came true, and shortly after Confederation, the new Dominion of Canada purchased the Hudson's Bay Company's charter lands. With the political future of the former Hudson's Bay Company lands determined, and £300,000 to be paid on December 1, 1869, Donald Smith prepared to travel west to consolidate his empire. It was at this time Smith learned that we Métis refused to allow Canadian "Governor" McDougall into the community and that the Provisional Government was established and headquartered in the Hudson's Bay Company's Fort Garry.

With this news, Smith demanded John A. Macdonald appoint him lieutenant-governor and provide him with troops to put down the so-called rebellion. Macdonald vetoed the proposal in these words: "Smith goes to carry the olive branch, and were it known at Red River that he was accompanied by an officer high in rank in military service, he would be looked upon as having the olive branch in one hand and a revolver in the other. We must not make any indications of even thinking of a military force until peaceable means have been exhausted. Should these miserable half-breeds not disband, they must be put down, and then, so far as I can influence matters, I shall be very glad to give Colonel Wolseley the chance of glory and the risk of the scalping knife."

It is my belief that Macdonald declined to send troops as he had his whole French caucus to think of. Although it would be popular in English Canada, he could lose crucial votes in Quebec if he sent troops to suppress the French-speaking Métis in the Red River. Appointing Donald Smith as Dominion Commissioner to inquire into the North-West troubles, Macdonald requested Smith to travel to Red River as an HBC superior and reconnoitre the situation — before revealing his Canadian commission.

Upon Smith's arrival in our community, I had him brought to me.

No namby-pamby Ontario bureaucrat or Quebec aristocrat, the old Labrador trapper demanded to know my intentions. Ignoring his bluster, I asked for his papers. He provided documentation indicating that he had come as Governor Mactavish's replacement as the head of the Hudson's Bay Company but nothing further. As Company representative he was made welcome, and I offered him the freedom of the community, under just one condition: I requested he acknowledge the Provisional Government and pledge not to take any action to overturn its authority. Initially, Smith refused, but when told his movements would be restricted, he did so solemnly pledge. His pledge was, I would soon learn, of no consequence to his conscience.

Immediately, Donald Smith began plotting to overthrow the Provisional Government. In this endeavour, he held clandestine meetings with prominent men, attempting to draw my councillors away from me. Using every resource available, including the great power of the Hudson's Bay Company, to which most of the population was in debt, he set up a program of bribery, seeking out those who were for sale. Pragmatic, Donald Smith acted like a man without principles. Not only did he break a solemn pledge, he also misrepresented his own power from Canada to me. In fact, this man's behaviour was so low and his greed and avarice so all-inclusive that in 1874, at the Special Parliamentary Committee on Causes of the Difficulties in the North-West 1869–70, he asked that the Canadian government reimburse him £500 for his bribes.

When Smith's interference in the internal affairs of our community became quite open, the other two unofficial commissioners, Thibault and de Salaberry, grew concerned that Smith "had been endeavouring to incite the different parties to hostile collision." Upon discovering concrete evidence of Smith's plots and confronting him with this evidence, I put him under guard. To relieve himself of this situation, he sent his secretary to Pembina for the hidden papers of his commission. Finally, with Smith's commission out in the open, I was able to begin useful negotiations. Ground rules were laid whereby Smith and I together called a large meeting of the population to determine the future of the people of the Red River.

Held outdoors, from the steps of the historic Hudson's Bay Company courthouse, which my father had once surrounded with armed men, and in the face of a major blizzard, with two thousand people attending, we put forward our arguments for the future of the Red River. Over the next two days, Donald Smith read a series of Royal Proclamations, the terms of his government commission, and numerous communications from the government in Ottawa promising to review our concerns. I, on the other hand, reviewed our experience to date with the Canadians and their "secret" negotiations to purchase the HBC title. I then proposed the different English-speaking and French-speaking communities establish constituencies to elect an equal number of French- and English-speaking representatives to lay out our demands to be negotiated with Ottawa. In the end, in a mass vote, mittens held high, my position held sway.

It was wonderful. As soon as we understood each other, we joined in common cause, seeking our just rights. Donald Smith and the other two commissioners had no option but to approve the decision of this democratic forum. I then requested this great convention re-establish the Provisional Government in preparation for the formation of an elected constituent assembly.

Political negotiations with Canada were now the key issue on our agenda. It remained to thoroughly study and agree on those claims, and make the pressing of the same as unanimous as possible. The Convention of Forty met in early February 1870 and drafted the following Bill of Rights which was soon adopted:

BILL OF RIGHTS 1870

1st. That, in view of the present exceptional position of the North-West, duties upon goods imported into the country shall continue as at present (except in the case of spirituous liquors) for three years, and for such further time as may elapse until there be uninterrupted railroad communication between Red River Settlement and St. Paul, and also steam communication between Red River Settlement and Lake Superior.

2nd. As long as this country remains a territory in the Dominion of Canada, there shall be no direct taxation, except such as may be imposed by the local legislature, for municipal or other local purposes.

3rd. That during the time this country shall remain in the position of a territory in the Dominion of Canada, all military, civil and other public expenses in connection with the general government of the country, or that have hitherto been borne by the public funds of the Settlement, beyond the receipt of the above mentioned duties, shall be met by the Dominion of Canada.

4th. That while the burden of public expense in this territory is borne by Canada, the country be governed by a Lieutenant-Governor from Canada, and a Legislature three members of whom, being heads of departments of the Government, shall be nominated by the governor general of Canada.

5th. That, after the expiration of this exceptional period, the country shall be governed as regards its local affairs as the Provinces of Ontario and Quebec are now governed, by a Legislature of the people and a Ministry responsible to it, under a Lieutenant-Governor appointed by the governor general of Canada.

6th. That there shall be no interference by the Dominion Parliament in the local affairs of this territory other than is allowed in the provinces, and that this territory shall have and enjoy in all respects the same privileges, advantages and aids in meeting the public expenses of this territory as the provinces have and enjoy.

7th. That, while the North-West remains a territory, the Legislature have a right to pass all laws, local to the territory, over the veto of the Lieutenant-Governor by a two-thirds vote.

8th. A homestead and pre-emption law.

9th. That, while the North-West remains a territory, the sum of $25,000 a year be appropriated for schools, roads and bridges.

10th. That all the public buildings be at the expense of the Dominion Treasury.

11th. That there shall be guaranteed uninterrupted steam communication to Lake Superior within five years; and also the establishment by rail of a connection with the American railway as soon as it reaches the international line.

12th. That the military force required in this country be composed of natives of the country during four years.

13th. That the English and French languages be common in the Legislature and Courts, and that all public documents and Acts of the Legislature be published in both languages.

14th. That the Judge of the Supreme Court speak the French and English languages.

15th. That treaties be concluded between the Dominion and the several Indians tribes of the country as soon as possible.

16th. That, until the population of the country entitles us to more, we have three representatives in the Canadian Parliament; one in the Senate and two in the Legislative Assembly.

17th. That all the properties, rights and privileges as hitherto enjoyed by us be respected, and that the recognition and arrangement of local customs, usages and privileges be made under the control of the local Legislature.

18th. That the local Legislature of this territory have full control of all the lands inside a circumference having Upper Fort Garry as a centre, and that the radius of this circumference be the number of miles that the American line is distant from Fort Garry.

19th. That every man of the country (except uncivilized and unsettled Indians) who has attained the age of 21 years, and every British subject, a stranger to this country who has resided three years in this country and is a householder, shall have a right to vote at the election of a member to serve in the Legislature of the country and in the Dominion Parliament; and every foreign subject, other than a British subject, who has resided the same length of time in the country and is a householder, shall have the same right to vote, on condition of his taking the oath of allegiance, it being understood that this article be subject to amendment exclusively by the local Legislature.

20th. That the North-West Territory shall never be held liable for any portion of the £300,000 paid to the Hudson's Bay Company, or for any portion of the public debt of Canada, as it stands at the time of our entering the Confederation; and if thereafter we be called to assume our share of said public debt, we consent only on condition that we first be allowed the amount for which we shall be held liable.

I argued against this last clause, and put forth an alternative motion to the effect that "all bargains with the Hudson's Bay Company for the transfer of this territory be considered null and void, and that any arrangements with reference to the transfer of this country shall be carried on only with the people of this country." In the English constituencies, my vehement repudiation of the sale was seen as rather "overstepping the mark." Largely, they wanted to smooth over old difficulties. My point was to recognize the sovereign right of the actual residents, most of whom did not even have patents on their farms. I also sought compensation for the exploitation of our lands and labour over the past two-hundred years. It was defeated by none other than my cousin, Charles Nolin.

My great ambition, to force Ottawa to come to terms, was now nearing completion. As special commissioner, Smith did not feel equal to the task of guaranteeing the approval of all the clauses of our Bill of Rights. So it was, he invited the Convention to elect two or three persons who would go to the capital of Canada and negotiate their acceptance by the federal administration and Parliament.

As a step in that direction, in order to have a responsible party to give the necessary credentials to the bearers of the people's claims, as well as to endow our government with the proper authority, it was deemed expedient to reorganize, complete and legitimize the Provisional Government. On January 26, 1870, when several of the English-speaking delegates grew concerned with our establishing a sovereign government, a distinguished deputation went to interview Hudson's Bay Company Governor Mactavish. They asked if he were still governor of the country. He gave an unequivocal response: "Form a government, for God's sake; I have no power or authority."

At this juncture, I wish to emphasize to this Inquiry that we did everything in our power to establish a loyal, British democracy in the North-West. On February 10, 1870, at the prorogation of the Convention of Forty, there was in Assiniboia, de jure and de facto, no other government than that which I presided over myself.

With McDougall having proven himself to be a reckless fraud, and former governor Mactavish relinquishing Hudson's Bay Company governance, our government, formed by delegates elected with the approval of Ottawa's representative, was legal and legitimate, though established only provisionally. To remedy this situation and formally establish our government, I called for the election of a legislative assembly. Thereafter, both the French-speaking and the English-speaking communities, minus the fringe element led by Christian Schultz's Canadian Party, elected representatives to our newly created Legislative Assembly of Assiniboia, named "Assiniboia" out of respect for the old governing Council of Assiniboia. Our legislature was free from all hindrances, and together we appointed an executive council, adjutant general, chief justice and clerk. With but one dissenting vote, I was confirmed as president of the Legislative Assembly of Assiniboia.

Representing a successful transition from martial law to legitimate, representative democracy, the Legislative Assembly of Assiniboia was the culmination of the work of the Provisional Government. Its primary focus, led by our leading constitutional expert, Reverend N.J. (Abbé) Ritchot, was to work on a constitution in preparation for negotiations with Canada. The Assembly went on to debate local issues, such as the building of public works, revising the judicial districts and even establishing a senate. With Donald Smith's agreement, and negotiations with Canada next on our agenda, our Legislative Assembly voted to send Father Ritchot, Judge Black and Alfred H. Scott as delegates to Ottawa to negotiate our entry into the Canadian Confederation with the understanding that the Legislative Assembly must sanction all agreements. Unfortunately, as our delegates prepared to leave, tragedy occurred and I was forced to deal with a renewed Canadian rebellion, and the court martial and execution of the Canadian, Thomas Scott.

COMMISSIONER: Mr. Riel please speak to the question: was Riel a murderer of Thomas Scott when he was executed in Red River?

RIEL: Our insurrection had been bloodless. We had defeated our enemies without a shot being fired. Now with the Provisional Government firmly established as the legal and legitimate government of our land, we were ready to take our place as an equal under the law of nations and to put our nation on a peacetime footing. As president, I announced that we were declaring an amnesty to those who would swear not to take up arms, and, with that guarantee, our troops too would be demobilized. It was at this very moment a tragic incident occurred. It was an incident of such magnitude and stupidity as to mar the general peace of the land. It is my opinion that it actually changed the course of Canadian history. I also believe it placed me in the position where I find myself this day.

West of our Red River Settlement, on the banks of the Assiniboine River, lies the little village of Portage la Prairie, a former staging area for the buffalo hunt out on the flatland prairie. As has been mentioned earlier, under the leadership of Major Charles Boulton, a group of men, posing as surveyors, had been gathering there. When the jailbreaks occurred, the Canadian road worker Thomas Scott and some of the other escapees made their way to Portage. Here, they rallied the men to join Christian Schultz who, after his breakout, had made his way north to St. Andrews where the remnants of Dennis' Canadians were ensconced.

Later, claiming he "reluctantly" accepted the role of leader, Major Boulton marched his men east along the frozen Assiniboine River, forcing a number of peaceful citizens to take up arms unwillingly. By the time they reached the parish of Headingley, they had recruited about a hundred men. From here Scott and a small band entered the town of Winnipeg, surrounding and entering a house where I was often to be found. Informed of this incident, our adjutant general, Ambroise Lépine, sent out his troops in search of the miscreants who had retreated back to Headingley and Boulton's forces.

The situation was most dangerous. We now knew that our enemies were marching towards Fort Garry from several different directions. Attempting to save the community from bloodshed, the prominent trader Andrew Bannatyne and I persuaded the remaining prisoners to promise not to bear arms. Once they signed, we set them free. Now, from here on, I must tell you that I am highly suspicious of the "official" versions relaying the chain of events that follow.

We do know that while waylaid by a vicious blizzard at the village of Kildonan, Boulton's men seized a local Métis woodcutter by the name of Norbert Parisien. Concerned he was a spy, or would tell about their whereabouts, the Canadians held him in their camp overnight. In the morning, we are told, Parisien escaped his captors and ran toward the frozen river. Once on the riverbank, Parisien is said to have seen a man riding hard across the river, coming towards him. Thinking the rider was one of his captors, Parisien allegedly seized a rifle lying on a sleigh pulled up along the riverbank and shot down the approaching rider. The insurgents then chased Parisien onto the ice where he was "roughly recaptured." Boulton later explained that when he intervened, Parisien's feet were tied together with a sash and he was being dragged across the ice by another sash, tied around his neck. Conveniently, Boulton fails to mention that the Canadians struck Parisien down with an axe and his head was split open.

Here again there is a great deal of confusion. One ridiculous report even claimed that Dr. Christian Schultz attended to Parisien's wounds, and Parisien died of pneumonia several weeks later. Boulton's version was that, on the following day, Parisien again tried to escape and was shot by his guard and died two days later. It is to be noted that no one was ever charged with the murder of Norbert Parisien or in the death of John Sutherland, the rider said to have been shot by Parisien. Critically, Major Boulton also failed to mention that John Sutherland, rest his eternal soul, was riding to the scene to inform the Canadians that I had set the remaining prisoners free and had offered them the opportunity to "form and complete the Provisional Government." Upon hearing of these horrible events, I then sent another message to the insurgents:

> War, horrible civil war, is the destruction of this country.... We are ready to meet any party; but peace, our British rights, we want before all. Gentlemen, the prisoners are out — they have sworn to keep peace. We have taken the responsibility for our past acts. Mr. William Mactavish has asked you, for the sake of God, to form and complete the Provisional Government. Your representatives have joined us on that ground. Who will now come and destroy the Red River settlement?

With their women, and especially Mrs. Sutherland, mother of John Sutherland, pleading, the vast majority of Boulton's men disbanded.

Conversely, on the evening of February 17, 1870, with the people of Winnipeg watching from their windows and rooftops, Major Boulton and a hard-core group of forty-eight Canadians marched openly and armed within sight of Fort Garry. With their movements giving the fort's lookouts the impression of a hostile manoeuvre, the alarm sounded. Adjutant General Ambroise Lépine, Treasurer William O'Donoghue and our Métis cavalry tore out through the gates of the fort and over the snow-covered fields, surrounding the Canadians and imprisoning them in Fort Garry.

Once again, our provisional government had narrowly escaped a civil war. Under a tribunal of war, we, the rightful government of the land, tried Major Boulton for his crimes. Since his arrival in the North-West, he had done nothing but organize and drill companies of forces intended to be used in a civil war. He had led a movement responsible for two deaths and almost fomented a civil war just after peace had been made possible by the establishment of the Provisional Government. Found guilty of treason, Boulton was sentenced to be executed by a firing squad.

Boulton would have been shot but for the intervention of Mrs. Sutherland. We allowed the pardon, but used this pardon to extract from Donald Smith a promise to assist in convincing the remaining English-speaking settlers to elect delegates to the Provisional Government's legislative assembly, the formation of which had been decreed by the Convention of Forty.

This was not the end of our problems. New troubles were expected to arise at any time. The chief of the Canadians, Christian Schultz, was still on the loose. He and his men had extracted a cannon from the old Stone Fort and were liable to put the lives of our citizens in danger. With our patrols out searching, Schultz's men began deserting. On February 21, Schultz, with the help of a half-breed guide, escaped to Minnesota.

Amongst the forty-eight Canadians we captured was the recalcitrant Thomas Scott. A troublemaker since he arrived in the community, he proved unmanageable in jail. After being in jail for two weeks, on March 1, he attempted a mass escape with other prisoners, endeavouring to rush the guards and force the doors. We subdued the prisoners, except for Scott, who remained belligerent. Put in chains, he struck his guards with his chains. When released, he immediately assaulted the captains of the guard. Called to the jail, I walked by a half-open door and he hurled himself at me cursing, "Ah! Son of a bitch, if I ever recover my liberty, it is at these my hands that you shall perish!"

It has been said that Scott was immediately court martialled. This is not the case. As president of the Provisional Government, I tried to avoid going to these lengths by holding an interview with Scott. I asked him to consider his position, and begged him, whatever his feelings, to behave quietly in prison. In this way, I said that I would have a reason for preventing him from having to appear before a tribunal of war, which is what the Métis soldiers were loudly demanding. Scott ignored this advice and persisted in his extreme conduct.

The situation was untenable. Scott's example was productive of the very worst effects on the other prisoners. The level of insubordination was such that it was difficult for the guards to withhold from retaliation. On March 3, 1870, Thomas Scott was summoned before a tribunal of war. He had taken up arms against the Provisional Government and had continued his provocations in jail, striking his guards, a captain, and attempting to attack the president of the Provisional Government. Accused of leading the other prisoners in a campaign of general insubordination and mutiny, he remained a threat to the lives of the guards and me and, if released, promised to continue making war against our community.

I wish to make it perfectly clear to this Inquiry that neither I nor Ambroise Lépine, who have both been charged with the murder of Thomas Scott, murdered Mr. Scott. In actual fact, Ambroise Lépine was the presiding officer at Scott's court martial, and I was called as one of the witnesses at the preliminary hearing and acted as translator during the actual proceedings. Under oath, the witnesses told how Scott, under arms, had rebelled against the Provisional Government, how he was guilty of "insubordination," had struck a captain of the guard and assaulted my person. Although I explained in English the evidence that had been given, Mr. Scott refused to make a coherent defence and treated the whole proceedings with utter contempt.

When the evidence had been given, all seven members of the court found Mr. Scott guilty. Four of them called for a sentence of death and two favoured exile. While the matter of exile was being discussed, Scott spoke, telling the tribunal: "If you escort me to the border I will be back at Red River before you." After this outburst, Ambroise Lépine, as presiding officer, declared that he would, reluctantly, agree with the majority. Thomas Scott was sentenced to death.

So it was that on March 4, 1870, Mr. Thomas Scott was lawfully executed by the Provisional Government of Assiniboia, the de facto government of the North-West, as recognized by the Dominion Commissioner to inquire into the North-West troubles, Mr. Donald Smith, and the other Canadian commissioners, J.B. Thibault, Charles de Salaberry and Bishop Taché. As this matter has had such a profound impact on my career, I would also like to enter into evidence the following from a personal letter sent from acting Prime Minister Sir George-Étienne Cartier to Lord Lisgar, the governor general:

> With regard to the murder of the poor man Scott . . . the Métis could contend that the deed was committed with the exercise of the local power of the de facto Government; that they cannot be made individually responsible for it, as it was to some extent the act of the community and the responsibility, if it lies with them to any extent, would lie more on the illegal deeds and several unauthorized invasions of the Canadians, who by their attempt at waging war against the settlers provoked the regretted deed.

It is not reasonable that an individual should be held responsible for an official act of a legitimate government. It needs to be further emphasized that after the execution of Thomas Scott, Schultz's men were dispersed. One by one, the prisoners in Fort Garry signed off on a peace bond and were released. Life came back to the communities and, as businesses revived, the settlement went from a state of extreme tension to one of tranquillity. A police force was established and the settlement was again quiet and peaceable. People felt more security in going about their daily lives than they had for some time. It was under these circumstances that I issued the following message:

TO THE PEOPLE OF THE NORTH-WEST (MAY 14, 1870)

Let the Assembly of twenty-eight Representatives which met on the 9th March, be dear to the people of Red River! That Assembly has shown itself worthy of great confidence. It has worked in unison. The members devoted themselves to the public interests and yielded only to sentiments of good will, duty and generosity. Thanks to that noble conduct, public authority is now strong.

To-day the Government pardons all those whom political differences led astray only for a time. Amnesty will be generously accorded to all those who will submit to the Government, who will discountenance or inform against dangerous gatherings.

From this day forth the public highways are open. The Hudson's Bay Company can now resume business. Themselves contributing to the public good, they circulate their money as of old. They pledge themselves to that course.

The attention of the Government is also directed very specially to the Northern part of the country, in order that trade there may not receive any serious check and peace in the Indian districts may thereby be all the more securely maintained.

The disastrous war, which at one time threatened us, has left among us fear and various deplorable results. But let the people feel reassured. Elevated by the Grace of Providence and the suffrages of my fellow-citizens to the highest position in the Government of my country, I proclaim that peace reigns in our midst this day.

The Government will take every precaution to prevent this peace from being disturbed. While internally all is thus returning to order, externally also, matters are looking favorable. Canada invites the Red River people to an amicable arrangement. She offers to guarantee us our rights and to give us a place in the Confederation equal to that of any other Province. Identified with the Provisional Government, our national will, based upon justice, shall be respected.

Happy country, to have escaped many misfortunes that were prepared for her! In seeing her children on the point of a war, she recollects the old friendship which used to bind us, and by the ties of the same patriotism she has re-united them again for the sake of preserving their lives, their liberties and their happiness. Let us remain united, and we shall be happy. With strength of unity we shall retain prosperity.

O my fellow-countrymen, without distinction of language or without distinction of creed, keep my words in your hearts! If ever the time should unhappily come when another division should take place amongst us, such as foreigners heretofore sought to create, that will be the signal for all the disasters which we have had the happiness to avoid.

In order to prevent similar calamities, the Government will treat with all the severity of the law those who will dare again to compromise the public security. It is ready to act against the disorder of parties as well as against that of individuals. But let us hope rather that extreme measures will be unknown, and the lessons of the past will guide us in the future.

Louis Riel, President

With Scott's execution, the leading Canadians — Schultz, Mair, Boulton, Dennis and numerous others, even members of the clergy — had all cleared out of our Red River Settlement, headed for Ontario. In Toronto, the Canada First Movement organized a huge rally and reception for the Canadian "veterans." Upon arrival, they were met by the mayor of Toronto and a large crowd of Orangemen, all loyal to the monarchy and bound together by their hatred of Catholicism, Indians, half-breeds, the Irish and now me. Schultz and company were said to have lathered up the mob with tales of my wickedness to the poor Protestant martyr, Thomas Scott. Amongst other wild tales, it was claimed that I buried him alive. Thereafter, travelling across southern Ontario, carrying a "hanging rope," the North-West veterans beat the drum and led a crusade against me, "the bloody western tyrant." Going from town to town garnering support for a racial war in the North-West, they found no lack of volunteers.

As this was occurring, on April 11, 1870, the duly constituted and invited delegates of the Provisional Government of Assiniboia reached Ontario. Upon arrival, two of the three delegates were arrested on an Ontario provincial warrant as accessories to the murder of Thomas Scott. Thankfully, Father Ritchot avoided capture and informed his superiors in the Church of the arrests. Subsequently, Prime Minister Macdonald had the delegates released, and our envoys reached Ottawa. Although Canada later tried to deny it, our North-West delegates were formally "recognized" by the Dominion government on April 26, 1870. Surprisingly, Macdonald was most magnanimous, and negotiations were quickly carried out, based almost entirely upon our Bill of Rights. A mutually satisfactory draft was completed on May 3, after some fifteen conferences, nine of them attended by Sir John A. Macdonald. The House of Commons passed the Manitoba Act on May 12, 1870.

Returning from Ottawa, Father Ritchot gave a full account of the negotiations to the Legislative Assembly of Assiniboia on June 24, 1870. Questioned on the implications of the various clauses, Ritchot reassured the Assembly that contrary to newspaper reports coming out of Ontario, the people of Canada were sympathetic to the Provisional Government. Satisfied that their rights had been recognized, Assembly vice-president, and my old school mate Louis Schmidt moved that the Legislative Assembly accept the Manitoba Act in the name of the people, and enter the Dominion of Canada on the terms proposed in the Confederation Act. Pierre Poitras seconded the motion and the Legislative Assembly of Assiniboia proudly ratified the Manitoba Act.

Prior to our adjournment, as president of the Legislative Assembly of Assiniboia, and the first "Premier" of Manitoba, I congratulated the people of the North-West on the happy issue of their undertakings and their moderation and firmness of purpose. I further congratulated them on having trust enough in the Crown of England to believe that ultimately they would obtain their rights. In the end, I congratulated our country on passing from under provisional rule to one of a more permanent and satisfactory character — the Canadian province of Manitoba.

As established, the province of Manitoba was limited to the immediate area surrounding the "settled" portion of the Assiniboia Territory, with the North-West Territories encompassing the great lone lands to the north and to the west. I had requested the name be "Manitoba" as it speaks of the voice of the great Manitou or the Great Spirit, which is already written in all hearts, and this suggestion was agreed upon in Ottawa.

I am proud to say that our little nation bargained in good faith with a larger nation and an equitable agreement was reached. It is my belief that these negotiations were extremely significant in the annals of Canadian history as, once again, they represented one of the key tenets of civilization: "No matter what the size of a nation, it has equal rights with all nations."

COMMISSIONER: Mr. Riel, please explain the significance of the Manitoba Act to the residents of the North-West.

RIEL: Gladly. Our provisional government had succeeded in every way; we held mass meetings leading up to the drafting of a Bill of Rights; we united the settlement; we presided over the appointment of delegates to negotiate the terms of the territory's entry into the Canadian Confederation; and we ruled in a fair and equitable fashion. On the other hand, the Canadian government, having tried diplomatic pressure, economic pressure and civil war, had failed. As a result, it had no choice but to recognize the democratic demands of our population. Most significantly, our Red River Settlement was no longer to be established as a colony, as originally envisioned by Macdonald, but was to enter the Canadian Confederation as the new Canadian province of Manitoba, with full rights in the Dominion of Canada, including Indigenous rights — as initially established by the Royal Proclamation of 1763. In addition, acceptance of religious and language rights in the Manitoba Act also signalled a nation built on principles of equality and inclusion.

The so-called Lieutenant-Governor William McDougall had departed in ignominy. With the Manitoba Act, a new lieutenant-governor was to be appointed to administer the colony and prepare for the transfer to Canadian jurisdiction. As there was no official to act as the head of the government in the intervening period, the Hon. George-Étienne Cartier, the acting head of the Canadian government — Macdonald being "under the weather" — suggested I continue in this role until the arrival of the new lieutenant-governor, A.G. Archibald. I agreed to this responsibility and carried it out until I was deposed by Colonel Wolseley.

In regard to the chief issue of land, we, the Métis and half-breed inhabitants, were to maintain the peaceable possession of lands now held. According to the agreement, further land, to the extent of 1,400,000 acres, was to be set aside for our children and future generations. We also negotiated the right to receive Catholic schooling, where numbers permitted, and the French and English languages were given official status. We had achieved recognition of our traditional rights, alongside the gaining of legitimate democratic institutions and rights. It is my belief that we were the first North American jurisdiction to provide recognition of Indigenous land and political rights. We looked to a bright future in the Canadian Confederation.

COMMISSIONER: Mr. Riel, with agreement on the Manitoba Act, you anticipated an orderly transfer to Canadian jurisdiction and were prepared to assist the new lieutenant-governor transfer jurisdiction to the Dominion of Canada. Can you please explain the events from your point of view.

RIEL: As requested, I carried out my duties faithfully, and the settlement once again reverted to its former life. Sending out its carts and dogsleds, the Hudson's Bay Company returned to its business, shops reopened and commerce returned. We eagerly awaited the new lieutenant-governor and prepared to welcome him and his party. As the time of his arrival approached, we began hearing from Métis working the lands west of Lake Superior that things were not as we expected. Contrary to our agreement with Canada, Colonel Garnet Wolseley and over four hundred hardened British regulars and a thousand Ontario "volunteers" were crossing the Canadian Shield on their way to Manitoba. Ostensibly, these troops were to accompany the new Canadian lieutenant-governor through hostile Sioux territory. The Sioux, however, were at peace in the "Grandmother's Lands," and Lieutenant-Governor designate A.G. Archibald was not with Colonel Wolseley.

As the Canadian forces drew near, Colonel Wolseley sent a declaration that he came on a mission of peace. We could clearly see that this was not the case when he also sent an undercover Irish intelligence officer, Captain William F. Butler, to reconnoitre the lay of the land, make local contacts and assess our military capabilities.

Captain Butler arrived in our community in the middle of the night and could not find his way about. When he was eventually found, I interviewed him, told him of our desire for a peaceful transition and sent him packing. Most interestingly, his evening's assessments, published later in *The Great Lone Land*, turned out to be a classic in the Anglo-Canadian adventure book genre.

In his book Butler described his impressions of me: "M. Louis Riel, President, Dictator, Ogre, Saviour of Society, and New Napoleon; as he was variously named by friends and foes in the little tea-cup of Red River whose tempest had cast him suddenly from dregs to surface. . . . He was dressed in a curious mixture of clothing — a black frock-coat, vest and trousers; but the effect of this somewhat clerical costume was not a little marred by a pair of Indian moccasins, which nowhere look more out of place than on a carpeted floor." Butler's language shows that he was completely unaware of the history of the Métis people and had little sympathy for them, their customary dress, or my participation in negotiating the Manitoba Act.

Warned of the malicious character of Wolseley's Canadian troops, Ambroise Lépine proposed that we block their access coming out of the Canadian Shield in the Lake of the Woods area. I rejected this. I relied on Bishop Taché's word. He had been personally assured by the prime minister that amnesty was to be granted. Acting at the request of the Canadian government, Taché assured me and the other leaders that ". . . all the irregularities of the past will be totally overlooked or forgiven; that nobody will be annoyed for having been either leader or member of the Provisional Government, or for having acted under its guidance. In a word, a complete and entire amnesty will surely be granted before the arrival of the troops." It was a difficult situation: Lépine was clearly right that we could use guerrilla tactics to stop Wolseley, but we had negotiated in good faith, and now we had to have faith in the agreement we signed with Canada. I felt we could not break our sacred word. That was until they were banging at the gates of Fort Garry, looking for my blood.

After months of slogging through muskeg and swamps, climbing rock faces and living on scanty rations, Wolseley's troops, cold and wet, reached the settlement in a mean and nasty mood. Contrary to his written declaration to our citizens, Wolseley and his troops marched into Red River with revenge in mind. As the soldiers rushed the front gate at Fort Garry, Ambroise Lépine, Will O'Donoghue, and I escaped via the back gate.

We were most brutally betrayed. Canada bargained and signed treaty with the people of Red River, then John A. Macdonald seized his opportunity to put the country under military rule. Colonel Wolseley and his troops entered our community with the intention of overthrowing the Provisional Government, arresting its leaders, and, if the Ontario volunteers had their way, lynching me. This was treachery of the first order.

After I and the other leaders narrowly escaped, martial law was proclaimed. As the new lieutenant-governor was not with this military expedition, Donald Smith, my old nemesis, now achieved his objective and was appointed acting governor in my stead. Life in our communities became hell. Shortly after the troops arrived, Elzéar Goulet, a member of Scott's court martial, was stoned and drowned in the Red River as he was trying to escape a hostile crowd of Canadians and soldiers. François Guillemette, a member of Scott's firing squad, was forced to flee to the United States where he was stalked by vengeful Canadians, overtaken and murdered. After our enemies attacked his horse, H.F. James Tanner was killed in a fall, André Nault was bayoneted and left for dead, and his daughter raped. It was a time of brutalization. Rapes, assault and battery were commonplace. The Canadian volunteers looted the taverns and created utter havoc in the community before the supply of liquor ran dry three days later. Canadian "squatters" indiscriminately moved onto Métis lands, threatening bloodshed to anyone who protested.

To the eternal shame of all Canadians, our community was brutalized and turned on its head by a community uniting in a racist jurisdiction that sought to establish Canadian hegemony over all aspects of life. Reporting to John A. Macdonald a year later, Lieutenant-Governor A.G. Archibald outlined the "persistent ill-usage" of the Métis by the Canadians: "many of them . . . actually have been so beaten and outraged that they feel as if they were living in a state of slavery. They say that the bitter hatred of these Canadians is so intolerable that they would gladly escape it by any sacrifice."

Although it may seem trivial in comparison to the abuses we faced, I would like to re-emphasize one other point. As previously discussed, amongst the many accusations hurled at me, and which I have asked this Inquiry to review, is my supposed "pillage" of the Hudson's Bay Company's Fort Garry. This accusation, although now minor in nature, reflects badly on the character of our government and the question of my conduct in the seizure of Fort Garry. I signed receipts for those supplies and monies we used to maintain civil society, while Colonel Wolseley's troops treated Fort Garry and the Hudson's Bay Company supplies as plunder. There is no comparison. We were upright in all of our dealings with the Company, conducting ourselves in an honourable manner throughout our tenure. The troops of Wolseley's 60th Regiment were responsible for wanton destruction. Discussing the creation of Manitoba, and the history of the Red River troubles, Manitoba historian Alexander Begg tells us that, "thinking that everything inside the Fort came under the head of spoils of war, the troops began a regular pillage on the stores of the Hudson's Bay Company."

With the members of our provisional government now in hiding, I set up a council in the little community of "St. Joe's" (St. Joseph) on the U.S. side of the border. Through Bishop Taché, I attempted to open negotiations with the military authorities. Neither Garnet Wolseley nor Donald Smith would discuss the situation with me or my council. Putting out a warrant for our arrest, Donald Smith declared us "outlaws."

Like the factors of old, Donald Smith ran the Company, the country and the government. Our legislative assembly was disbanded, and any number of depredations were allowed to be perpetrated. The new lieutenant-governor, A.G. Archibald, did not arrive until September 1870, and initially refused to acknowledge the members of the previous government. He would speak only to Bishop Taché. A good number of the Canadian volunteers who had arrived with Wolseley stayed behind, and it was these bandits who would intimidate Métis families to abandon their farmsteads.

COMMISSIONER: Mr. Riel, in 1871 the new province of Manitoba faced an Irish-American Fenian invasion. Please explain to this Inquiry your role in this affair.

RIEL: It needs to be remembered that our old Red River Settlement had been a very cosmopolitan community. Although we French-speaking Métis made up the majority of the population, we had our English-speaking cousins, the half-breeds, as well as the old HBC functionaries and the descendants of Selkirk's settlers, and some Quebecers, including the priests, living in the community. Throughout our struggle for recognition of the Provisional Government, we also had a significant number of Americans actively involved in our discussions. We knew that amongst them were American operatives, as well as outright annexationists working through official and unofficial channels. These included Oscar Malmros, James Taylor and the legless American speculator and annexationist Enos Stutsman, to name but a few. Also, two key Minnesota politicians, the notorious "Sioux fighters," Governors Ramsey and Sibely, saw the North-West as theirs for the taking, and kept particularly close tabs on what was happening in the Red River Settlement. Previously, back in the year of the Canadian Confederation, Republican Senator Ramsey had tabled a motion in Congress offering the Hudson's Bay Company $46,000,000 for Rupert's Land and the North-West Territories. The motion did not pass, but the sentiment remained.

We were basically helpless at this time: our people were being brutalized, and I was in hiding in the U.S. where American friends kept me safe as assassins fanned out looking for my blood. Deciding that drastic action was necessary, I crossed back over the border to meet secretly with forty of my Métis brothers in Father Ritchot's rectory in St. Boniface. After lengthy consultations, we decided to prepare a "Memorial and Petition of the People of Rupert's Land" to be sent to President Grant, stating:

> Not a single pledge given by the English and Canadian Governments to
> our people, and to the Government of the United States, has been kept

or performed. On the contrary, each and every one as set forth in this memorial, has been ruthlessly and revengefully violated and trampled upon.

It was at this point our former treasurer, William (Bill) O'Donoghue, insisted that American annexation was the only answer. Concerned with being "swallowed-up" by the American juggernaut, I vehemently rejected that position, explaining that what we wanted was only for President Grant to apply pressure on Prime Minister Macdonald to implement the amnesty as negotiated in the Manitoba Act and as my bishop continued to promise. O'Donoghue derided me for my naïveté. Slapping my face, he called me a coward, and stomped from the room. That was the last I saw of him. But it was not the last I heard of him.

With the help of Enos Stutsman and other Americans, O'Donoghue reworked the memorial to make it read as if we Métis were in favour of annexation. In late December 1870, O'Donoghue was granted an audience with President Grant. Although Grant was not convinced that the people of the Red River were as keen on American annexation as O'Donoghue intimated, he listened "very kindly" and went about making his own plans for the North-West, clearing the Indians out of the right-of-way of his Northern Pacific Railway.

Next, O'Donoghue went to New York, meeting with General John O'Neill, the president of the Council of the Fenian Brotherhood. Unsuccessful in his call for another Fenian invasion of Canada, O'Donoghue returned to St. Paul and made his way west into the Dakotas. Promoting a new "Republic of Rupert's Land," he attempted to garner Métis support for a revolt against the Canadians.

At this time we also knew that back in the East, General John O'Neill received a visit from a presidential intimate, the Philadelphia banker, Jay Cooke. Famously, Cooke had financed the Union Army by selling bonds to "Tom, Dick and Harry," and was now a director of the Northern Pacific Railroad, along with President Grant. Amongst their plans was a Northern Pacific feeder line from the Minnesota border up into the Red River Settlement. Although O'Neill's last two Fenian invasions in Niagara and New Brunswick had been total fiascos, O'Neill had a change of heart after this meeting in regards to an invasion of Manitoba. O'Neill also now had the money, enthusiasm and four hundred Springfield rifles with which to invade. Enlisting the two Civil War veterans, General J.J. Donnelly and Colonel Tom Curley, O'Neill moved the field of operations to Minneapolis, Minnesota.

We Métis kept tabs on Bill O'Donoghue and his activities in the Dakotas. We knew what he was up to as he made no secret of his activities, or his disdain for me. He talked openly of invasion and sweeping the Canadians from the North-West. What we did not know was that John A. Macdonald knew of the impending invasion as well. He had been monitoring the Fenians since the end of the American Civil War. Concerned about further possible invasions, and with the help of the British Secret Service, Macdonald had his ace spy Henri Le Caron working right alongside O'Neill as a major in the Fenian army. Le Caron knew O'Neill's plans and where his money was coming from. Reporting to the commissioner of the Dominion Police, and head of the Canadian secret police, Judge Gilbert McMicken, Le Caron revealed to the judge that the money for the invasion came from Grant's "bagman," Mr. Jay Cooke.

With this information, Macdonald informed newly arrived Lieutenant-Governor Archibald in Manitoba of the potential invasion and Canada's inability to send troops to the North-West. With Wolseley's troops having returned to Ontario, Archibald asked Bishop Taché to feel out the mood in the Métis communities in regard to an American invasion. Taché told him that I was the only person capable of dealing with this crisis. So it was that, with a warrant sworn for my arrest and an Ontario bounty of $5,000 on my head, I was asked to protect Manitoba from an American invasion. Knowing that an American invasion would most certainly not recognize our Métis and Indian rights, I quickly agreed to stand with the Canadians. Ambroise Lépine then called out three hundred of his men to defend the Red River community against any American invaders. With our men under arms, I purposefully paraded my Métis cavalry before the entire English-speaking male population of Kildonan. My point: to prove our powerful Métis force was ready to defend the community as true Canadians.

On October 5, 1871, O'Neill, O'Donoghue and some thirty recruits crossed into Manitoba, taking over the Hudson's Bay Company's border post. Here, they waited for the Métis reinforcements that O'Donoghue had recruited to republicanism. None came. As Ambroise and our brigades swept south towards the border, U.S. Captain Lloyd Wheaton and a troop of U.S. cavalry crossed the international border, extracting O'Neill and his men and escorting them back across the border to Fort Totten. Meanwhile, our Métis scouts captured Bill O'Donoghue attempting to evade the U.S. cavalry. They took O'Donoghue to the border where he was handed over to Captain Wheaton. As the incident occurred in British North America, the Americans laid no charges, and the conspirators all walked free. Thereafter, Bill O'Donoghue would fade from memory, a school teacher in Minnesota until his early death.

The Fenian attack was a dismal failure, but its implications were profound. At the local level, my point was made. If we had wished to do so, we Métis could easily have supported the Fenians and overthrown the Canadians. By supporting Lieutenant-Governor Archibald, I attempted, once again, to demonstrate the willingness of the Métis population to be true Canadians — with the rights and responsibilities of Canadians — including defending Canada from invasion. In an honourable move, Lieutenant-Governor Archibald came over to St. Boniface to review our Métis troops. After doing so, he thanked Ambroise for our contribution to Canada and shook my hand, although he consciously did not address me by name. Such petty hypocrisy! I used this occasion to obtain from Archibald a written promise of amnesty. Which proved to be meaningless.

Our reality is that although John A. Macdonald recognized the right of the people of the Red River to form a government, what he did not recognize was the right of our people and government to continue our right to peace and security. What we had not agreed to was that our land be occupied militarily, our leaders arrested or forced into exile, and our people subjected to the ignominies of the hostile Canadian forces. We had not agreed to the series of measures over the next few years that deprived us of the land which the Manitoba Act said was ours. Nor did we agree to our rights being trampled, our schools dismantled and our language virtually extinguished from the streets of the new city of Winnipeg, as our people scattered to the wind.

I can state categorically that under the pretext of legality, Anglo-Canadian colonialism seized political power and put an end to the self-rule of the people of the Red River and our democratic rights. I had fathered the patriation of the North-West, as a British colony, into the Canadian Confederation, but was exiled and forced to flee my homeland for my efforts. In this regard, I wish it to be firmly established that neither I nor our Métis forces rebelled. Neither my government nor I renounced our allegiance to the British Crown. Let it be known that Sir John A. Macdonald also admitted this fact on December 16, 1869, in his report to the Committee of the Privy Council where he said that this resistance "is evidently not against the sovereignty of Her Majesty or the government of the Hudson's Bay Company, but to the assumption of the government by Canada."

COMMISSIONER: Mr. Riel, there has been a great deal of confusion in regard to Métis scrip lands and the policies of the Canadian government. Would you please speak to these issues?

RIEL: Under the Manitoba Act "assuring to the settlers in the Province the peaceable possession of the lands now held by them," I would have this Inquiry note that although the Hudson's Bay Company had been delinquent in the distribution of title, the right to remain on our homesteads was recognized by Canada. The challenge that arose was that we Métis could not obtain legal title or scrip to our lands until Dominion surveyors finished sectioning the land — a job which took three years. This legal lapse allowed for the wholesale expropriation of Métis family farms by Canadians claiming title. According to the Manitoba Act, additional scrip lands were also to be made available "to the extent of 1,400,000 acres thereof for the benefit of the families of the half-breed residents." Here, however, was the biggest swindle of all. Scrip lands were administered in a most devious fashion. Family plots were often on non-contiguous lands or separated by extreme distances. Moreover, over the next decade the Manitoba government, in particular, passed a series of legislative changes, altering the rules of distribution of allotment, and creating wide-scale confusion over who owned which parcel.

Many times, land reserved for the Métis would be apportioned to an immigrant family before the scrip was even issued to the Métis family. In the majority of cases, the confusion led to the sale of scrip by the Métis to speculators. Donald Smith, Christian Schultz and other men of note acquired large land holdings during this period. As a consequence of the legislative amendments and actions by speculators and squatters, we, as a people, became dispossessed and dispersed. As a result, our Métis people began a mass exodus, leaving the Red River area for the U.S. or the Saskatchewan country to the west. I personally never received my legal land allotment and have asked to have this recognized by this Inquiry.

COMMISSIONER: Thank you, Mr. Riel. The second session of this Inquiry is now in recess. Upon reconvening, we will receive the third part of your testimony.

PART III

Amnesty, Exile
& Revelation

COMMISSIONER: Mr. Riel, please begin by speaking to the "Amnesty Clause" and its role in the Manitoba Act.

RIEL: When the treaty or the Manitoba Act was made between the people of the Red River and the Canadian government, there was, as I have mentioned, a question of amnesty. Our original Bill of Rights, as sent to Ottawa by the Provisional Government for negotiations, included a provision guaranteeing that an amnesty would be granted "... that none of the members of the Provisional Government or any of those acting under them be in any way held liable or responsible with regard to the movement, or any of the actions which led to the present negotiations." This was the *sine qua non* of any agreement. Throughout the negotiations, one of the key points made by our delegation was that before the Canadian government would send a governor into Manitoba, an Imperial amnesty should be proclaimed so as to blot out all the difficulties of the past. We had every reason to believe the amnesty was coming, as amongst Commissioner Thibault's papers were five hundred copies of the following from the Queen's representative in Canada, Governor General Sir John Young, and dated December 6, 1869:

> And I do lastly inform you, that in case of your immediate and peaceable obedience and dispersion, I shall order that no legal proceeding be taken against any parties implicated in these unfortunate breaches of the law.

With this promise by the governor general, our Red River delegates went to Ottawa with an amnesty as an integral part of the terms of our joining the Canadian Confederation. Wrapping up the successful discussions, the Canadian delegates left the impression with our delegates that an amnesty would be granted upon successful completion of negotiations. The Queen, they said, would then grant the amnesty. Negotiations were completed. We waited. No amnesty.

The Manitoba Act received royal assent May 12, 1870 and went into effect July 15, 1870. Tragically, there was no amnesty in the final version. It had been surreptitiously removed by the prime minister after negotiations had been completed. Later the Canadians claimed that since it was irrelevant to the actual process of forming a province, it was not included in the official Manitoba Act. It is my belief that the Canadian government had no intention of declaring an amnesty. John A. Macdonald did not have the political will to declare an amnesty. He allowed it to be negotiated and then slyly withdrew it from the final agreement. This deception and the later aggression by Colonel Wolseley were the result of the racist fervour that swept Protestant Ontario at this time. This is the same racist zeal that followed and often directed European colonialism in its conquest of the New World. Ideas about racial superiority poisoned Europe and were imported into the New World, until Canada too had its own rapacious breed of racism, as exemplified by the Canada First Movement and the attempted expunging of Indigenous title. It was this movement that ensured that there would be no amnesty for me and the other members of the Provisional Government, and which indirectly and directly influenced government policy.

COMMISSIONER: Mr. Riel, please explain the role of the Canada First Movement in preventing an amnesty from being declared for yourself and the other members of the Provisional Government.

RIEL: It was in April 1868 that the Macdonald Cabinet minister, D'Arcy McGee, the Irish-born "orator and prophet" of the union of the British colonies in North America, was assassinated. Presumably, he was shot by a member of the Irish Brotherhood, the Fenian movement, for his work to link the Catholic Irish and Anglo Protestants in order to make for a strong Canada in close alliance with Britain. A Father of Confederation, and bon vivant associate of Prime Minister Macdonald, McGee was seen as a "nationalist," and as such was given Canada's first state funeral, an affair of grandeur and pageantry. With all the traditional pomp and ceremony of Britannia, McGee's funeral was designed to ignite a patriotic fervour. It was also an occasion to bring together the Anglo-Canadian nationalists of the Canada First Movement.

As was explained earlier, Canada First was the name and slogan of a movement originating in Ottawa in 1868 to promote British Protestant nationalist sentiment in Canada. Among its founding members were prominent Canadian business and political leaders, including such Canadian luminaries as R.G. Haliburton, Henry Morgan, William Foster, G.T. Denison and the poet Charles Mair. Believing that they were the descendants of the Aryan tribes of northern Europe, "the Northmen of the New World" believed they were destined for greatness. Determined to carry on from where McGee, the first martyr of Canadian colonialism, had fallen, they planned to tread a glorious path, showing Canadians, and the world, the superiority of their race in North America. Following this racist ideology, Canada First sought to use their version of racist nationalism as the basis of unifying Canada, under the British Ensign, in their own interests. They also had a superordinate goal: the colonization of our homeland, the Red River country and the whole Great North-West.

Like all reactionaries, they needed a war to glue their country together, in this case, a war in the North-West. They felt we "miserable half-breeds" would be no problem. But life is never as simple as a racist's dream. When they launched their offensive through Christian Schultz and his Canadian Party, we Métis outmanoeuvred them, politically and militarily. They were furious that the province of Manitoba was established in the image we crafted, and not that of Orange Ontario, or Canada First. Only through political deception and military occupation were they finally able to reverse our victory and attempt to dismantle and destroy the Métis culture and presence in the Red River area.

Thomas Scott was their second martyr, and the *cause célèbre* of the Canada Firsters. With our delegates negotiating with John A. Macdonald and the Canadian Cabinet, Colonel Denison threatened to seize the Toronto arsenal if an amnesty were proclaimed. Mob violence was incited and the Orange Lodge carried out a massive anti-Riel campaign of racist hate-mongering across Ontario and the eastern townships of

Quebec. Liberal politicians, such as George Brown and Edward Blake, supporters of Canada First, also called for "the end of French domination in Manitoba." Not daring to move one way or the other, Prime Minister Macdonald bowed to their demands and let the amnesty question linger. Caught in a bind, the Canadian government then attempted to shift responsibility for the amnesty to the Imperial government. For the next five years, while my people and I suffered, the Imperial government also dithered. Even American President Grant petitioned them for an amnesty, to no avail. Amnesty would only be granted five years later, when it was no longer in their interest to keep me as the chief villain in the land.

COMMISSIONER: Mr. Riel, as a Canadian province, Manitoba was involved in the federal election of 1872. Although initially you were not a candidate, please explain your role in this election.

RIEL: Canada's second federal election was held in 1872. Prior to this, an Ontario provincial election was held in 1871. It was a racist nightmare. The central issue of the "murder of Thomas Scott" successfully elected Edward Blake and the provincial Liberals. One of the first provincial bills passed was reconfirming an initial $5,000 reward for my arrest that Blake had personally issued leading up to the election. Even the Manitoba provincial legislature protested against Ontario's interference in its internal affairs. In the French-speaking parishes of Manitoba, meetings opposing the imposition of the Ontario reward were held. Lieutenant-Governor Archibald reported that our people were "determined that the parties against whom the rewards were directed should remain in the country, and that the people should protect them from any attempt to arrest them." Also, coming out of these meetings, the call was made for me to run in the upcoming Canadian election, an idea I found attractive.

In the month of February 1872, as the Canadian election loomed, our newly appointed archbishop, my old mentor, Bishop Taché, came to my mother's house to tell me that the authorities in Lower Canada wanted Ambroise Lépine and me to cross to the other side of the U.S. border until the present crisis passed. They wanted us to "lie low" and leave the country during the upcoming general election for the Canadian Parliament. I knew that Taché meant that the leaders of the Conservative Party, John A. Macdonald and George-Étienne Cartier, wanted us out of the way. Taking lessons from the Ontario election, they sought to prevent the Liberal Party and the newspapers in Ontario from using the "murderers of Thomas Scott" as a federal election issue. I told Archbishop Taché that if the crisis concerned me only, it would be in my interest to leave, but as my crisis is also that of my Métis people, I will let them decide. This did not sit well with the archbishop. He was determined that I go, and was relentless, as only an archbishop can be.

As I have explained earlier, Taché had been a "second father" to me, and it was extremely difficult for me to oppose his wishes. Knowing that I could not appeal to his reason, I told him that if he commanded me to go, and took the responsibility of my leaving my people in the crisis, I would go. I also used this opportunity to tell his lordship that I was broke. Having no means of making an income, I had to rely on my people to help feed my mother and my siblings. I reminded him that the Canadian government owed me money for my administration during the transition and also for the work they had asked me to do during the Fenian invasion, for which they had never paid me. I also told him they owed me something for my reputation — that they abused every day.

Agreeing that Lépine and I needed to be paid, the archbishop offered us £10 a month to stay on the other side of the line. This was ridiculous: it did nothing for our families who would be home alone. Finally, after consulting with Ottawa, Taché agreed that they would give £800: £400 to Lépine, £400 to me. This comprised £300 to me personally, £300 for Lépine, £100 for my family, £100 for Lépine's family. In addition, the newly confirmed Conservative candidate for Winnipeg, Donald Smith, put up an additional £600 to be rid of us. On our way to cross the border, having said goodbye to our families, Lépine and I met the archbishop at the chapel of St. Vital. Here I told him: "I will take this money as part of what they will have to pay me one day. If the one who wants me to go away was here, and if I were to treat him as he is treating me, this little sack of gold ought to go through his head."

We went to St. Paul. Although we were under assumed names, we still found ourselves unsafe when Christian Schultz and other Canada Firsters were spotted in the neighbourhood of our rooming house. When two Métis youth reported being offered $50 to steal my papers, we were forced to vacate and hide out. Knowing that we were being hunted by dangerous men, we slipped out of St. Paul and rode to the Dakotas. Soon after, we made our way back to St. Joe's. At this point, Lépine decided to return to his farm and take his chances. I could not risk the threat to my family and stayed in hiding in the border country of the Dakotas, awaiting the results of the election.

COMMISSIONER: Mr. Riel, great changes occurred as a result of the Canadian election of 1872, with implications for all of Canada as well as for your career and the North-West. Would you please speak to these changes?

RIEL: Yes, the implications of the 1872 Canadian election were significant. It shook the very heart of the Canadian political structure as established by John A. Macdonald. Whereas Ambroise Lépine and I had reluctantly accepted money to vacate ourselves from influencing the federal election of 1872, money that we did not consider to be illegal, it still left us with a bad taste considering its source. As I was to discover, however, the money paid to us was tiny in comparison to what was paid in Macdonald's signature project, the Canadian Pacific Railway. Moreover, I found that I was myself asked to play a part in the politics surrounding the financing scandals of the railway and the actual election machinations as they took place in Manitoba with George-Étienne Cartier's candidature. The history is complicated but important, and it will take me some time to clarify what happened.

Prior to the Canadian Confederation, the British Foreign Office considered the building of a British transcontinental railway as a critical component of the empire's defences: an Imperial highway, a thin "red line" blocking American expansion into the North-West and linking London with Cathay. With backing from London, it also became a key component of Macdonald's Canadian Confederation. As is well known, one of the conditions of British Columbia joining Confederation was the building of a railway by the newly constituted Dominion government.

Two rival financial syndicates sought to gain the construction contract. The first was Hugh Allan from Quebec, president of the Allan Shipping Line and a director of the Grand Trunk and the Northern Colonization railways. The second was the Interoceanic Company, headed by Toronto Conservative Senator David Macpherson. Seeking financiers to back his bid, Allan went south to the United States where the post-Civil War railway market was hot. Here he talked with the American financier Jay Cooke and a number of his investors. Cooke, an American expansionist, financier of the Fenian invasion of Manitoba, and a director and key financier of the Northern Pacific Railroad, was diametrically opposed to the construction of a competing Canadian railroad line.

Of like mind, Hugh Allan also had little interest in an all-Canadian railroad route. With Cooke's backing, he hoped to slip a line down into Michigan, bypassing the rugged Canadian Shield, to connect with the Northern Pacific heading west. It did not take long before Macdonald heard rumours of Allan's scheme to skip south. Warning Allan that he had to agree to an all-Canadian route, Macdonald was also adamant that Allan's American directors were not appropriate. Under these circumstances, Allan simply removed the names of his American backers from his board and bought some new Canadian associates, including the HBC's Donald Smith, who came on board for a consideration of $100,000.

With Macdonald suspicious, and Macpherson's Toronto syndicate promising to build an all-Canadian line, Allan grew anxious that he would not win the contract. He knew that he had to put pressure on Macdonald, and to do this he would have to make Macdonald vulnerable in the upcoming election. How to do this? It was but a minor problem for Allan's friend, Jay Cooke, who had spent his career bribing senators and congressmen. Spending extravagantly, Cooke and Allan set about sabotaging Macdonald's election campaign, supporting the Liberal Party and applying particular pressure on Macdonald's weakest link, his Quebec lieutenant, George-Étienne Cartier.

As Allan's dirty-tricks campaign gained momentum, public opinion slipped away from Cartier, as did twenty-seven of his forty-five Quebec Conservative caucus. Cartier was caught, and he knew it, as did John A. Macdonald. Now desperate, Macdonald agreed that after the election Allan and his syndicate would receive the railway charter. This outraged the Ontario wing of the Conservative Party. Senator Macpherson offered a compromise. He proposed to jointly build the railroad, his stipulation was that there be no American investors. Allan agreed, simply putting his American partner's shares in his own name.

Macdonald's election was still in jeopardy. In crisis, he had Cartier promise Allan the presidency of the new company. Still concerned that Senator Macpherson would not go along with this new arrangement, Allan forced Cartier to put the offer in writing. Cartier conceded, sealing his own fate and, as it turned out, destroying his once glorious career. Now having signed his life away, Cartier looked for payback. Cartier asked Allan to help in the election campaign. When Allan asked Cartier how much he wanted, he was told that it could be up to $100,000. Allan wanted that in writing as well. Two letters were produced, one had Cartier promising Allan the presidency, and the other was for financial assistance of $50,000. In the end some one hundred and fifty Conservative candidates received up to $360,000 in support.

Macdonald just barely won the election, and his own seat. Cartier was soundly defeated, even though Allan had given him $20,000 personally and forwarded another $30,000 to the Cartier Central Election Committee. This was cash money to buy votes in the streets, taverns, churches, wherever. Unfortunately for Cartier, his political machine had been so corrupted that although money had been distributed far and wide, when it came time for the actual vote, mysteriously, man after man put up for the opposition candidate. Cartier had been sold out: a secret Liberal supporter working on his Central Election Committee had rigged the election. Desperately needing Cartier in his Cabinet, John A. Macdonald searched for a vacant parliamentary seat, a seat where a "Frenchman" could win.

I apologize for the long historical account but without it, one cannot understand how I then became involved. Due to geographical considerations, and Manitoba's recent entry into Confederation, the federal election was delayed in Manitoba and was scheduled to take place two weeks after the general Canadian election. With the general election over, my obligation to remove myself from Canada was over as well. Although living in hiding, I was nominated as a candidate in the new federal district of Provencher. No longer bound by my promise to vacate the country, I accepted the nomination. There was also one other candidate, an Anglo-Catholic lawyer, Henry J. Clarke, a member of the Legislative Assembly of Manitoba. Now with Cartier needing a seat in the House, Prime Minister Macdonald called upon Archbishop Taché to influence both Clarke and me to step aside and allow Cartier to run in our place.

As a youth in Montreal, I had corresponded with George-Étienne Cartier. He was a French-Canadian hero who, as a young man, had gone into exile in the United States after the rebellions of 1837–38. Now as deputy prime minister and leader of the Quebec caucus, I saw him as our only hope to resolve our North-West crisis. After negotiating a number of vital concessions, I agreed to step aside and let Cartier run in my stead. In return, the archbishop promised an amnesty that would provide immunity from prosecution to all members of the Provisional Government, and that Cartier would personally guarantee the fair distribution of the 1.4 million acres of land promised to the Métis in the Manitoba Act. Coincidently, Clarke stepped aside and was shortly thereafter made acting premier of Manitoba.

With no other candidates in the running, Cartier won the Provencher election by acclamation. He was, however, no longer the great statesman or orator of the past. As rumours of election irregularities built, Cartier was a fallen man. Morally beaten down, he was too ill to deal with any of the problems of his constituents and died before returning to Parliament. With the death of Cartier went all hope of his exercising his enormous power to see to amnesty or the distribution of Métis lands.

Now I need to turn to another dimension of our Métis situation after the 1872 election. Our optimism for a better deal for the Métis was now at a low ebb, especially when our first lieutenant-governor, A.G. Archibald, who earnestly attempted to implement reasonable and fair government in an atmosphere of extreme racial and civil tension, was called back to the Maritimes following Canadian complaints that he had shaken the "bloody hand" of Louis Riel after the Fenian invasion.

Archibald was replaced by Alexander Morris, who had been John A. Macdonald's law clerk prior to Confederation. As an elected Member of Parliament, Morris steadily worked his way up the political ladder in Ottawa. As Macdonald's minister of internal revenue, he played a key role in diverting funds for the prime minister's railway projects. Now Morris had been chosen to open the North-West, signing treaties with the Indians and replacing the conciliatory Lieutenant-Governor Archibald. Appointed chief justice of the Manitoba Court of Queen's Bench and acting lieutenant-governor, Morris exercised his own authority over the province's courts and legislative process. Although fluently bilingual, Morris refused to speak French, "quietly enforcing" English practice and English law whenever possible. Still legally bound by the Manitoba Act, Morris complained bitterly of "a conflict of authorities and practices" — the old Assiniboia ideas in conflict with those of Ontario and Quebec.

It is my contention that Morris also had another responsibility. Under the watchful eye of John A. Macdonald, he was to facilitate the arrest and trial of Louis Riel and Ambroise Lépine. I became especially concerned when Morris chose my old political rival, Henry J. Clarke, as the new Manitoba attorney general. Through the appointment of Clarke, Morris let it be known that he would look favourably upon the prosecution of the "murderers of Thomas Scott" as Clarke had so often bragged he would do.

It was at this juncture that another brash young Ontario lawyer, Francis E. Cornish, set out to make a name for himself. His plan was to capture and prosecute Ambroise Lépine and me, and pick up the $5,000 reward for our capture. Calling in one of our former prisoners, euphemistically known as "Farmer," Cornish gathered his "evidence," which he presented to Attorney General Clarke, who then formally charged Ambroise Lépine and me with the murder of Thomas Scott. These illegal warrants, added to the reward already posted by Ontario Liberal leader Edward Blake, were ample enticement for large numbers of

Canadians to scour the countryside looking for us. I barely escaped an ambush, but Ambroise Lépine, an innocent man, let himself be captured.

When Frank Cornish heard that Lépine was back home, working on his farm, he sent two policemen, Jack Ingram and John Kerr, along with others, to arrest Lépine. With the farm surrounded, the two policemen found Ambroise working in his yard. Served a warrant, he did not resist and allowed himself to be arrested, without physical violence. Taken to Winnipeg he was charged with murder and held without bail, until there was a change in attorney general, and then he was finally released on his own recognizance and $8,000 bail.

Please excuse me, as I must interject a classic Canada versus Métis conflict of views at this point. As always, historical interpretations diverge. The noted historian, Auguste-Henri de Trémaudan's *Histoire de la nation métisse dans l'ouest canadien* (History of the Métis Nation in Western Canada) tells us Ambroise Lépine, "built like a Hercules, only remarked laughingly to the pygmies who came to lay hold of him, that if he felt like it, he could break the two of them together over one of his knees, as he did with the fork handle he held in his hands." Yet, when you hear the tale from the Canadian side, Ingram and Cornish both earned their reputation that day. Ingram claimed that he executed the capture through the simple expediency of "walking up to Lépine, putting him off guard by greeting him as he would an old friend, then knocking him out with a well-placed left hook to the head." This is, of course, utter nonsense, but it paid off handsomely in their subsequent careers. Ingram and Cornish shared in the $5,000 reward for bringing Ambroise Lépine to trial. Later, when Cornish ran and was elected the first mayor of Winnipeg, he made Ingram his chief of police.

With the arrest of Ambroise Lépine, I was no longer safe in St. Boniface. With Canadians fanning out across the countryside searching for me, I would spend forty-five days living in hiding, my whereabouts secret to all but the most trusted few. Camped on the prairie knolls, it was a period of deep reflection, intense contemplation and prayer. Over time, I gained solace and strength reading of Biblical King David hiding from the Philistines before emerging victorious. David gave me strength and it is for that reason I have adopted his name, Louis "David" Riel.

In this climate of racial fear and intimidation, some five hundred frustrated Métis and their supporters gathered outside the cathedral in St. Boniface in October 1873 and officially nominated me as their candidate in the Provencher by-election. Under my community's protection I came home where, shortly after, I was visited by Henry Clarke, who once again sought the federal seat. Clarke came to try to dissuade me from running as a candidate in the by-election. According to him, I was "too divisive." When I declined his kind offer, he became very upset and in a fit of rage offered to fight a duel at twelve paces. Once again I declined Mr. Clarke's offer, and he was escorted from my home, now confirmed as my mortal enemy.

I won the nomination by a landslide and, surrounded by my Métis friends and family, I was proclaimed the new Member of Parliament for the federal riding of Provencher. Giving thanks to God, we hoped this would lead to better days. Here, finally, was my opportunity to take our issues directly to Ottawa. Yet, with a warrant out for my arrest and a price on my head, I dared not travel without my Métis protectors.

The newly elected Conservative Member of Parliament for Pembina had no such problems. As a Member of Parliament and head of the Hudson's Bay Company, Donald Smith was now able to influence the political as well as the economic affairs of Manitoba and Canada in his own interest, and his interest was now trade, transportation and communication. As a "clean" Conservative, not connected, or involved with, the payments that Hugh Allan made to Macdonald in what became known as the "Pacific Scandal," Smith now orchestrated the downfall of his prime minister and his government, and seized control of the CPR by ousting Hugh Allan. Unfortunately for Smith, as he consolidated his hold over transportation and trade in the North-West, the bottom fell out of the credit market. In the "Panic of 1873," one of the worst of the cyclical economic collapses, the leading American banking firm of Jay Cooke and Company found itself overextended and went bankrupt, leading to a major collapse in railways, banks and manufacturing businesses internationally. The great capitalist empires, the United States and Britain, built on credit, hollowed out, leading to the world economic depression that would last until 1879, and even longer in Britain.

COMMISSIONER: Mr. Riel, as the elected Member of Parliament for the federal riding of Provencher you faced a number of extraordinary challenges. Please inform this Inquiry of the nature of these challenges and their implications for your career.

RIEL: With my election to the House of Commons, I determined that I had to make my way to Ottawa, to Parliament Hill and into the House of Commons. Surely, I believed, once I took my seat in the Dominion Parliament I could claim sanctuary and let the House decide my innocence or guilt. Once there, refuting the lies and misrepresentations of our enemies, I would bring forth the documentary evidence of our negotiations with Canada, nation to nation. This way I would prove, once and for all, that Thomas Scott was not murdered by a number of individuals but legally executed by a legitimate government, a government recognized by Canada.

With the new government in place, in the spring of 1874, I secretly left Manitoba under an assumed name and travelled through the United States and up to Ottawa. In Ottawa, joined by Jean-Baptiste Romuald Fiset, my Quebec schoolmate and Liberal Member of the House, I made my way into the Parliament buildings. Bundled up in my winter coat and scarves, I signed the Members Register. Slipping aside, I watched to see what would happen when the clerk discovered that it was I who had signed the register. Almost immediately there was a great commotion, with calls for the guards to bolt the doors. Realizing that I was going to be hunted down, I escaped from Parliament Hill, hurriedly made my way across the Ottawa River to Hull, Quebec, where I went into hiding. I had caused a great tumult. The Orangemen were in the streets rallying against me, and troops and police were everywhere, searching high and low.

In the halls of Parliament, many of the backbench Quebec Liberal MPs rallied around Fiset. They called for my admittance to the House of Commons with full immunity to state my case. On the other side of the House, the Ontario Orange faction was not slow to act either.

Prior to his defeat, Prime Minister Macdonald had struck a "select committee of the House of Commons to inquire into the causes of the difficulties that arose in the North-West in 1869–70." Chairman of this select committee was MP Mackenzie Bowell, the grand master of the Orange Association and a future Canadian prime minister. Following my signing of the register, Bowell quickly convened the Committee and moved, seconded by the rookie MP for the riding of Lisgar in Winnipeg, Dr. Christian Schultz, to expel me from my seat in the House of Commons. I would like to have their motion entered into evidence:

> That Louis Riel, a Member of this House for the Electoral District of Provencher, in the Province of Manitoba, having been charged with murder, and a Bill of Indictment for the said offence having been found against him, and Warrants issued for his apprehension, and the said Louis Riel having fled from justice and having failed to obey an Order of this House that he should attend in his place on Thursday, the 9th day of April, 1874, be expelled this House.

The implications for my career were such that I was in a double bind. Although called upon to defend myself, I could not go back to the Hill because hundreds of soldiers, police and vigilantes were looking for me everywhere. On the Hill, MPs of dark complexion were closely scrutinized in case I might be returning to the House in disguise. With Bowell's motion, I was not only officially expelled from the Canadian Parliament but in acute physical danger. I had to make a series of midnight rides deep into Quebec to escape from my enemies.

COMMISSIONER: Mr. Riel, the arrest and subsequent trial of Ambroise Lépine for the murder of Thomas Scott had profound ramifications for Lépine, yourself and Canada. Please review Mr. Lépine's trial and explain its impact across Canada.

RIEL: The arrest and trial of Ambroise Lépine was a heavy blow to me personally. I knew Lépine's trial was as much about me as it was Lépine. It also stirred up ethnic tensions anew. Divisions in Manitoba grew deeper with our two major ethnic communities growing further and further apart. In Ontario, the Orangemen were gleeful and saw this as but a prelude to putting Louis Riel on trial; in Quebec, anger grew at what was seen as a great injustice to a francophone hero.

With support from our Métis community, Mr. Joseph Dubuc under-
took Lépine's defence along with Joseph Royal, who also served as
Manitoba's provincial secretary. Prior to the trial, during the preliminary hearing, both men sought to have the charges quashed, producing
evidence that proved that although Ambroise Lépine had reluctantly
voted for Scott's execution, he had not been present in the Fort Garry
courtyard when the execution took place. Their plea was overruled. As
the trial loomed, with a strong defence team in place, a conviction on the
bogus charge of murder was doubtful. At this critical juncture, Lieutenant-Governor Morris dumped Henry Clarke as attorney general and
appointed Joseph Dubuc as Manitoba's new attorney general.

Conveniently, an attorney general could not prosecute a case he had
been hired to defend. Effectively sidelined, Dubuc was forced to take
himself out of the trial completely. Further, with Clarke removed as
attorney general, he too was removed from the Lépine trial. This allowed Frank Cornish, the only other lawyer in the province with
enough knowledge of the case to conduct the prosecution, to be appointed Crown Counsel.

Joseph Royal now stood for the defence alone. Seeking support, he
sent out a call for help to our friends in Quebec. Joseph-Adolphe Chapleau, a prominent criminal lawyer and up-and-coming Quebec parlia-
mentarian, was approached to take up the defence with Royal. With the
intensity of feeling aroused in Quebec by the arrest and trial of Ambroise Lépine, and the lingering amnesty question, Chapleau was easily
induced to accept the offer.

After numerous delays, mostly regarding the court's jurisdiction over
crimes committed before the territory became a part of Canada, the
trial was finally heard by Chief Justice Edmund Burke Wood and a jury
of twelve: six English-speaking and six French-speaking jurors. Royal
and Chapleau based their case on the argument that the Provisional
Government of Assiniboia had been a de facto government, and that the
Métis court martial derived its authority from this fact. They also argued that the Manitoba court had no jurisdiction to try offences committed in the Hudson's Bay Company's territories prior to the admission
of Manitoba into the Canadian federation. Justice Wood would not

accept the latter argument and, when requested, refused to permit the correspondence and "private" letters of George-Étienne Cartier and John A. Macdonald relating to the amnesty question, as well as others, from being summoned and introduced as evidence. This effectively prevented the defence from proving that the Canadian government had given formal, written recognition to the delegates of the Provisional Government as a de facto government.

The case for the Crown, in the hands of Francis Cornish and his partner, a local lawyer by the name of Stewart Macdonald, involved a series of former prisoners providing wild tales of the torture and abuse they suffered in jail, leading to Scott's resistance and his subsequent execution. Throughout the trial there was little care for the normal rules of evidence. Chief Justice Wood had his own interpretations and, when there was an objection, continually favoured the Crown. Adding to the challenges, it was also a bilingual trial in which the defence was French-speaking and the Crown English-speaking. At any given time, the judge, and half of the jury, were relying on translations that were not always clear or accurate. In the end, on November 2, 1874, the jury found Ambroise Lépine guilty of aiding in the murder of Thomas Scott. Judge Wood admonished Ambroise Lépine for his "savage crime" and sentenced him to hang on January 29, 1875.

Ambroise Lépine's death sentence was another tremendous shock, both in the Métis community in Manitoba and in Quebec, where a Manitoba amnesty was widely supported. In response to the xenophobia and chauvinism running at a fever pitch in Anglo-Protestant Ontario, the predominantly Catholic and French-speaking peoples of Quebec rallied and sought to protect this valiant fighter for Indigenous, French and Catholic rights in Western Canada. The anger and indignation in Quebec was such that the Quebec legislature passed a unanimous resolution asking the governor general to grant an amnesty. The newspaper *Le Nouveau Monde* called on the French-Canadian ministers in the Liberal Cabinet to seek a stay of proceedings and immediately secure an amnesty, or resign. Petitions poured into the offices of the federal Cabinet ministers, and the archbishop and six bishops of Quebec added their prayers.

With this tragic turn of events, I now spent my time speaking in support of amnesty for Ambroise Lépine in the rural parishes of Quebec and the Franco-American communities in the northern United States. But alas, nothing changed. Liberal Prime Minister Mackenzie, like Macdonald before him, was caught between the support he received from Protestant Ontario and that from Catholic Quebec. Paralyzed, Mackenzie refused to intervene. Our appeals and petitions for commutation of Lépine's sentence went nowhere, until December 1874, when the defence succeeded in getting André Nault and the others off as accessories to the murder of Thomas Scott. Now we had grounds for appeal. However, this fortunate news was followed by a wave of negative reaction and anger in Ontario, once again paralyzing Prime Minister Mackenzie.

In Manitoba, the provincial government, as initially established by Governor Archibald back in 1870, was defeated in a non-confidence motion. With the fall of this government, which included many of those who had worked with us in the early days, both French- and English-speaking, a new "Canadian" order was officially ushered in. With large numbers of Ontarians moving to the new province of Manitoba, the new government began the systematic process of disenfranchising the rights of its Métis citizens.

COMMISSIONER: Mr. Riel, at this point in your career your compatriot Ambroise Lépine had been sentenced to hang for the murder of Thomas Scott. Would you now explain how it was that amnesty was finally granted.

RIEL: Although the amnesty issue was resolved rather unsatisfactorily, thank God, it saved Ambroise Lépine from the gallows. To understand how this occurred we need to step back and examine the events surrounding his trial and sentencing. As has so often been pointed out in this Inquiry, Prime Minister Macdonald had promised both Bishop Taché and Lieutenant-Governor Archibald that the amnesty pledged in the negotiations leading to the Manitoba Act would be given in good faith. From our point of view, this was clearly understood.

However, with Ambroise Lépine sentenced to hang, our last lingering hopes for amnesty lay in Mackenzie's Liberal administration acting upon the evidence being collected at a select committee of Parliament struck to investigate the amnesty question. Included in the evidence presented to this bipartisan commission was Taché's authoritative pamphlet: *The North West Difficulty: Bishop Taché on the Amnesty Question.* Citing the prime minister's numerous promises of an amnesty for all involved in the Provisional Government and its activities, the archbishop provided evidence that, despite the ambiguity of Prime Minister Macdonald's statements, and all his denials on numerous occasions, he had solemnly promised that an amnesty would be provided the members of the Provisional Government.

But no, ignoring the findings of the select committee, the old Scot, Mackenzie, refused to take a stand that might upset his explosive Ontario constituencies. Cowed, his Quebec caucus were caught with divided loyalties between the demands of their constituents and their Liberal prime minister. The prime minister prevailed and none revolted. The people of Quebec were outraged, calling their representatives traitors. Talk of betrayal, independence and the revolution of 1837–38 could be heard.

Two weeks before the scheduled execution of Ambroise Lépine, the Queen's representative, Lord Dufferin, intervened, commuting Lépine's death sentence. The colonial secretary approved Dufferin's assumption of responsibility. His one amendment was the request that the forfeiture of political rights be added to the commutation of the death sentence. Accordingly, Lépine's death sentence was commuted, reduced to two years' imprisonment and permanent deprivation of his political rights. This saved my dear friend's life. However, with an outstanding warrant for my arrest for the "murder of Thomas Scott" still waiting to be executed, I remained in acute danger and there was still no permanent settlement of the Manitoba Question.

When Parliament met in February 1875, Prime Minister Mackenzie finally took the initiative and introduced a motion providing that "a full amnesty should be granted to all persons concerned in the North-West (Manitoba) troubles for all acts committed by them during the said troubles, saving only L. Riel, A.D. Lépine, and W.B. O'Donoghue. . . . That in the opinion of this House, it would be proper that a like amnesty should be granted to L. Riel and A.D. Lépine conditional on five years' banishment from Her Majesty's Dominions." Although my French-Canadian friends in the Canadian Parliament demanded an unqualified pardon without the banishment — which carried with it the implication that Lépine and myself were criminals — Mackenzie's bill passed. Because Will O'Donoghue participated in the Fenian Raid of 1872, he was excluded from the amnesty. Rejecting banishment, Lépine remained in jail to fulfill his two years, and I was banished from Her Majesty's Dominions for five years. It was a hollow victory. This bill removed the threat of hanging, but gave me only the freedom of the outlaw. I would be a man without a country for the next five years.

COMMISSIONER: Mr. Riel, having reviewed your career up to this point, we would request that you now inform this Inquiry as to the nature of your "exile."

RIEL: Exile is hell. It is a cruel and unusual punishment. Forced from the centre of my universe, my home and my family, I was now a refugee, itinerant in the eastern United States. Always concerned about assassins, I kept moving, a dark shadow travelling from parish to parish, from safe house to safe house. Hunted like an elk, I never knew if it was safe to sleep in the same bed two nights in a row. I ate with my back to the wall and tried never to turn my back on strangers.

As I said, exile is hell. With no prospects of employment or, consequently, money, I had no choice but to rely on the generosity of my hosts in the Catholic community. It was during this dark time of emotional distress and vulnerability that my spirits were lifted by a letter from the gracious Bishop Ignace Bourget of Montreal, whom I had met as a student in Montreal. Replying to a letter I had sent seeking his guidance, the bishop wrote back, telling me that "God has given you a mission which you must fulfill in all respects." I understood this to mean that it is my duty to love and protect my Métis nation, and through them to know Jesus Christ.

With the good bishop's message close to my heart, I travelled the northern parishes of New York and Maine, speaking to our Quebec brothers and sisters forced to cross the border in their economic exile. I told them of their French-speaking brethren in the Canadian North-West. I told them we had land and need of their numbers to maintain a vibrant French-speaking Western Canada.

COMMISSIONER: Mr. Riel, there is a great deal of confusion regarding your health and well-being in exile. There have been numerous accusations that your religious revelations at this time indicate "insanity." Would you please speak to this issue.

RIEL: Thank you. Accusations of "insanity" have stained my good name. As I indicated very early on in my testimony, no issue is more important to me than the charge that my actions were those of an insane man. As we have seen earlier, at my trial my own lawyers pronounced me "insane." Also, in the same vein, included in the six charges of high treason at my trial was the overall accusation that I was "moved and seduced by the instigation of the devil." As a foundation for British jurisprudence, I find this highly disturbing because it relates directly to the other base accusations that I am a man of evil intent: an imposter, a deceiver. Unfortunately, all of this relates directly to my lifelong relationship with the Roman Catholic Church. As boy and man, I have loved my church. Nonetheless, over my career, in Manitoba 1869–70, and especially in my exile, this relationship became fraught with ambiguity.

Pardon me while I make a short excursus. In that fateful fall of 1875, while I was living the life of an exile, itinerant in the northern U.S., I received a most welcome invitation from my expatriate former schoolmate, Edmond Mallet. It was an invitation to visit him in Washington, D.C. A Civil War veteran, Edmond is well connected amongst the ruling circles in Washington, and so I was fortunate to be invited to attend the opening session of the Congress of the United States as presided over by President Ulysses S. Grant. An august occasion, it was made even more so for me, when, on December 6, 1875, I was given a private meeting with President Grant.

Brought to the White House under an assumed name, I met the president, who was most gracious and well aware of events in the North-West. I spoke of the difficulties our people were having with the Canadian government and told the president of my dream of establishing francophone communities in the North-West. Listening, the president expressed interest in the plight of the various peoples, but no concrete plans were discussed. As I was about to leave, the president suggested I take out American citizenship and carry on my work in the United States. Although I did not consider taking out American citizenship at the time, years later in 1883, I became an American citizen.

I readily admit that I was somewhat nervous before the American president. My command of the English language is not what it could be, and I feared that my earlier relations with the United States might cast a long shadow over the meeting. Our seizure of political power in the North-West in 1869 had offered the American annexationists a golden opportunity, another Texas. Back then, Grant had even sent Jay Cooke into the Red River to investigate a right-of-way for their Northern Pacific Railway. Then, when the American consular representative openly advocated intervention, I stuck with "British rights" instead of "American republicanism." In light of all this, the president was most gracious. Because of my nebulous situation with the Canadian government, it was felt best that this visit between the president and me was left unrecorded.

On the sixth anniversary of establishing the Provisional Government — my proudest achievement — I was still in the American capital, Washington, D.C., when something miraculous happened as I attended Mass at St. Patrick's Cathedral. I suddenly felt in my heart a joy which took such possession of me that to hide from my neighbours the smile on my face I had to unfold my handkerchief and hold it with my hand over my mouth and cheeks. After these consolations had made me rejoice about two minutes, I was immediately struck by an immense sadness of spirit. I prudently bore in silence the almost insupportable sadness I was experiencing in my soul. But that great pain, as great as my joy, passed away in just as short a time. And in my spirit remained this thought: "Are the joys and pains of man short on this earth?" I felt as if I had been in communication with the greatest of spirits and felt that my God had anointed me. After this I knew my destiny. It was then that I knowingly took up my role in the biblical sense. Henceforth, I lost all fear of my enemies and strove to take my rightful place in the world as prophet of the New World.

When it was over, I attempted to explain this experience to my friend Edmond Mallet. He was flabbergasted and expressed his concern for me, telling me I must rest. Then, when Father Primeau and Church officials heard of my experience, they were shocked and scandalized. They would not hear of it. Revelation? I must be ill. I must be mad. They became so concerned that I was moved from Washington up to New England, then spirited into Quebec. Penniless, physically exhausted and disbelieved, I was taken to the home of a distant uncle where I was put to bed, ill.

Here lies my critical question. Was this Divine experience madness? Did I suffer a mild psychosis from exhaustion? Or, was this a miracle, a sign given by God that I truly am the prophet of the New World? I believe the latter. Such experiences are not unusual in our world, or historically. How else do people know their role in life other than from revelation — of whatever kind that revelation may be? We Indigenous peoples of the New World have always gone on vision quests and searched our souls for the meaning of life. In our world, Cree Chief Maskepetoon (Broken Arm) had a spirit vision of his future role as peacemaker between the Cree and the Blackfoot nations on the Western Plains. In other words, revelation is a true blessing and not an unknown phenomenon in our world, or yours. Did Joan of Arc not follow the light of revelation? How did Moses get the Ten Commandments? Others too have claimed revelation, including the man who gave his life to free the slaves, John Brown. Revelation is all around us. Why must I be condemned for mine?

On March 6, 1876, shortly after a visit by Joseph-Charles Taché, brother of my archbishop, Alexandre Taché, I was taken for a night ride to Saint-Jean-de-Dieu Hospital at Longue Pointe, Quebec. Without my knowledge, I had been decoyed to an asylum where I was held by force under the name "Louis R. David." Officially, no one knew I was at Longue Pointe. Nevertheless, after an incident where the bars on my window were tampered with, concerned it was the work of my enemies,

I was transferred to the Saint-Michel-Archange Asylum in Beauport, Quebec. At Saint-Michel I was admitted under the name Larochelle.

When I objected to being incarcerated once again, I was told I must stay "for my own protection." Right from the start, I was abused. As I was being processed, and my belongings were being inspected, a nun grabbed my precious book of prayer and, when I objected, she ripped out my sister's beautiful inscription and signature. Furious, my protests led to isolation and lockdown. To those who care for personal details of this period, I readily admit that at times I was physically and spiritually cowed by the institutional experience. I was violated physically, mentally and spiritually. At times, I was forcibly constrained, confined in straightjackets, manacles, even their disgusting crib-beds. I was a prisoner in a madhouse. I was not allowed to correspond with my family, friends or my former constituents. Most disturbing, throughout my confinement, my poor mother was left in limbo, not informed where her son was, or if I was safe, or even alive.

I rebelled, I went on hunger strikes, and tore off my clothes. I did hard time, weeks of solitary confinement. Getting out of solitary, I would go through another round when a simple request, a basic human need, would be denied. I lost chapel privileges for the slightest infraction. For every denial of right, I told myself I would endure and demand justice, only to be subjected to the vilest abuse again and again. A visiting British physician called our Holy Catholic asylum "a chamber of horrors."

Like many prisoners of conscience, I was initially intimidated, but I found that they could jail my body but not my soul. In solitary confinement, I saw the light of our New World rise in the Great North-West. I came to an understanding that our world, the Métis world, with its synthesis of two cultures, is the true New World. We are a new nation, our legacy the harmonious merging of the old and new, the best of both worlds. This proud legacy became my new reality. My task? The ridding from our lands of old bigotries, intolerance, religious prejudice, injustice and the yoke of colonialism. Through my tortures, through my pain, my vision clarified. I now knew, most clearly, my mission, and what I must do.

Not only was I to minister to the need of my people for a homeland

and their rights, but also it was necessary to establish a successor to the corruption of the Holy Roman Catholic Church here in the New World. We, the peoples of this New World, would create a new Catholicism based on the teachings of Christ, not Caesar. To accomplish my goals I now hid my true feelings and thoughts, and became a model inmate.

Finally, Archbishop Taché visited me. It was a strange visit. I thought I was under the Inquisition. He drilled me on what I "thought" I saw, and how it was all an "illusion" on my part and best rejected. He demanded a regime of prayer and penitence. On my part, although we had had many disagreements, I believed we were united in our love of our people. I asked to be released. My request was simple. "Be my liberator. I want to reach the United States." But Alexandre Taché, my second father, did not assist me. He left me languishing. Not only did he not release me, in the cruelest cut of all, he took a letter to my mother which he never delivered.

On January 23, 1878, after almost two years, I was released and taken south to the United States where I stayed with friends in Upstate New York. One last note in regards to the asylums: I feel it is necessary to inform this Inquiry that I was not alone in being held against my will at either Longue Pointe or Beauport. It was not uncommon for people to be held in these institutions on the instructions of a highly placed source, as long as the appropriate fee was paid. In an article in the Hudson's Bay Company magazine *The Beaver*, quoting the *Montreal Star*, we are told, "the fact of the matter is there is not a person in this city, high or low, rich or poor, that could not, by shrewd management and the liberal use of money, be sent to Longue Pointe."

COMMISSIONER: Mr. Riel, after being released from the asylums of Quebec, were you able to resume your career in Manitoba?

RIEL: Sad to say, as much as I treasured the idea of returning to St. Boniface to take up my scrip lands and live a peaceful life in the service of the Lord, it was impossible. My exile from Canada still had a number of years to run. After a short time recovering in Upstate New York, I followed my calling and went to St. Paul to see Bishop Ireland, who was in charge of resettling Irish Catholics from the urban slums to Catholic missions in the American West. I had hoped to entice the bishop to expand his settlements to the French Canadians working in the mills and factories in the American Northeast. When this fell through, I hurriedly travelled up the old Métis cart trail through the Dakota Territory to Pembina to reunite with my family and friends.

After so many years and so many changes, it was a joyful but sad reunion. My dear mother was aged with worry, while our extended family, like many of our Métis families, had been dislocated. Some had received scrip and some had not. Searching out their plots, they had found non-contiguous, divergent properties that were barely accessible. Delays and the general unsuitability of the properties saw many Métis selling their titles for a song and starting over again out in the Saskatchewan country, or going west into Montana.

In discussions with family members and friends, such as Joseph Dubuc and Ambroise and Maxine Lépine, I became familiar with the political changes that had occurred after the Canadian government seized the Red River and sent me into exile. With the influx of Ontario settlers, our provincial legislature was now an Anglo bastion of reaction, with a minority French-speaking bloc. Laws were being passed, or amended, dismantling or nullifying the provisions of the Manitoba Act, each piece of new legislation withdrawing the French and Métis fact little by little or lot by lot.

After my ousting, various colonial institutions were put in place to tighten federal control over the North-West. The original, temporary North-West Territories Act of 1869 — under which the region was governed by an appointed lieutenant-governor and his appointed council — was altered numerous times. In 1875 the Act was amended to consolidate Canadian legislative control over policing, Indian treaty negotiations, railway construction, settlement and the deeding of land to settlers. The 1875 Act also limited the number of councillors to five members, while providing for the gradual addition of elected members as population growth warranted. Prince Albert would be the only constituency with the requisite population.

Technically, the North-West Council was to act as the representative council of the people of the North-West Territories to the Canadian government. Yet, with appointed representatives, it was little more than the old Hudson's Bay Company governing model back in place. Edgar Dewdney's territorial government had the authority to pass regional ordinances dealing with matters such as public health, roads, inheritance and alcohol control. Ultimately, though, the federal government could amend or cancel any ordinance passed by the territorial government. Further, it was an English-speaking institution being imposed on our French-speaking population from above. Amongst the council members dismissed as a cost-cutting measure was our Métis representative, Pascal Breland. ·

On the national front, I learned that the Pacific Scandal had deepened the economic crisis, and that Mackenzie's Liberal government was in deep financial and political trouble. As a result of British and Canadian meddling during the American Civil War, the key Reciprocity Treaty with the United States had not been renewed. At the same time, Great Britain's push for "free trade" had wiped out Canada's preferential markets with the United Kingdom. With both American and British markets and revenue sources having dried up, Canadian producers of staple products and manufacturing were in crisis and Canadian railway construction ground to a virtual halt.

In the North-West Territories, the economic crisis was enduring. All sectors of the population had been hit hard. Most desperate were the Indians. With the virtual elimination of the buffalo, they were destitute. On August 15, 1876, two thousand Plains and Woods Cree and Assiniboine camped outside Fort Carlton on the North Saskatchewan River to "treaty" with Canadian Treaty Commissioner Alexander Morris. With his brass band and presents, Morris promised money and gifts and a square mile of land to farm for each family. According to Morris, Treaty No. 6 would bring prosperity: "All along that road I see Indians gathering, I see gardens growing and houses building; I see them receiving money from the Queen's Commissioners to purchase clothing for their children; at the same time I see them enjoying their hunting and fishing as before, I see them retaining their old mode of living with the Queen's gift in addition."

William Henry Jackson played an important part in gathering support
for settlers' rights on the Saskatchewan. He was the editor of *The Voice of the
People*, secretary of the Settlers Union and personal secretary to Louis Riel.
He was made an honorary Métis and given the name Honoré Jaxon.

Métis leader Gabriel Dumont (ca. 1880), a renowned buffalo hunter and warrior, the "Prince of the Plains," led Riel's forces against Major General Middleton as Adjutant General of the Provisional Government of Saskatchewan in 1885.

Major General F.D. Middleton, Commander-in-Chief of the Canadian militia, was defeated by the Métis in the battle at Tourond's Coulee (Fish Creek). With overwhelming numbers and firepower, his troops overran the Métis defences at Batoche on May 12, 1885, while the general retired for lunch. PHOTO: GLENBOW ARCHIVES NA-680-1.

Louis Riel, age forty, as a prisoner outside the guard tent, Batoche, North-West Territories, 1885, after his surrender to Major General Middleton. This is a poor but rare photo of Riel on the battlefield. PHOTO: GLENBOW ARCHIVES NA-363-53.

Pîhtokahanapiwiyin, Poundmaker, was a Cree chief and the adopted son of
Isapo Muxika (Crowfoot). He was known for his role as a "peacemaker,"
stepping in to prevent bloodshed numerous times in battles with the
North-West Mounted Police. After surrendering to Major General Middleton
in 1885, he was convicted of treason and sentenced to three years in Stony
Mountain Prison. Falling seriously ill, he served only one year and died
some four months later. PHOTO: GLENBOW ARCHIVES NA-1681-4.

Mistahimaskwa, Big Bear, was a powerful and charismatic Cree chief who sought to resolve peacefully the problems between his people and the Canadian government. Although he attempted to stop the murders at Frog Lake in the Saskatchewan uprising, as chief, he was found guilty of treason and sentenced to three years in Stony Mountain Penitentiary. Like Poundmaker, he fell seriously ill and was released early and died soon thereafter. PHOTO: ONTARIO ARCHIVES PA-2882-2.

Donald Smith is seen here driving the last spike on the Canadian
Pacific Railway, Nov. 7, 1885, nine days before Riel's execution. Appointed
by John A. Macdonald as Dominion Commissioner, he had worked
unsuccessfully to overthrow Riel's Provisional Government at Red River.

PHOTO: GLENBOW ARCHIVES NA-218-2.

After the execution of Louis Riel and the untimely death of his wife
Marguerite, their children, Jean-Louis (age six) and Marie Angelique
(age five), lived with the Riel family in St. Boniface, Manitoba. Marie
Angelique died in 1897 at age fourteen, the result of illness. Jean-Louis
died in 1908 at the age of twenty-six, the result of a riding accident.

PHOTO: LIBRARY AND ARCHIVES CANADA PA-139072.

With little or no options, most of the chiefs signed treaty, transferring 300,000 square kilometres to Canada — the largest land treaty in the continent's history. Herded onto their arbitrary reserves, they gave up the life they had known as a free people for a life of dependency. They would know no prosperity. The Indian Affairs Department would ignore their treaty promises, using the North-West Mounted Police, which was founded in 1873, and the law to reshape their tribal cultures and family structures.

COMMISSIONER: Thank you, Mr. Riel. The third session of this Inquiry is now in recess. Upon reconvening, we will receive Mr. Riel's testimony regarding his part in the North-West Resistance.

PART IV

The North-West Resistance: Saskatchewan

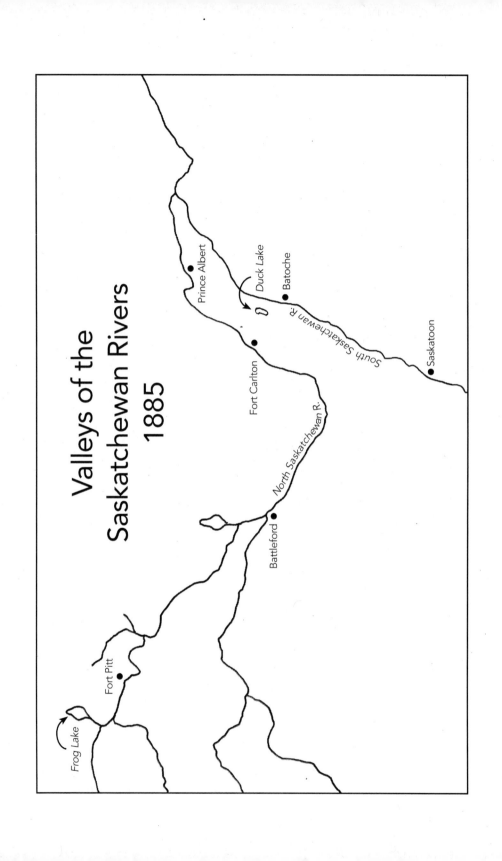

Valleys of the
Saskatchewan Rivers
1885

Prince Albert

Duck Lake

Batoche

Fort Carlton

South Saskatchewan R.

Saskatoon

North Saskatchewan R.

Battleford

Fort Pitt

Frog Lake

COMMISSIONER: Mr. Riel, upon your return to the West, you have been accused of a grand conspiracy planning an Indian and Métis invasion and takeover of Western Canada. Please provide this Inquiry with an overview of your work on the plains at this time, as well as the reaction of the Canadian and American authorities.

RIEL: While I was visiting with my family in the Dakotas, a Sioux "tobacco man" came to see me. He was a messenger who came from Chief Sitting Bull. The great chief sought me out as an intermediary. After defeating General Custer and the U.S. 7th Cavalry at the Battle of the Little Bighorn, Sitting Bull and his followers, including nine hundred lodges of Yankton Sioux, sought refuge in the low rolling Wood Mountains of southern Saskatchewan. With dwindling supplies of food on the northern prairies, the Blackfoot, Assiniboine and Cree had left their barren reservations and were now congregating in these same hills. With extreme competition for the remaining buffalo, the arrival of the Sioux was a concern to all, especially when inter-tribal raids began, which the North-West Mounted Police ignored, creating even greater tensions.

Under the pretext of a horrible massacre of Assiniboine Indians by American whiskey traders in the Cypress Hills, Prime Minister Macdonald sent his newly formed police force into the North-West to protect the "Redman." A noble motive, indeed, but unfortunately this was not Macdonald's true motivation. Establishing his new police force on the model of the much-hated Irish Constabulary, Macdonald initially sent them west to Saskatchewan to dismantle Gabriel Dumont's "little government." Thereafter, the North-West Mounted Police continued to monitor Métis activities on the Saskatchewan, right up to and beyond their attack on us at Duck Lake in March 1885.

Although still banished, I left the Dakotas, slipping into Canadian territory on August 2, 1879. Meeting with Sitting Bull and other Sioux leaders, I suggested a treaty of peace to resolve inter-tribal conflicts and to work together for improved rations. After this meeting, my Métis tobacco men visited the camps of the Cree and Blackfoot. Shortly after, Sitting Bull met with Crowfoot, chief of the Blackfoot nation. As a result, a peace pact was smoked between the two old foes. A similar pact was already made between Crowfoot and his adopted son, Poundmaker of the Cree. We, the Métis, were bonded by blood with all of these peoples. It is interesting to note that the "illegal" meeting between Sitting Bull and me was held without the knowledge of the NWMP, although Inspector S.B. (Sam) Steele claimed that the officers and men of the force were aware of every move of the Sioux — from the date of their arrival until 1881, the time of the surrender to the Americans of Sitting Bull and the last of the hostile Sioux.

While in the Wood Mountains, I also met with Red Stone, the leader of the Wolf Point Assiniboine. After this meeting I crossed back into Montana without any problems. Upon hearing of my visit to the Wood Mountains, I am told Superintendent Walsh of the North-West Mounted Police rushed to the area, hoping to catch me in the country illegally. Walsh later claimed that Red Stone and I had signed a document declaring the land belonged to the Indians and their brothers, the half-breeds, and that I, Louis Riel, was their true and rightful chief. Walsh also claims he persuaded Red Stone to withdraw from what he called "Riel's conspiracy."

This conspiracy theory is a total fabrication. It would be amusing if it were not so dangerous. Does Walsh actually believe it would be necessary for Red Stone and me to create such a document? Relations between our peoples have been cemented by the pipe and verbally honoured for over a century. Walsh also claimed to have extracted pledges of fidelity from Sitting Bull and other important chiefs. What he actually did was further subjugate the people, withholding food and then discontinuing the sale of arms and ammunition necessary for the hunt.

I state categorically that the role played by the North-West Mounted Police in Indian and Métis affairs was not honourable. With food in short supply, the closure of Fort Walsh in the Cypress Hills forced those in the "Grandmother's Country," in other words, the Indians in the Canadian North-West, back onto their isolated reserves. Sweet promises were overshadowed by semantics — if it was not on a treaty paper, it was naught.

Superintendent Walsh played on his power to feed or starve the Sioux and the other Indigenous peoples to his advantage. He used the presence of the Sioux on the Canadian side of the border to pretend that Canadian policy towards the Indians was more honourable than American Indian policy, and also to exaggerate his personal usefulness in the North-West. Walsh was not alone in this type of devious behaviour. With the hide hunters working for James Jerome Hill's Great Northern Railway slaughtering the buffalo in the Dakotas and Montana, the boundless southern herds no longer foraged north in the spring. Then in the fall of 1879, the grasslands along the Saskatchewan–Montana international border were torched. A massive prairie fire ensued across hundreds of miles of prairie. Although everyone knew they were attempting to starve Sitting Bull out of Canada, the American Army denied all responsibility. So it was that food became a major weapon of war and peace. With the fires having blocked the northern herds, next to no buffalo came north — ever again.

The next spring, on the fledgling reserves, seed was again late in coming and the promised oxen, ploughs and harrows remained in short supply. Even hand tools, shovels and rakes were unavailable. The situation was untenable. The Indians were desperately attempting to scratch the earth, with little result. With near starvation on their reserves, and no other options, Indian Commissioner Edgar Dewdney now encouraged Crowfoot of the Blackfoot, Sweet Grass, Thunderchild, Strike Him on the Back and Little Pine of the Eagle Hills Cree, as well as some Stoney chiefs, to take their people south of the border into American territory where the last of the buffalo stands were located.

Across the Saskatchewan country, the Indians left the reserves with the last of their tipis and travelled south into the Sweet Grass Hills of Montana. That country, from north of the Missouri River to the burnt-out international border, was the last major buffalo range in the whole North-West. It was also part of the Wolf Point and Fort Belknap Indian Agencies, home of Assiniboine and Yankton Sioux and Nez Perce refugees from Chief Joseph's heroic attempt to outrun the U.S. cavalry and reach the "Grandmother's Country." Joseph never made it. With his people decimated, he famously said that he would "fight no more, forever."

Living in that wild country as *chef du camp* of about 150 Métis buffalo-hunting families, I was asked to attend a meeting of the nations of the North-West dealing with broken promises on both sides of the U.S.–Canadian border. It was of such importance that even Sitting Bull slipped into Montana to attend. Speaker after speaker emphasized that the treaties were a colossal failure. In the U.S., those Indians who remained off the reservations were being hunted down and murdered by the cavalry. In Canada, those who had honoured their treaty now saw the Whiteman's promises as false.

Each speaker pointed out how the Indian nations and tribes were dealt with in a most high-handed and outrageous fashion, how every effort was made to subjugate them, including war and starvation. The treaties with the Long Knives and the Red Coats had to be renegotiated. They needed to know they could again live in a land where their children would grow up healthy, and the ancestors and animal brothers were there to comfort and feed them for evermore. I told my brothers that we Métis, too, had been duped out of our lands and that our sacred Manitoba Act treaty had been violated. For us, the key question remained land, our birthright. All were in agreement. It was time to renegotiate the treaties. When asked, I agreed to assist in this matter.

Now I must deal with a number of lies that came out of this meeting. There have been many claims that I used the meeting to attempt to form a military alliance, to launch a war of aggression against British possessions in the North-West. Chief amongst those making this claim was one named Jean L'Heureux, interpreter for Walsh of the North-West Mounted Police, as well as for Crowfoot. Both L'Heureux and Walsh have taken credit for breaking the unity we were attempting to establish. Contrary to their assertions, the meeting was a success. Strengthening working relations between our various peoples, this meeting was the forerunner of the great councils of 1884.

In the spring of 1880, shortly after our great meeting, Colonel Walsh of the North-West Mounted Police and General Miles, the infamous

American Indian fighter, colluded against us. Our Métis camp on the Milk River was dispersed at the armed "request" of American officials. The Cree, closest to us, were rounded up by the American military. Their weapons were confiscated, as were their horses and carts. Disarmed and dismounted, they were escorted back across the border. In a much weaker position to press for their rights, they returned on foot to the dismal reserves they had left the previous spring. Even the great chief, Big Bear, who embarked upon a marathon walk visiting and talking to find a just solution for his people, was finally forced onto a reserve after this treachery. I am sorry to report that hunger and desperation eventually forced Sitting Bull to return to the United States, surrendering on July 20, 1881. Leading the Ghost Dance Movement, he was killed during an attempt by Indian agency police to arrest him on the Standing Rock Indian Reservation in 1890.

My enemies have said that establishing unity was impossible as Crowfoot, Big Bear and Sitting Bull regarded me and my projects with some suspicion. This position is absurd. The degenerate L'Heureux, acting as an informant for both the Canadian and American military, had attempted to misinterpret my intentions to Crowfoot, but Crowfoot was no fool and never deviated from his role as leader of his people. In his lifetime he had seen over two-thirds of the Blackfoot nations wiped out by smallpox and liquor, and he was cautious lest his people be deprived of the meagre rations that kept them barely alive. He made his decisions in the interest of his people and was an honourable man. It was not suspicion of me that thwarted unity; it was outside factors such as the police and their agents: starvation and destitution.

One last point on this matter is appropriate. The accusations that Sitting Bull regarded me, the leader of the Métis, with suspicion is easily disproved in a speech he gave to General Terry of the U.S. Army at a meeting in the Cypress Hills of Southern Saskatchewan in 1877. I would like to enter Sitting Bull's full speech into evidence of his high regard for the Métis:

> For 64 years you have kept me and my people and treated us badly. What have we done that you should want us to stop? We have done nothing. It is the people on your side who have started us to do these depredations. We could not go anywhere else, so we took refuge in this country. It was

on this side of the country that we learnt to shoot, and that was the reason I came back to it again. I should like to know why you came here. In the first place I did not give you the country, but you followed me from one place to another, so that I had to leave and come over to this country. I was born and raised in this country with the Red River half-breeds, and I intend to stop with them. I was raised hand-in-hand with the Red River half-breeds, and we are going over to that part of the country, and that is the reason that I have come over here. That is the way I was raised, in the hands of the people here, and that is the way I intend to be with them. You have got ears and you have got eyes to see with, and to see how I live with these people. You see me, here I am. If you think I am a fool you are a bigger fool than I am. This house is a medicine house. You come here to tell us lies, but we do not want to hear them. I do not wish any such language used to me, that is tell me such lies in my Great Mother's house. Do not say two more words. Go back to where you came from. This country is mine, and I intend to stay here, and to raise this country full of grown people.

During this period, I was honoured to work with the great Indian leaders of legend: Sitting Bull, Big Bear, Poundmaker, Crowfoot and the others. They are all men of great integrity. Placed in an impossible situation, their "only friend" the buffalo obliterated, they counselled their people to take up the new life. Seeking to learn agriculture, to educate their children and to save their people from starvation, they negotiated with dignity and as much of the pomp and ceremony of old as was possible. Yet, what did they receive in turn: inadequate resources, poor lands and colonial appropriation that was mean-spirited and meant to "take the Indian out of the man." I had no choice but to help them.

COMMISSIONER: Mr. Riel, although your banishment from Canada ended in 1880, you chose to remain in the United States. Please inform this Inquiry as to your reasons for staying in the United States, and the nature of your work there.

RIEL: I stayed in the United States, in Montana, as that is where I found I was most urgently needed. With the post-Civil War railway boom, and the Union Pacific crossing the continent, settlers were rapidly pouring into the former Indian territories west of the Mississippi, ploughing up the grasslands and planting crops. Farther north, as James Jerome Hill's Great Northern pushed its way west from Minnesota, the Montana outback was truly the last American frontier. Living with the last of the buffalo hunting Métis in this area, I would have to say that nearly all the scum of the American West were now congregated in the lawless area outside Fort Benton, the last port of call for the keelboats on the Missouri River. Rustlers, wolfers, buffalo hunters, card sharks, prostitutes and killers, they all sought the anonymity of a land with little or no law. With these vultures preying on the Indians and our Métis, devastation was near.

With destitution staring them in the face, I was called to the open ranges of Montana to live with the last of the buffalo-hunting Métis out on the prairie. Theirs was a life of absolute poverty, a life I shared for three years. Never sure of food, hounded by the military, and preyed upon by the whiskey traders, my people were headed for extinction. I could not let that happen. My main concern was in gaining influence to stop the "rot-gut" whiskey trade. Ink, turpentine and tobacco juice were added to homemade alcohol and sold to the Indians and Métis out on the plains in exchange for their furs, horses, guns and women. The debauchery was contagious and relentless, with nearly all the prairie peoples suffering from the vicious trade in these poisons.

In March 1883, I took out my American naturalization papers. With American citizenship, I was able to work for the physical and spiritual redemption of my landless people. Encouraged by the words of President Grant, I took a petition to General Miles asking for a reservation, schools and agricultural implements for our people. Although we Métis were the first settlers in Montana, the first to build a church, the first to run a school and to form a choir or library, our petition was refused. I then attempted to take a notorious whiskey trader to court. The case was summarily thrown out.

Joining the political party of the late emancipator Abraham Lincoln, I participated in the state election in support of his Republican Party. Pressing for legislative action to fight the whiskey trade, I sought to register legitimate Métis voters, many of whom, although the original Montana settlers, were barred at the polling station doors by the colour of their skin. We lost by a landslide. In May of 1883, charges of illegal election practices were brought against me by influential members of the ruling Democratic Party. Arrested, I was thrown in jail in Choctaw, Montana, until my friends could make my bail. During my incarceration, I wrote a little poem describing politics in Montana, "... your principal men ... throw in jail the half-breed, as if, having lost the Negro, their rage had to have a new feed." It was the old racist pattern continued. We Métis were again denied our rights as human beings because of our race.

With no land to call our own, ours was a nomadic life subject to the whims of man and nature. Yet it was amongst these people I found true happiness. I was blessed, and found and married my true love, Marguerite Monette *dit* Bellehumeur.

My joy in starting my own family was immense. As it turned out, we were given but three wonderful years together, in which I felt as though I knew the reason for existence: life begets life. We had a son, Jean-Louis, then a beautiful daughter, Marie Angelique. With the responsibility of a family, I took a job teaching school for the Jesuit Fathers at St. Peter's Mission on the Sun River in Montana. It was a period of quiet joy. We lived life as others did, each day passing in natural serenity and familial love.

In this atmosphere, I worked quietly at collecting the names of the Montana Métis originally from Red River, who, like myself, had not received their Manitoba scrip as per the Manitoba Act of 1870. I also had an added claim for compensation for my work as acting governor for which I had not been paid. My goal was to present our petitions to the authorities in Winnipeg and take my family home to meet their relatives. It was not meant to be, for once again my Métis nation called, this time to the Saskatchewan country to the north.

COMMISSIONER: Mr. Riel, please provide this Inquiry with an overview of the political and economic conditions that led to your travelling to the Saskatchewan country in 1884.

RIEL: Over the years while living in Montana, I received numerous visitors, many of whom carried letters from friends and family either in Manitoba, or from those who had gone to live in the Saskatchewan country. Many complained about the lack of progress in receiving titles to the lands guaranteed by the Manitoba Act. Others who had settled along the South Saskatchewan River had been petitioning the Macdonald government for years about their riverfront lots. Surprisingly, in 1878 Alexander Mackenzie's Liberal government sent out a survey team that laid out 71 river lots along the South Saskatchewan River south of the growing little town of Prince Albert. Although this was first seen as a most encouraging development, politics and economics would soon get in the way.

With the Canadian economy in a shambles, and the popularity of Liberal leader Mackenzie at rock bottom, John A. Macdonald made his comeback. With his National Policy putting Canadian industries behind a high tariff wall, Macdonald appealed to both the workingman and the businessman. He won the 1878 federal election. In 1879 he took on the additional portfolio of minister of the interior, which included the role of superintendent general of Indian affairs, in charge of the Indian Department. Amending the Dominion Lands Act of 1872 in 1879, Macdonald introduced a Parliamentary Bill recognizing Canada's obligations to extend the same scrip land privileges as had been granted to the Métis and half-breeds in Manitoba to eligible Métis and half-breeds in the North-West Territories. It was bait, nothing more. "Old Tomorrow" coveted that land and would deal with this issue again only when he had troops steaming westward to throttle the Métis and Indians of the North-West in 1885.

Macdonald was fortunate in that his re-election coincided with one of the temporary upturns in the world economy. With lenders having cash to invest in railroads, it did not take long before the "Canadian" forces behind the International Finance Society/Hudson's Bay Company offered to build Macdonald's transcontinental railroad. Headed by George Stephen, president of the Bank of Montreal, and his cousin, Donald Smith, Chief Commissioner of the Hudson's Bay Company from 1871–1873, and now an elected member of the Company's board of directors, their new Canadian Pacific Railway Company also included another unique individual, James Jerome Hill, the Canadian-American entrepreneur of the Great Northern Railroad. Unbeknownst to most Canadians, Hill would change the destiny of the Canadian North-West — strictly in his own interest.

In the context of the Canadian economy, what is noteworthy is that although the CPR was founded as a private company, it actually followed the American model, a key component of which is colonization. The sale or distribution of lands to settlers, fee simple or homesteads, was big business. In the United States, the building of the Union Pacific and then the Great Northern railways opened the settlement of adjacent lands, and helped amass some of the greatest fortunes known to man. Hill of the Great Northern became a virtual feudal lord, controlling the distribution of settlers, his serfs, over vast portions of the former buffalo country of the Dakotas, Montana and Idaho.

In Canada, John A. Macdonald's biggest asset was the 300,000 square kilometres that Morris had acquired by treaty with the Cree. However, vacant lands produce no revenue, and the property owner was desperate to see a profit. Macdonald looked to emulate the American model, and the construction of the CPR became the dominant economic venture of the day. With the hiring of William Cornelius Van Horne, an American railway contractor experienced in the American Civil War, vast amounts of track were laid. As construction of the CPR was reaching the prairies, a meeting was held in St. Paul, Minnesota, where the three key directors of the CPR, Smith, Stephen and Hill, arbitrarily changed the route of the Canadian Pacific Railway from the settled lands of the North Saskatchewan corridor to the grasslands of the arid southern prairie. Secretly surveying an alternate Kicking Horse Pass route through the Rocky Mountains, they now proposed to change the route of the CPR to run directly across the prairie just a hundred miles north of the U.S. border. When they proposed the new route to Macdonald, he readily agreed. Ignoring the needs of the northern settlers, this line opened up the southern Saskatchewan prairie to settlement and provided a more direct route through the Rocky Mountains to the Pacific coast.

This Inquiry will recall that during the "Panic of 1873" the global economy went into depression and railway construction ground to a halt. Unfortunately for Macdonald and the CPR capitalists, the global economic upturn of the early 1880s was short-lived. Money dried up and another crisis followed. Macdonald's precious Canadian economy once again began to slide off the rails. Production in the industrial east was stagnating, and the brief CPR boom was tremendously overextended, with no credit and no new orders. In response, Macdonald's government went into recession mode and began searching for redundancies. This "cut-back" would be felt in all government departments, and would have a most devastating effect on the Indians on the reserves. When an assistant deputy minister came to the North-West on a cost-saving mission, reviewing reserve expenditures, he called for a leaner and meaner disposition of resources, which has been characterized as "feed one day, starve the next."

On the Saskatchewan, the initial survey of Métis riverfront farms was cancelled. The decree was issued that no more river lots were to be surveyed. The rest of the country was to be subdivided into townships. Father Vegreville, a priest in the area, wrote, "these inflexible limits, right-lines and parallels will traverse fields, pass through houses, cut off farm houses from the fields connected with them. What serious hardships, what deplorable results must flow from all this?"

All of this news was devastating. With no easy access to Ottawa, the only appeal was to Lieutenant-Governor Dewdney's Territorial Council. In late 1881, Lawrence Clarke, Hudson's Bay Company factor, and regional representative on the Council for the District of Lorne (Prince Albert), met with the deputy minister of the interior with a list of requests for redress from his constituents, both Métis and settler. Clarke reported back that the Department of the Interior promised to provide patents to homesteaders of 160 acres, with a pre-emption on an additional 160 acres at $1.00 per acre — on both odd and even sections. This offer was available to those settlers already on the land, although it did not apply to the half-breeds or the Métis. Nor was there any mention of their scrip lands, as negotiated in the Manitoba Act and guaranteed by the prime minister. Métis requests for both title to their farms and recognition of their Indigenous title lands were ignored. With no action taken, in September 1882, the Métis submitted another petition:

> Having been so long regarded as the masters of this country, having de-
> fended it at the cost of our blood, we do not consider that we are asking
> too much when we call on the government to allow us to occupy our
> lands free from the regulations by making free grants of land to the
> Métis of the North-West.

It was of no consequence. Surveyors began dividing the lands in the parish of St. Louis, just south of Prince Albert, using the square rectilin-ear system. A year later, the thirty-six families of the parish found that their land and village site, which included a church and a school, had been sold to the Prince Albert Colonization Company. This was expro-priation, as had happened in Manitoba, yet the Métis were once again powerless. Please note that amongst others, one of the directors of the Prince Albert Colonization Company was Mackenzie Bowell, the MP who orchestrated my expulsion from the House of Commons and would go on to be a short-lived prime minister.

With dissension growing, in the spring of 1883, the Dominion Sur-vey sent Mr. William Pearce out to deal with the question of land pat-ents in the North-West. Townships were surveyed and many settlers around Prince Albert received formal title to the lands they occupied. The English-speaking half-breeds around Prince Albert also got to keep their original river lots. However, it did little for the South Sas-katchewan Métis. Although Pearce reviewed claims throughout the area, he did not investigate the southern St. Laurent river lot claims of the Métis along the South Saskatchewan River. After considerable com-plaints, he finally hired a French-speaking assistant who took deposi-tions, which Pearce carried back to Ottawa. Fully aware of the Métis river lot farms along the South Saskatchewan River, Mr. Pearce did not deal with the problem:

> In the neighborhood of Duck Lake, though the lands were surveyed and
> open for entry since August 1881, in March (1885) not 25% of the claim-
> ants had made entry — even though in the autumn of 1883 the assistant

agent at Prince Albert visited all the claims he could ascertain, told the claimants on what particular quarter section their claims were situated, and urged them to come forward and make entry.

"Quarter sections!" Pearce's report verifies that the Government of Canada proposed to impose the rectilinear survey across the west, denying the Métis what they saw as their inalienable birthright. The truth of the matter is that even though the Canadian government recognized Métis Indigenous title in 1870, and again in 1879, it reversed itself and refused to recognize it on the ground. All the Métis asked was for a re-survey of their farms now designated as quarter-section parcels. Through this simple expediency, the problem of a survey transposing the boundaries of pre-existing parcels would have been solved. The Canadian government did not refuse to do this; it just did not do it. In the language of the Church, a sin of omission. This type of behaviour was a repeat of the experience we had had on the Red River in the late 1860s and through the 1870s. At this juncture, the Métis of Saskatchewan had absolutely no reason to trust the government of John A. Macdonald. The conclusion must be drawn that the Métis were treated differently from others in the area, and that the government did so consciously and with a definite reason, which I put down to that old Hydra: racism.

COMMISSIONER: Mr. Riel, thank you for that background information. Please inform this Inquiry as to the request you received from the Saskatchewan territory in 1884.

RIEL: On June 4, 1884, our sweet life in Montana changed when I was asked to come to the Saskatchewan. On that day, I received a distinguished delegation from the Saskatchewan country to the north. Gabriel Dumont, Moise Ouellette, Michel Dumas and James Isbister came to see me. They came representing the Métis of the south branch of the Saskatchewan River, the English and Scots mixed-blood half-breeds and the Settlers Union in the Prince Albert area in the Canadian North-West Territories. Stymied by the Canadian government's refusal to deal with the land question, they presented me with a request emanating from a meeting held in the Saskatchewan River country:

. . . the French and English natives of the North-West knowing that
Louis Riel has made a bargain with the government of Canada in 1870,
which said bargain is contained mostly in what is known as "the Manitoba Act," we have thought it advisable that a delegation be sent to said
Louis Riel and have his assistance to bring all the matters referred to in
the above resolutions in a proper shape and form before the government
of Canada, so that our just demands be granted.

I was extremely heartened by their long trip across the prairie to see me.
These were the true pioneers of Saskatchewan, men of renown.

Having received visitors and letters informing me of the plight of the
Métis in the North-West Territories, I knew of their concerns. It was a
repeat of Manitoba. Denied their rights, they were concerned their
lands would be overrun by Canadian settlers — again. After a night of
warm conversation, and a period of prayer and reflection at Mass the
next morning, I made the decision to return with them to the Saskatchewan country to provide assistance in their constitutional campaign for
rights. It was then also my plan to return to Manitoba where I would
stake my personal claims to monies and lands owed me, as well as file
the claims of the Montana Métis to their scrip lands in Manitoba. After
visiting family and friends, I planned to take my family back to Montana to watch my children grow, and carry on my work in the United
States. Once again, it was not to be.

We travelled across the short-grass Saskatchewan prairie through
June 1884, just as the prairie grasses grew lush, and the chokecherry and
Saskatoon berries budded-out in the ravines. Herds of *eabri*, the prong-
horn antelope, seemed to fly across the endless landscape, delighting the
children. But there were no buffalo, just bones. Amongst my hosts,
there was a profound sadness and anger as they travelled day after day
with no sight of their "only friend."

Our arrival in the valley of the "Little Sister," the beautiful South
Saskatchewan River Valley, on July 8, 1884, was a time of great joy. From
up and down the river, people congregated, and my wife, my children
and I were warmly welcomed into the bosom of our Métis nation, old
friends and new. I can truly say it was one of the happiest days I have
known. Initially we stayed at Moise Ouellette's little house overlooking

the east bank of the South Saskatchewan, before moving in with my cousin Charles Nolin at his place between St. Louis and St. Laurent. As I have reported, Charles and I had not seen eye to eye in Manitoba, but here he had been a key proponent in inviting me to the Saskatchewan. Shortly afterwards, we were able to settle into Ouellette's once again where I dedicated my time to my people and their problems.

Please understand, contrary to the assertions of my enemies, I did not think of war. I crossed the line without arms and without ammunition. I came to petition for my people, and for myself, in the hope of obtaining something, if not complete satisfaction. I had been asked to assist in achieving representation on the North-West Council, free patents for Métis lands, and recognition of our Indigenous title and improved management of Indian affairs. These were all questions we had previously resolved with the passage of the Manitoba Act in 1870.

COMMISSIONER: Mr. Riel, your work in the Saskatchewan involved constitutional matters. Please inform this Inquiry of the nature of this work and the individuals with whom you worked.

RIEL: Over the next eight months, I worked amongst my Métis brethren, as well as with a young Canadian by the name of William Henry Jackson, a man whom history has "willfully forgotten." On our part, we loved him and gave him the Métis name, Honoré Jaxon.

Unequivocally, I can tell you William Henry Jackson, the "white rebel," is a man John A. Macdonald and his ilk want the world to forget. Acting as secretary of the Settlers Union during the crucial months of 1885, Will Jackson played a key role in our constitutional struggles. Ontario born, he was our Henry David Thoreau, a man of principle who lived his beliefs. Our dear friend Honoré Jaxon would pay a heavy price for his involvement in the Métis movement and for our friendship, but through it all he has stayed forever true to our cause. I am going to diverge for a moment to give some detail about the work that Will Jackson had already done in unifying the people of the Saskatchewan to petition for their rights. I do this to show that well before I came, the people of the Saskatchewan were looking for ways to gain representation from an uncaring government.

I first met William Henry Jackson, along with his brother Thomas Eastwood and their father Thomas Getty Jackson, in July 1884, shortly after my arrival in the Saskatchewan. A settler family of Methodists, the Jacksons are of the Wesleyan tradition, believing in free will in spiritual matters and justice for the oppressed on the temporal plain. Thomas Eastwood was the first apothecary in the North-West, with a drugstore on River Street in the town of Prince Albert. Thomas Getty Jackson had a homestead and repaired agricultural equipment on the side. In 1882, to the chagrin of his parents, young Will dropped out of university in Toronto to join his family in the West.

Times were tough. As has been noted, the promised CPR rail line had been arbitrarily moved south and would bypass the Saskatchewan River Valleys for the southern plains. On the land, early frosts and abysmal crops meant little surplus produce was harvested. Moreover, there was no means of transportation for what there was. Many of the settlers were having trouble keeping body and soul together. When a Settlers' Rights Association organizer came north from Qu'Appelle, the Jacksons went to hear him tell a crowd of some 150 farmers about the myriad of grievances down on the southern prairie, ranging from lack of land patents and low commodity prices, to the absence of democratic representation. Everyone here had pretty much the same grievance, plus the "goddamn CPR." By the end of that evening, young Will was elected secretary of the newly formed Prince Albert branch of the Settlers Union.

As secretary of the Union, Will visited the farms in the Prince Albert area, where most of these folks readily joined up. He then went calling on the English-speaking half-breeds along the North Saskatchewan. These prairie descendants of the Scots, in particular the Orkney Islanders, were, like the rest of us, called "half-breeds" for having married Indigenous women. It could be said that they suffered a more subtle form of racism than their French-speaking cousins.

Will quickly gained the support of James Isbister, the influential original half-breed settler in the Prince Albert area. A great conversationalist, Isbister, speaking English, Gaelic, Cree, Dene and Michif, had spent years as an interpreter and buffalo hunter for the Hudson's Bay

Company. He also has the distinction of being Saskatchewan's first true farmer. Back in the summer of 1862, he cleared, ploughed and planted wheat on a plot along the riverbank. His success led to several other half-breed families setting up farms alongside his on the North Saskatchewan. The area became known as Isbister's Settlement, a name that lasted until a Presbyterian Church minister by the name of James Nisbet arrived in 1866. Nisbet had come to establish a mission for the Cree. Of English descent, Nisbet named his mission after Queen Victoria's late husband and consort, Prince Albert. As more Anglos heard of Isbister's success and moved into the neighbourhood, the English name stuck.

With his success recruiting in the Prince Albert area, Will Jackson began to travel south into the outlying districts: Red Deer Hill, Davis, MacDowall, Birch Hills and on down to Carlton and to the Duck Lake-Batoche region where he met the Métis, including the leader of the Saskatchewan Métis, Gabriel Dumont, who was also sympathetic, having been petitioning the Canadian government since the early 1870s.

With the first territorial election for the Territorial Council looming, the Hudson's Bay Company factor Lawrence Clarke was the delegated incumbent. To oppose Clarke, Will Jackson founded a little broadsheet newspaper, *The Voice of the People*, dedicated to the struggle against the monopolies and oligarchies which were "fastening their relentless talons upon the vitals of this infant country." In his third issue he published a purloined copy of the HBC's fur prices. This document, clearly showing Lawrence Clarke's exorbitant "over-plus" profit margin on furs, infuriated the "boss of the Saskatchewan" who, although he still won the election, lost most of the Métis vote he had previously counted as his own.

Membership in the Settlers Union grew until there were representatives in each of the Lorne districts, including some in the French-speaking Métis community as well as the English-speaking half-breeds. Each district was gathering local resolutions and seeking action by the Canadian government. Although letters of request were sent to newly appointed Lieutenant-Governor Dewdney, there was no response from Regina or Ottawa. Local conditions continued to be ignored. It was at that time Gabriel Dumont and James Isbister called a council of the

French- and English-speaking Métis, which passed a resolution to call on me to come north and assist in gaining constitutional rights.

With the delegates coming to see me, Ottawa and Regina finally took notice. Numerous reports from Lawrence Clarke, Inspector Crozier and others warned the prime minister of the consequences of not dealing with the half-breed land questions and the dangers of allowing me to re-enter Canada — dangers which Macdonald knew only too well from past experience.

When I arrived in the Saskatchewan, Will Jackson was already known as the voice of opposition to corruption and nepotism in the North-West, the "rabble-rouser" who had shamed the "boss of the Saskatchewan." Making common cause with the English-speaking half-breeds and the Métis, he really upset the powers that be. Frankly, they saw us Métis as "inferior beings," and young Will Jackson, breaking down racial and religious barriers designed to keep the population divided, was, if you will pardon the expression, seen as a real "pain in the ass." Personally, I found him delightful. Despite the difference in age and background, we had much in common and enjoyed each other's company. Immediately upon our first meeting, we both saw the necessity and the advantages of joining forces.

Our first joint meeting was held in the English-speaking settlement of Red Deer Hill. Addressing the folks who gathered in both French and English, I outlined the difficulties under which the peoples of the North-West were struggling. Providing a summary of the various forms of constitutional agitation, I was warmly received. Will spoke of the need for a broad representative convention. As a result of the success of this initial meeting, I was invited to address a mass meeting of farmers, settlers and town folk in Prince Albert. I hesitated. P.A. is a white-Anglo town, and most of these folks came originally from Ontario. Concerned that the old Ontario antipathy towards me was still strong, and not wanting to sow even a germ of division to weaken our basis of unity, I declined. However, they would not take "no" for an answer. A petition was drawn up and signed by eighty-four people from all walks of life. Even Father André wrote me, telling me to come, and "come quickly." In the end the meeting was a great success. I received a warm reception, as did the other speakers.

After that meeting, Will Jackson began to set up representative committees whose duties were to call local meetings and consolidate the lists of grievances to be sent to a new and expanded central committee of the Settlers' Rights Association. Announcing our intention to hold a general convention of delegates from across the North-West Territories, we heard grumblings of opposition from a number of sources. Some said we were going too fast and that we were not allowing the government time to meet all our needs. Others complained that I was an outside agitator and we were a couple of dangerous radicals. With the voices of our opponents rising, Will issued the following declaration to the citizens of Prince Albert and the District of Lorne:

> We are starting a movement in this settlement with a view to attaining provincial Legislatures for the North-West Territories, and, if possible, the control of our own resources that we may build our railroads and other works to serve our own interests rather than those of the Eastern provinces. We are preparing a statement of our case to send to Ottawa as a matter of form. We state the various evils which are caused by the present system of legislation.

He hit a nerve and wild rumours began to fly. Patrick Laurie, the publisher of the influential *Saskatchewan Herald*, called for my removal as a foreigner interfering in Canadian affairs. Shortly after this editorial, I received a note asking me to ride over to St. Laurent. Bishop Grandin, the vicar of the missions of the North-West, had arrived and wished to see me. Once there, Bishop Grandin introduced me to a Mr. Forget, the secretary to the Territorial Council. Mr. Forget informed me that he came as a representative of Lieutenant-Governor Dewdney, and that he had arranged this meeting to offer me a position on the North-West Council.

Surprised, and somewhat taken aback by this statement, I asked if there were any positions open on the Council at the present time. Forget told me that Raoul Bréland had volunteered to step down and let me take his place. When I asked if Bréland were not performing his duties satisfactorily, I was told, "yes, but. . . ." I then explained to Mr. Forget that I could not possibly accept this offer as it would be an injustice to

Bréland. Forget immediately responded, "A seat in the Senate, perhaps?" When I said that I doubted that even he could deliver such a prize, Bishop Grandin said, "Leave it with me. I will see what can be done."

After Mr. Forget departed, I looked forward to spending time with the bishop. He was in no mood for conversation, however, and sternly began to lecture me. Through Père André, the Church had spent years dealing with these same issues, and André had the ear of the government. I had only been working on them for less than a year, and the bishop warned me that he did not want to see our movement "cross the line."

I told the bishop that I had no intention of starting a revolution and only sought what we had been promised in the Manitoba Act. I then asked the bishop if he would sanction a new religiously based organization designed to meet the needs of our Métis people. I told him that the title that came to mind is l'Union nationale métisse Saint-Joseph, named after the patron saint of the Métis, St. Joseph. Fortunately, he was impressed with the idea and said he would sanction the organization, provided I agree to the conditions we had already discussed. Which I gladly did. I am proud to say that the Union nationale métisse Saint-Joseph du Manitoba remains to this day at the heart of the Métis nation.

Next, Père André and a member of the North-West Council, D.H. MacDowall, came to visit me. They wished to discuss my future plans. I told them much the same as I had told Bishop Grandin. I had come to the Saskatchewan at the request of the residents to assist in their constitutional campaign to gain representation and to alleviate their concerns over land title and issues arising from the Manitoba Act. Upon completion of this work, I planned to attend to my personal claims and that of others presently living in Montana. Asking me pointed questions, they wanted to know what my personal claims were with the Canadian government. Not so subtly, they were attempting to arrange a personal payout, separating my personal claims against the government from my work in the agitation. It was shades of Bishop Taché's palace and Macdonald's bag of gold all over again.

In exchange for returning to Montana, they sought to strike a bargain where they would relay a claim to the lieutenant-governor seeking anywhere from $35,000 to $100,000 for my work in Manitoba. Much has been made of this attempted bribe. All kinds of figures have been thrown around, but the most interesting aspect of the whole thing is that when they submitted a request to pay me for past services to Lieutenant-Governor Dewdney, the government did not even respond. John A. Macdonald had other plans.

So, for absolute clarity on this issue: it is true that I had come to Saskatchewan planning to work on my own claim as well as to work for democratic reform. But I never considered giving up one for the other. In my mind the two were inseparably bound. After this, when I asked my Métis people if I should return to Montana, they insisted we stay on with them. Our family was their family.

As the press became even more outrageous, the papers began calling for military intervention to keep the Indians on the reserves, the deportation of the itinerant exiled Sioux from Canada, as well as my arrest. Even Will Jackson, who had united the agricultural sector but vocally opposed the deportation of the Sioux and other racist measures, saw his support in the countryside plummet. Racial fear began to spread its tentacles as rumours spread. Will pleaded for a suspension of judgement about concerns based on old biases. He told the citizens worried about Indian war that "there is no danger of Indian troubles as long as we can keep Riel in the country." Will's position deteriorated further when he told a public meeting in Prince Albert that "the North-West belongs to the Indians and not to the Dominion of Canada." That has always been my position, but I believe Will Jackson was the first Caucasian to ever utter those bold words. Now he was condemned as "an Indian lover" and my right-hand man.

Will and I spent our time from August until December 1884 working together to relieve the condition for all sectors of our North-West population. During that time I spoke with the Cree and Assiniboine leaders about what the Indian Agent Robert Jefferson, a friend of the Cree, called their great "Cree Strikes of 1884." After this, we met with Big Bear at the Jackson family home in Prince Albert, where I agreed to support their campaign for "one who speaks for all."

As I have previously explained, Will Jackson and I were able to gather a list of grievances and requests representing the interests of all classes in the North-West. These requests included the following: responsible government; the setting aside of two million acres of land to provide funds for the relief of distress amongst the Indians; the purchase of machinery and seed grain for the Métis; and the immediate issue of patents. We also requested that works and contracts of the government of the North-West be given as far as practicable to residents therein, as well as a number of other issues. We organized these requests into one great Petition of Rights which we sent to Secretary of State Joseph-Adolphe Chapleau and the Canadian government on December 16, 1884.

We were buoyed when Chapleau acknowledged receipt of our petition. However, as time elapsed, we were perplexed that the government said nothing about what they intended to do with our requests. I can tell you that all was not goodness and light around us, either. We had worked hard to ensure that we had consensus regarding the resolutions and our requests, so as to have general unanimity on our petition within the various linguistic communities. Then, Father Fourmond, the priest at St. Laurent, produced another petition in which he asked Ottawa to subsidize support for the day school run by the Faithful Companions of Jesus at St. Laurent. In Protestant Prince Albert this second petition was very damaging. The Protestants did not want money going to religious schools, certainly not Catholic schools. Almost immediately, I was accused of being behind this second petition. This was a real slap in the face concerning our work to unify the various communities. Taken aback, I was most angry at the clergy for breaking the growing unity of Catholics and Protestants in the North-West.

In February 1885, two months after receiving our petition, Macdonald's Cabinet informed Lieutenant-Governor Dewdney that a commission of three members were to be appointed, not to negotiate but to enumerate those who did not participate in scrip under the Manitoba Act. In another slight to the authors of this petition, Will Jackson and me, this message was passed from Governor Dewdney to Père André and then on to his pious acolyte, my cousin Charles Nolin. By March 1,

1885, with no action but a stale promise and more and more police moving into the neighbourhood, we could conclude that the Canadian government was not only ignoring our petition but preparing to arrest me.

COMMISSIONER: Mr. Riel, what evidence do you have that Prime Minister Macdonald was not genuine in attempting to ameliorate the circumstances in the North-West and in actuality was planning your downfall?

RIEL: As I have indicated, it was always my intention to go to the Saskatchewan to help the population peaceably obtain those rights we had been guaranteed by the Manitoba Act. But Sir John A. Macdonald, Canada's Father of Confederation, prime minister, minister of the interior and superintendent general of Indian affairs, the one man with power to create change, ignored our Petition of Rights and ordered another study. I ask you: what kind of father is this? Snubbing the needs and the grievances of all sections of the population, he ignored his responsibilities, and when he did act, he did so in a covert and malicious fashion. His reasoning soon became evident.

Remember, after winning the federal election of 1882, Macdonald pumped vast sums of money into the CPR, virtually giving their syndicate the southern prairie from Portage to Calgary. Then, in the autumn of '83, with massive amounts already spent, and huge orders placed, the company ran short of working capital. The directors asked Macdonald for another government loan of $22 million, which they received. However, by the winter of 1884 this money, too, was gone. With government coffers depleted and no credit, the Canadian Pacific Railway teetered on the brink of bankruptcy, as did the career and reputation of Macdonald.

With creditors calling in their debts, directors Smith and Stephen clamoured for additional financial support. Although politically sympathetic, Macdonald dared not provide more money in a time of national downturn. Nor could he risk handing over more capital to the country's richest men. Running out of options, Macdonald signed over expanses of previously laid, government-financed track to appease company creditors. Yet railway debts continued to mount. By February of

1885, with the workers not being paid, and strikes up and down the line, Sam Steele and the North-West Mounted Police were called in to suppress the CPR workers and keep the trains moving. A new solution to keep the company afloat was desperately needed. It is my contention that Macdonald knew exactly what he had to do. He would use the railway crisis to launch the second phase of his fifteen-year war in the North-West.

This premise, that the prime minister wanted a war, is based on a number of facts. First, and I am not being egotistical in stating this, was his hatred of me — a hatred which I truly consider to be of a pathological nature. Why is this? It must be remembered that as a young man, twenty-four years of age, I prevented his long dreamed-of colonial government from being established in the North-West, and I also defeated William McDougall and his Canadian forces in war. Not only that, I had the province of Manitoba created in the interests of the actual inhabitants and not the band of speculators in Ottawa, Montreal and London. I outfoxed the fox, and the old racist could never stomach losing to a "breed." I am told his pet phrase for me was "that gone coon." So, not only was John A. Macdonald looking to eliminate me, he knew that after fifteen years of petitioning, the Métis were no longer willing to wait for title to their farms. An order in council to survey river lots south of St. Laurent would easily have removed this irritant.

The developing unity of the Indians across the North-West was also a deep concern. The American cavalry was embroiled in wars all across their West. Here in the Canadian North-West, there had already been armed standoffs and food riots in the Qu'Appelle, and war had been narrowly averted after then Superintendent Crozier disrupted Poundmaker's Thirst Dance in the Eagle Hills during the past spring. On top of all of this, Will Jackson and the Settlers Union had organized a broad agrarian protest movement of settlers and farmers with plans underway to hold a North-West Rights Convention in Brandon, Manitoba, in the spring of '85. The farmers were now demanding provincial status and representation in the Canadian Parliament. They were demanding real democracy, not government by decree. Macdonald would have none of it.

COMMISSIONER: Mr. Riel, we now come to what is perhaps the most critical question of your career. Did you rebel on the Saskatchewan in 1885?

RIEL: Mr. Commissioner, although my work in bringing Manitoba into Confederation has been grudgingly recognized, my career in Saskatchewan has most often been portrayed as being wild and crazy, yet we spent eight months in constitutional struggle before we were attacked by the police at Duck Lake. It was at this point we formed a provisional government for our own protection. For me to answer your question honestly, I would have you rephrase this question. Did Louis Riel rebel in the Saskatchewan, or did John A. Macdonald consciously plan to instigate an armed conflict in the North-West? That is the question which I will answer shortly, but before I do I wish to convey the following facts.

Over the winter of 1884–85, with police patrols now originating from both Fort Carlton and Prince Albert, police activities and harassment on the roads and trails ratcheted up in our neighbourhoods. The police constables were constantly stopping and threatening Métis travellers. In Prince Albert, the campaign to rally public opinion against the "ogre Louis Riel" grew ever more virulent. Lieutenant-Governor Dewdney wrote to the prime minister bragging of having turned the northern press against me. But most crucially, it would be Hudson's Bay factor Lawrence Clarke who would light the fuse.

Returning to the Saskatchewan from meetings with Macdonald in Ottawa and Lieutenant-Governor Dewdney in Regina, Lawrence Clarke met a group of Métis, including Napoleon Nault and Michel Dumas, who inquired of him what answer the government was going to make to our petitions. Claiming to have passed a camp of five hundred policemen coming north to capture Riel and Dumont, Clarke told them the only answer they would get would be bullets. With Clarke's declaration, this news spread like wildfire. Our men hurried home to get their guns and came to Batoche ready to defend Gabriel and me.

With the police rumoured to be on their way, I sought the support of Père André and the Church to intervene, but the old priest refused to give me his support. Now we had no choice. We had to respond or run, and we were not about to run, as we were more afraid of the hell into which the Mounted Police and their government were openly seeking to drive us than of their firearms which, after all, could only kill us.

Following the centuries-old military tradition of the plains, Gabriel Dumont organized the Saskatchewan Métis into the buffalo brigades of old. Determined to proceed, Will Jackson and I began preparations to call the constitutional convention. It was at this point, when André and I were at loggerheads, that Charles Nolin proposed that, as March 19 is St. Joseph's Day, and St. Joseph, being the patron saint of the Union Métisse, a novena, nine successive days of prayer, be held leading up to our saint's day. His argument was that whatever decision was then made would surely be in accordance with God's will. Being a religious people, seeking guidance, we agreed. However, as the novena progressed into its third day, Father Fourmond concluded his sermon warning those congregated that he would deny the sacraments to all who, in the present circumstances, took up arms. I was furious. It was an inappropriate warning in the midst of a devotional service. Rising from my seat, I walked to the altar rail. Pointing at Father Fourmond, I denounced him. "You have turned the pulpit of truth into the pulpit of falsehood. . . . You talk politics now; you foster discord. We are sick and tired of the things you say." Nolin now stood, and turning to the assembled Métis, he pleaded for them to support Father Fourmond. He wanted us to agree to send Père André to Ottawa. Seeing André's hand now at play, I had had enough and walked out, followed by all but Nolin and the priest.

On the steps of the church I called our people to the constitutional convention. When Will Jackson attempted to take this news to Prince Albert, he found the road blocked by the police and was forced to return to Batoche rather than surrender his documents. On March 13–14, 1885, we met, and no longer able to call a constitutional convention, we established a provisional government to defend our rights. With a large gathering of Métis, three white delegates and both Sioux and Cree representatives in the hall, I chaired the meeting. Telling those assembled that the government threatened our liberty and our lives, I pointed out that the purpose of dispatching and reinforcing the Mounted Police was to confirm their government spoliation and usurpation of the rights and liberties of all classes in the Saskatchewan, except for their resident oppressors, the Hudson's Bay Company and the land speculators. Petitions had been ignored, speculators were seizing Métis lands, and the Hudson's Bay Company, with its low fur prices, was deliberately impoverishing the Métis people. This could not go on without dark consequences.

I then moved that, as the government had neglected to settle Métis claims for fifteen years, and although it had repeatedly confessed their justice by providing for their adjustment in the Dominion Land Act, the meeting should assume that the government had abdicated its functions through such neglect. Proposing that we proceed to establish a provisional government, a government that bases its program upon the demands of all sections of the population, I asked for discussion. After a brief dialogue, all were agreed, and the Provisional Government of Saskatchewan was there and then formed. I then moved that the Provisional Government pass a resolution that the Canadian government should immediately appoint a commission to deal with the Métis land claims, and pledge itself to deal with the questions affecting settlers and Indians. On obtaining reasonable guarantees that this would be done, the Provisional Government would disband.

Having repudiated the Canadian government, our provisional government of Saskatchewan then set forth its program in a Revolutionary Bill of Rights of the Saskatchewan, representing the position of our varied peoples. Based on eight months of constitutional work by Will Jackson and me, it was our basis for negotiations. No hostile movements were to be made, unless word was received from Ottawa refusing to grant the demands formulated in the Bill of Rights. Bloodshed was to be avoided, unless the provocation amounted to a matter of life and death for the settlers. In the meantime, the authority of the Dominion of Canada would be repudiated and supplies collected to provide against the emergency of war. Immediately after the meeting we began to place a levy on the freighters and settlers for just such an emergency. Gabriel Dumont, elected adjutant general, turned his attention to the Indians, and tobacco men were sent out in all directions informing them of what had been done.

I find it interesting that our Saskatchewan Bill of Rights seems to have disappeared from Canadian history, as if it never existed. Sent to Ottawa and Regina from the Provisional Government of the Saskatchewan of 1885, it is not to be found in the private or public papers of John A. Macdonald or Lieutenant-Governor Edgar Dewdney. It has magically disappeared. An advisor to Canada's Conservative prime minister has even slanderously accused me of deliberately burning the Saskatchewan Bill of Rights shortly before the Battle of Duck Lake, because I felt it to be too "incriminating." This is an absurd position. We did not burn the Bill of Rights. It was the culmination of eight months of intense constitutional work up and down the Saskatchewan River Valleys. We had met publicly and openly, and had collected the opinions and resolutions of all sectors of the population. There is absolutely nothing incriminating in the Bill of Rights. It still today calls out for implementation. I now proudly present this Saskatchewan Bill of Rights to the Canadian people, as it was found reprinted from the *Regina Leader*, Evening Edition, on April 21, 1885:

THE REVOLUTIONARY BILL OF RIGHTS
OF THE SASKATCHEWAN, 1885

That the half-breeds of the North-West Territories be given grants similar to those accorded to the half-breeds of Manitoba by the Act of 1870.

That patents be issued to all half-breed and white settlers who have fairly earned the right of possession on their farms.

That the Provinces of Alberta and Saskatchewan be forthwith organized with Legislatures of their own, so that the people may be no longer subject to the despotism of Mr. Dewdney.

That in these new Provincial Legislatures, while representation according to population shall be the supreme principle the Métis shall have a fair and reasonable share of representation.

That the offices of trust throughout these Provinces be given to residents of the country, as far as practicable, and that we denounce the appointment of disreputable outsiders, and repudiate their authority.

That this region be administered for the benefit of the actual settlers and not for the advantage of the alien speculator.

That better provision be made for the Indians, the Parliamentary grant to be increased and lands set apart as endowment for the establishment of hospitals and schools for the use of whites, half-breeds and Indians, at such places as the Provincial Legislatures may determine.

That all the lawful customs and usages which obtain among the Métis be respected.

That the Land Department of the Dominion Government be administered as far as practicable from Winnipeg, so that settlers may not be compelled, as heretofore to go to Ottawa for the settlement of questions in dispute between them and the land commissioner.

That the timber regulations be made more liberal and that the settlers be treated as having rights in that country.

Not only has the original copy of the Revolutionary Bill of Rights disappeared, the colonial press has asserted that the Provisional Government of the Saskatchewan was established on March 19, 1885. This is not the case. March 19 was significant as it was the last day of the novena and, on that day, the Feast of St. Joseph, patron saint of the Métis, William Henry Jackson was baptized and given his Métis name: Honoré Jaxon.

There is another point that needs clarification as it has been deliberately distorted by Anglo-Canadian officials and scholars. The Provisional Government was the political arm of the movement for democracy in the North-West. It has been deliberately misconstrued as being synonymous with the Exovidat, the religious assembly of the ex-communicated Roman Catholics under arms. The Provisional Government had its own program and agenda, as did the Exovidat, which was our religious council guiding our actions. The term "Exovidat" is a neologism derived from the Latin *ex*, from; *oved*, flock — "from the flock." The term Exovidat designated our association as an instrument of the people, a gathering of equals to serve God's will.

March 19, 1885, is significant as it is also the day the sacraments were actually denied all those who took up arms to protect Gabriel Dumont and me. After morning prayers that day, when I requested the use of St. Antoine de Padoue church for a meeting, the priest, Father Moulin, denied my request. I asked him again and that is when he told the congregation that the Oblates would refuse the sacraments to all those under arms as well as their families. Angrily, I brushed him aside. Crossing myself, I declared "Rome has fallen. . . . Providence, which has foreseen this miraculous movement, has prepared this church to serve as our stronghold. . . . St. Antoine de Padoue is going to become celebrated in history as the birthplace of the emancipation of the North-West." Henceforth, I took up my duties and led prayer and administered the sacraments to my people. That evening the Exovidat elected twelve from "the flock" to guide our religious practice.

The second point requiring clarification and emphasis is that, contrary to colonial opinion, the Provisional Government of the Saskatchewan was not "out for blood." Inspired by the Métis tradition of self-government on the plains it was a response to an imminent attack against the Métis people and me. The Provisional Government worked out the strategy and tactics of the movement for democratic rights and was willing to negotiate these rights. As we have seen, the Canadian government, and those forces behind it, had no interest in negotiations. Their program once again called for the dispossession of the Métis people, the obliteration of the Indian race, and feudal status for the farmers and settlers of the North-West.

The third point needing emphasis is that John A. Macdonald knew from experience that I was capable of uniting the various groups in the North-West around a democratic program. The proof was the Manitoba Act of 1870, and my election to the Canadian Parliament on three separate occasions. Macdonald was determined to use whatever means it took to stamp out that democratic program.

COMMISSIONER: Mr. Riel, is it your contention that the Canadian prime minister, John A. Macdonald, actively sought to start a war in the North-West?

RIEL: Yes, it remains my contention that the war in the North-West hinges on John A. Macdonald's personal vendetta against me and the financial crisis facing the Canadian Pacific Railroad. Worried about my presence in the Saskatchewan, John A. Macdonald saw that the

Canadian Pacific Railway would enable his government to put a strong military force rapidly in the field. As I see it, his plan was to instigate a clash, and then call on Parliament to raise the money to send troops into the North-West over the near-bankrupt CPR. Once this was achieved, he could raise more money for the railroad with endorsement by the Canadian Parliament.

On March 21, 1885, with our provisional government calling for Canadian commissioners to come and negotiate, Macdonald, rather than call in mediators, convened a meeting with the minister in charge of the Canadian militia, Adolphe-Philippe Caron. Also at that meeting were William Cornelius Van Horne and British Major General Frederick Middleton, commanding officer of the Canadian militia. It was at this meeting, before a shot had been fired, that Macdonald began dedicating his resources to war. The immediate task was the transportation of troops and supplies out west over the still incomplete CPR line. Van Horne had done just this in the American Civil War, and pledged to do so again — in record time. So it was that Major General Frederick Middleton was mobilized to proceed to Red River on March 23. Recognizing the need for a large-scale force to prevent a full-scale uprising, Middleton summoned troops from every province of the Dominion. Officially, once assembled, Middleton commanded over 5,000 military personnel as well as 2,600 logistical staff.

I can state categorically that all of this was but a part of a longer-term scheme, as shortly after my arrival in the Saskatchewan, in the spring of '84, Macdonald wrote Donald Smith "secretly" requesting use of the HBC's now redundant Fort Carlton to house a troop of North-West Mounted Police in the lands between the North and South Saskatchewan Rivers. Now with Superintendent Crozier of the North-West Mounted Police headquartered in our territory, and Lawrence Clarke's suggestion that more Mounted Police were coming north from Regina, I sent off urgent requests for Canadian commissioners to come and resolve the situation. As in Manitoba, fifteen years earlier, a commissioner with the right credentials could have greatly assisted in resolving the impasse.

We knew that Joseph Royal was desirous of acting as a mediator. Not only had Royal been counsel for the defence in the trials of Ambroise

Lépine and André Nault, he had since had a distinguished career in Manitoba where he had been superintendent of education and the provincial secretary of the executive council. Twice elected as the Conservative Member of Parliament for my old seat, Provencher, Royal was a man who understood our issues and was an excellent choice for a mediator. Then, when he was preparing to leave Winnipeg for Batoche, we understand that he was unaccountably called back, disallowed by the prime minister who refused to send any government representative to negotiate with us. Macdonald, and later Major General Middleton, vowed there would be "no appeasing of rebels." Unconditional surrender was to be Canada's answer to constitutional and extra-constitutional agitation henceforth.

COMMISSIONER: Mr. Riel, there has long been debate in regard to who fired the first shot at the Battle of Duck Lake between the Métis and the North-West Mounted Police. Please provide this Inquiry with your evidence regarding the battle at Duck Lake.

RIEL: As I have already indicated earlier in this Inquiry, at my trial, I was charged with six counts of high treason.

> Louis Riel, then living within the Dominion of Canada and under the protection of our Sovereign Lady the Queen, not regarding the duty of his allegiance nor having the fear of God in his heart, but being moved and seduced by the instigation of the devil as a false traitor against our said lady the Queen, and wholly withdrawing the allegiance, fidelity and obedience which he should and of right ought to bear towards our said lady the Queen . . . and did levy and make war against our said Lady the Queen . . . and did then maliciously and traitorously attempt and endeavour by force and arms to subvert and destroy the constitution and government of this realm as by law established. . . .

The first and fourth of the six charges relate to my activities at the battle at Duck Lake, which has often been misrepresented in the Canadian press as a Métis ambush. As a participant, I wish to clear up any misconceptions that may still linger.

On the 18th of March, 1885, on orders from Ottawa, Commissioner

Irvine left the NWMP barracks in Regina and began marching north with ninety men. On his march, Irvine received a dispatch from Superintendent Crozier dated the 19th, advising him that we had seized supplies from various stores in St. Laurent. Crozier next sent the half-breed scout Joseph (Joe) McKay Jr. to Prince Albert with a dispatch to NWMP Captain Moffat calling on him to enroll eighty volunteers to come and augment Crozier's forces at Fort Carlton. A meeting of the citizens of Prince Albert was hastily held with Captain Moore reading the dispatch. After a series of loyal speeches delivered by Lawrence Clarke, Charles Mair and other prominent citizens, some eighty men were sworn in to go to Fort Carlton. The universal impression was that nothing more than a show of force would prove necessary. That afternoon, Prince Albert volunteers left in sleighs and clippers to reinforce Superintendent Crozier at Carlton.

Between Fort Carlton on the north branch of the Saskatchewan River and Batoche on the south branch is the little community of Duck Lake, a long-time Métis and Indian trading centre. With the expansion of the Anglo merchants into the rural areas over the last few years, it was now home to several shops, the most prominent being Hilliard Mitchell's hardware store. Mitchell, with whom we were on friendly terms, attempted reconciliation, keeping in close touch with both Crozier and me. On March 20, Crozier sent Mitchell, along with Joe McKay, to Batoche with a proposal that he and I hold a personal interview at an appointed rendezvous between Batoche and Carlton. With reports of volunteers being organized to reinforce Carlton, and the police from Regina coming to arrest Gabriel and me, I sensed a trap and replied with the following:

St. Antoine. N. W. Ter., March 21, 1885

To Major Crozier, Commander of the Police at
Forts Carlton and Battleford.

Major:

The Councilors of the Provisional Government of Saskatchewan have the honour to communicate to you the following conditions of surrender: You will be required to give up completely the situation which the

Canadian Government placed you in at Carlton and Battleford, together with all Government properties.

In case of acceptance, you and your men will be set free on your parole of honour to keep the peace. And those who choose to leave the country will be furnished with teams and provisions to reach Qu'Appelle.

In case of non-acceptance, we intend to attack you. When? Tomorrow, the Lord's Day is over, and to commence, without delay, a war of extermination upon those who have shown themselves hostile to our rights.

Messrs. Charles Nolin and Maxime Lépine are the gentlemen with whom you will have to treat.

Signed (Riel and nine councillors)

With an emphasis on our use of the word "extermination," this document was not only used against me at my trial, it has since been used to condemn me as a megalomaniac murderer. It is harsh language indeed, and in hindsight, I can see that the choice of the term "extermination" was unwise. Nevertheless, please allow me to explain. Since the Hudson's Bay Company had moved its longtime commercial operations from Fort Carlton up to Prince Albert over the previous year, Fort Carlton had become a paramilitary barracks in the heart of our territory. Now it was being reinforced by police and volunteers from both north and south. We could not let this happen as it left our community vulnerable to a coordinated police attack.

From our experience fifteen years earlier in Red River, we knew that we could not let our enemies surround and annihilate us. When Canadian designate Lieutenant-Governor McDougall declared war on us, we had to block the border and remove Schultz and company from "Fort Schultz" in the heart of our community for the same reason. Then, when we believed Garnet Wolseley's declaration of peace, he and his troops overran our community and we suffered the terror that came with occupation and its long-term results: murder, rape and pillage. For the safety of the community, we knew that the police must leave. We were determined to neutralize this threat, hopefully through our rhetoric, if not our blood. I hoped our stern reply would impress upon Crozier our determination that, if necessary, we would drive them from our country by force.

Having force-marched through the remnants of the winter snow, Commissioner Irvine and his ninety men reached Prince Albert on the afternoon of March 24, 1885. Irvine's intention was to proceed at once from Prince Albert to Carlton, but the people in the district believed that the situation had already ceased to be immediately dangerous. Accordingly, Irvine held back his exhausted and sometimes snow-blind men and spent the evening in Prince Albert.

It was under these circumstances that the English Métis under James Isbister and some white settlers met at St. Andrew's school in the Halcro Settlement to discuss the situation. Their meeting sent the following resolutions to us at Batoche:

1. That while heartily sympathizing with the French in their endeavors constitutionally to get redress of their many grievances, we cannot endorse the present attitude in taking up arms for that purpose, and we hereby beg of them not to shed blood.

2. That the opinion of this meeting is that had the Government been just with the settlers, this disturbance would never have been.

3. And further, had the influential citizens of Prince Albert joined the movement, instead of ignoring it, had they advised the Government instead of inciting against the people, it is the opinion of this meeting that the government would have settled all grievances long ere before this.

4. That we, the English Half-breed and Canadian settlers, while advocating peace and remaining completely neutral as resorting to arms, do not for one moment, lose sight of our grievances and will henceforth use all lawful means for the redress of the same.

I replied as follows:

Reponse aux Métis Anglais de St. Catherine's et de St. Andrews:

Gentlemen, please, do not remain neutral. For the love of God help us to save the Saskatchewan. We sent today [24 March 1885] a number of men with Mr. Monkman to help and to support, as it is the just cause of the aboriginal half-breeds.

Public necessity means no offence. Let us join willingly. . . . If we are well united our union will cause the Police to come out of Carlton as the hen's heat causes the chicken to come out of the shell. A strong union between the French & English Half-breeds is the only guarantee that there will be no blood shed. . . . Let us avoid the mistakes of the past.

On March 26, 1885, under a white flag of peace, with thirty Métis and five Indians in our party, Gabriel Dumont rode out from the little village of Duck Lake on the road to Fort Carlton. When he arrived, Crozier was nowhere to be seen. Instead, Sergeant Stewart and Joe McKay with a couple of teams and a number of volunteers and policemen showed up. They had been sent to get the supplies out of Mitchell's store in Duck Lake. Stopping the head team, driven by Mr. Neilson, later sheriff of Prince Albert, Gabriel insisted the convoy return to Fort Carlton. Sending his scouts back to report to Crozier, McKay threatened a standoff. Gabriel then spoke to Mr. Neilson and suggested he turn his team around or we would impound it or worse. Reluctantly, he agreed to turn his team and the police headed back to Fort Carlton.

When McKay's scout reported back that the Métis had blocked the road, Superintendent Crozier prepared to move out with his full contingent and cannon. However, just as he was about to leave, Mr. Neilson and the convoy returned with the message that we came under the flag of peace and sought an interview with the superintendent. Crozier pulled his men up, but Lawrence Clarke and others called on him to carry on and show the half-breeds who was in charge. When Crozier suggested waiting for Irvine's reinforcements, Clarke made disparaging remarks regarding the commander's manhood, convincing Crozier that his force, three times ours, with a cannon, could easily teach this Louis Riel and his Métis rebels a lesson. With Joe McKay in the lead, Crozier commanded his men to their destiny.

That same morning, March 26, with a number of his men still snow-blinded or ill, Commissioner Irvine left Prince Albert, taking eighty-three non-commissioned NWMP officers and men from Regina, in addition to twenty-five volunteers. A short distance from Fort Carlton,

Irvine received a dispatch informing him that Crozier was advancing on Duck Lake. With this news, Irvine hurried forward in hopes of taking command and restraining Crozier and his forces until the situation was reviewed.

It was at this juncture that I joined Gabriel and our men. I carried no weapon, but the Cross of our Lord, Jesus Christ. Having encountered the police and knowing of their desire to retrieve the supplies still at Duck Lake, we blockaded the road and waited for the police to return. Upon seeing us, Crozier pulled up. He had his men bring forward his seven-pound cannon, behind which he placed a line of sleighs, twenty-eight in number, strung out across the road. With his men taking up a threatening attitude behind the sleighs, Isidore Dumont, Gabriel's elder brother, went forward with Chief Aseeweyin waving the white flag of peace. Joe McKay, with Crozier close behind him, rode over towards Isidore and Aseeweyin. Unarmed, the old chief waved his flag. Pointing to McKay's weapons, and the men with the cannon, he asked McKay in Cree, "Where are you going with so many guns, grandson?" As Aseeweyin was speaking, McKay reined up his horse, drew his revolver and fired point-blank, hitting the old chief in the face. Turning, McKay then shot Isidore Dumont off his horse. At the same time, Crozier shouted out to his men, "Fire away, boys!"

Furious, Gabriel yelled out his command and the rest of our men dropped and melted into the bush. Crack-shot buffalo hunters, our men began to pick off the police in their tunics, blazing red against the white of the snow.

Relying on his cannon to scatter our men, Crozier ordered three sighting rounds, after which the gunner rammed the shell before the shot. Misloaded, it was useless. With the cannon out of action, Gabriel prepared to charge the police. Then he was hit with a bullet grazing his skull. With our leader down, I could see our fighters were confused and in shock, but not for long. Dazed and angry, with blood streaming down the side of his face, Gabriel picked up his carbine, *Le Petit*, and let off three quick shots. As he did so, he called out to his concerned comrades, "As long as I have not lost my head I am not dead." Cheering, his men renewed their fire.

Seeing their mates getting badly shot-up, Crozier's troops and volunteers were astonished. Recoiling behind their sleighs, they had no place to hide, and our Métis sharpshooters were picking them off, one by one. With no shelter, and their numbers dwindling, the men started shouting at Crozier. He was flummoxed, his cannon was plugged and his troops pinned down. Realizing the hopelessness of his situation, Crozier finally gave the order for his men to rehitch their horses to the sleighs and cutters and retreat.

As they started to retreat, I could see Gabriel was too wounded to mount his horse. But his men were looking to their horses, preparing to obliterate the retreating Canadians. Blood had been shed, our emissaries shot down and our leader wounded. I knew what would follow. Holding aloft the Cross of Christ I spurred my horse to the front, calling out: "For the love of God, no more killing. . . . There is already too much bloodshed." It was at that point that God intervened. All firing ceased. With the Canadians in retreat, we dropped to our knees, thanked our Lord for our victory and asked that he receive the souls of our martyrs. Recovering Canadian arms and ammunition, as well as a wounded Canadian, we placed their dead in a nearby log shack safely away from predators. We then returned to Batoche with Gabriel tied to his horse, fortunate in that his wound, although severe, was not life threatening.

I would like to make a further point in regard to Canadian history and this battle. Although the numbers are often reversed, we in fact were forty in number, and fought against approximately 120 North-West Mounted troops and volunteers. Many Canadian accounts have some two hundred Indians attacking Crozier and a little troop of police. The reason for this fiction is the ignoble defeat of Crozier and the discrepancy between the number of Métis and Indians killed and the number of Canadians who were killed in this first battle. If one is to believe the old standard Canadian version of this story, the one used in the schools (Gage's New Historical Series, 1928) for nearly a century, "A Métis waved a dirty white blanket and Crozier with Constable 'Gentleman Joe' McKay, his interpreter, and another man went forward to parley. Dumont's men raced for the shelter of the shacks while the police force drew up their sleighs in a barricade across the road and led their horses to the rear. . . . In the no man's land between the two forces one Métis grappled with McKay, while another, dropping to his knee covered him with his gun. Seeing there was no likelihood of a real parley, Crozier snapped out an order. As he turned, an Indian grabbed his shoulder. Gentleman Joe McKay whipped out his pistol and shot the man covering him. It was the first shot fired in what became known as the 'Riel Rebellion of 1885.'"

It is also true that my role in this battle has been satirized and demeaned. What kind of lunatic carries a cross into battle? I carry a cross into battle as I am a soldier of God, just as our Métis people are soldiers. We are not aggressors. As a nation, our military history is one of self-defence. We first learned of war in Quebec, and then again as we moved west in the early years of inter-tribal warfare on the plains. In the "fur-trade wars" we defended ourselves and our territory from the encroachment of Lord Selkirk and his governors. Cuthbert Grant, captain general of the Métis, led us at the Battle of Seven Oaks in 1816, and thereafter the valiant Father Lafleche held high his cross at the Battle of Grand Coteau in 1851. In that legendary battle, our Métis buffalo hunters defeated some hundreds of Sioux warriors with such bravery and military precision that our Sioux brothers sought peace. We still honour that peace today.

Gabriel Dumont was fourteen when he fought at the Battle of Grand Coteau. From then onward he has been a leader. Through his youth, Gabriel led Cree raiding parties, and he was the supreme hunt captain through the last of the great Métis buffalo hunts. Through it all, Gabriel, a man who never attended school, advanced and expanded the tactics of plains fighting to its highest development. All of Gabriel's men respect him and consider themselves to be his soldiers.

Returning now to the battle at Duck Lake: did God allow me to perform a miracle and stop the slaughter? I truly believe so. It was his will that allowed me to prevent a massacre, for justice was on our side. The war had begun, and tragically the dead included many prominent individuals from Prince Albert who had volunteered to join Crozier. It is to be noted that Lawrence Clarke, who had goaded Crozier to attack, had quickly fled once the shooting began, even leaving behind his sumptuous lynx fur coat.

COMMISSIONER: Mr. Riel, although you won the first battle, you must have realized how vulnerable your situation was. Why did you continue to fight?

RIEL: What choice did we have? We had been attacked, and as we have always done, we would defend our homes, our lands and our way of life. The day following the battle, I drew up our combatants in two lines and, after reviewing them, I addressed them, calling out: "God bless Gabriel Dumont, and thank God for having given you so valorous a leader."

We did not gloat but passed the day praying for our dead, whom we buried at St. Laurent. Gabriel then suggested sending a prisoner with a letter promising safe conduct to the police to come for their dead. When our messenger, an innocent Canadian, reached Fort Carlton, he was seized as a spy. Commissioner Irvine had arrived with his troop of police and volunteers shortly after Crozier's ignoble retreat. Taking over command of the fort, Irvine had his troops evacuate on the next night, March 27, as a fire "accidentally" broke out consuming most of Fort Carlton's buildings. When Irvine and his troops arrived back in Prince Albert, they were without the bodies of those who had died in the battle. The citizenry were both shocked and outraged. They were shocked at the police being beaten by the Métis, and outraged that they returned without the bodies of their beloved.

Nor were the police in any hurry to retrieve the bodies, even though I had personally assured the safety of those sent to retrieve them. After a number of inordinate delays, three men were finally sent out to recover the bodies of the dead police and volunteers. Our Métis elders gave what assistance they could to Irvine's emissaries. We also restored to them the wounded policeman whom they had left behind and we had captured. With these duties completed, Gabriel took defensive measures and burned all the buildings at Duck Lake, except the mill. We then retired to a defensive position at Batoche to heal our wounds and carve out our future. I would have this Inquiry note that in his subsequent report, Commissioner Irvine wrote as follows: "I cannot but consider it a matter of regret that, with the knowledge that both myself and command were within a few miles and en route to Carlton, Superintendent Crozier should have marched out as he did."

I also want to assure this Inquiry that we understood only too well that although we had won the Battle of Duck Lake, we were now in a most precarious position. Entrapped, we had been forced to defend our lives, land and culture, and God had given us a victory. We truly needed his Divine guidance. It was clearly a time of prayer and contemplation. With the priests sidelined, we now met as the Exovidat, a "flock" of twenty seeking guidance and intervention. The majority of our Exovidat were Métis. It also included, however, the Sioux Chief, White Cap, two French-Canadian members and Honoré Jaxon. Our ultimate goal in the service of Jesus Christ, the Son of God and only Redeemer of the world, was that of Moses: to lead our people to a promised land of peace.

With this tragic war forced upon us, the North-West as we had known it was torn asunder. Short months previous we had achieved a multiracial alliance, all seeking to work together to meet the needs of our communities. Now with blood having been spilled and a siege mentality prevalent, our half-breed cousins were neutralized, and we had lost the last of the support we had amongst the settlers. Martial law was in place in Prince Albert. Guards and pickets were posted around the perimeter of the town, and volunteers were drilled in the streets. Although the half-breed settlement adopted a course of strict neutrality, they were no longer trusted and were seen as potential spies or saboteurs in the town they had founded. When the half-breed elder James Isbister returned to Prince Albert from Halcro Settlement, where he sought to mediate the dispute, he was immediately jailed as a "suspected rebel." In addition to Isbister, Thomas Scott, Henry Monkman, Charles Bird, Caleb Anderson and Fred Fidler were also imprisoned as suspected rebels. All of these men had been involved in the English Métis political movement over the past few years. They had not been with us at Batoche or Duck Lake, yet now their neighbours were turning them in.

COMMISSIONER: Mr. Riel, the Duck Lake battle was but the beginning of your war. Please elaborate and inform this Inquiry of the conflicts that ensued and your role in each.

RIEL: By the time of the battle at Duck Lake, Major General Middleton and his field force were already steaming west on the CPR. From Winnipeg, Middleton was to have his force disembark at Troy Station in southern Saskatchewan, and there assemble to march north against us at Batoche. Lieutenant Colonel William Otter was sent farther west to disembark at Swift Current Station from whence he was to march north to reinforce the police and civilians huddled in Fort Battleford, fearful of an attack by Poundmaker and the Eagle Hills Cree. Major General T.B. Strange was to take his troops west to Calgary, march north to Fort Edmonton, and then head eastwards along the North Saskatchewan River to "corral" Big Bear's band, or any Indian or Métis attempting to flee west from Battleford or Batoche.

Our scouts, the local carters hired to move the Canadian supplies, reported that to intimidate the people, Middleton's army purposefully snaked its way through the reserves in the Qu'Appelle Valley. With massive quantities of supplies, hundreds of troops mounted and marching, followed by carts and wagons carrying cannons and two Gatling guns, the troops swept into the Métis village of Lebret, where they found a ghost town, the people having all fled to the safety of the Touchwood Hills.

Gabriel Dumont had excellent intelligence as to Middleton's movements, even obtaining diagrams and maps outlining the structure of the Canadian camps. With his knowledge of the countryside, Gabriel longed to ambush, harass and wear down the troops out on the prairie. And, it is true, we could have pinned down Middleton's troops, spooking them with a string of "coyote" hit-and-run attacks: Indian-style warfare. Praying for mediation, I would not allow it.

Over my career, I have oft-times been rebuked for refusing to allow Ambroise Lépine the opportunity to block Wolseley's troops coming off the Lake of the Woods back in 1870. I have also been criticized for refusing Gabriel's request to take the battle to Middleton. Yet what is my role? When the war was brought to our lands, we defended ourselves. It should be noted that I was closely allied with Poundmaker and wrote to him, calling on the Cree to dislodge the police from Fort Battleford. But while Poundmaker was waiting for Big Bear, Colonel Otter attacked

Poundmaker's camp at Cut Knife Hill. Under the leadership of War Chief Fine Day, the Cree soundly defeated the Canadian forces, with Poundmaker, "the peacemaker," preventing a retaliatory massacre of the retreating Canadians. As I had done, Poundmaker refused to take advantage of the Canadians when they were wholly vulnerable. That engagement would be the end of Poundmaker's war. He was treated as I was: charged with treason felony along with Big Bear and Chief One Arrow. Found guilty, they were all sentenced to Stony Mountain Penitentiary where each contracted pneumonia. Although released, each died shortly thereafter. One Arrow never made it home to Saskatchewan and died and was buried at the cathedral in St. Boniface.

COMMISSIONER: Mr. Riel, you have also been accused of taking a leading role in the battle at La coulée des Tourond (Fish Creek). Please review your role in this battle for the Inquiry.

RIEL: A first point of clarification. I was not at the battle at La coulée des Tourond. Our scouts had reported that Middleton's army had now passed Manitou Springs, and the salt flats near Watrous, and were headed to Clarke's Crossing on the Saskatchewan, where the general planned to split his forces to attack Batoche from both sides of the river. As we had no communications with the outside world, and no Canadian contact or commissioner on the horizon, I knew we had no choice: General Middleton had to be stopped. And stopped he would be.

Our military leader, Gabriel Dumont, knew where to spring the trap. To reach Batoche from Clarke's Crossing, Middleton's troops would have to cross Tourond's Coulee at the base of a steep ravine where, over the eons, the Cree and then the Métis had constructed a "buffalo jump." Chasing the great beasts, the hunters drove them over the edge of the ravine twisting down towards the South Saskatchewan River. A natural trap, the trail the Canadians would use entered the coulee, then circled up the ravine and back onto the parkland prairie. At the point of the jump, the bank jutted out high above the valley bottom. With Gabriel's marksmen hiding in the creek bed and on the slopes, soldiers looking out along the rim were exposed.

Leaving some thirty men to guard Batoche, Gabriel and I rode south with two hundred men preparing to confront the advancing Canadian Army. Our troop was a mixed lot, made up of Métis as well as Cree, Saulteaux, Assiniboine (Stonies) and Sioux warriors. Armed mostly with buffalo rifles, shotguns and pistols, we made our way south. On our way, we were overtaken by two Métis scouts. They reported there were indications that the police in Prince Albert were planning a night raid on Batoche. Although only a rumour, it had to be taken seriously. Taking a small group of our fighters back with me, I returned to defend Batoche. It turned out to have been a false alarm; the "gophers" stayed in their burrow and we spent the night in prayer asking God for Divine guidance.

Approaching the coulee, Gabriel had his men move off the road below and onto the game trails leading to the bluffs above the creek. Seeking the element of surprise, our warriors made their way in small groups, leaving no tracks for Canadian scouts. They were to dig into the wooded slopes at the base of the ravine where they had a clear line of fire on the ridge above. Meanwhile, Gabriel and twenty horsemen moved into the trees behind the slope, planning to launch a horseback attack on the soldiers once they were pinned down on the trail. Fortunately for Middleton, the trap failed. Canadian scouts came across one of Gabriel's men not yet dug into the forest. As the man began to run, one of the scouts took aim. Instinctively, Gabriel shot the scout and then, with the Canadians opening fire, he and his little cavalry made a dash into the bush.

With shots having been fired, the curious Canadians, many of whom were raw recruits, moved to the rim of the ravine and began shooting wildly into the dense bush. They were lined up like ducks in a row. Our Métis soldiers, nearly invisible in the bush, fired back, picking off the soldiers silhouetted against the prairie skyline. Middleton's cannons were useless, for they could not aim at such a downward angle. The battle lasted through the day. Desperately short of ammunition, our Métis warriors made every shot count until they ran out of supplies. Gabriel then used the last bit of daylight to fire the prairie grasses up the ravine. As the fire roared up the hill, he sent his scouts forward to harass and spook the Canadians into retreat. It worked: Middleton pulled his forces back to safety as Gabriel and his men disappeared onto the prairie.

Gabriel lost four men with two wounded. With ten men killed and another forty wounded, Middleton had lost one soldier in ten. As one combatant said to me: "We prayed all day, and I think prayer did more than bullets." Later, while interrogating me, Middleton told me he figured our numbers were in the hundreds. We had fewer than fifty men just metres away.

Gabriel had given us a victory and time to prepare our defences at Batoche. General Middleton spent the next two weeks "licking his wounds" and waiting for reinforcements prior to finally making his move north and into the heart of the Métis homeland, Batoche.

COMMISSIONER: Mr. Riel, please inform this Inquiry about the Battle of Batoche.

RIEL: I am not a military man. Our war chief was Gabriel Dumont. Where I sought salvation both on the material and spiritual plain, Gabriel would lead us in our war. Truly, this is his story, but I will tell you what I know.

Having licked their wounds, the Canadians now took their revenge on Gabriel and his neighbours. With the HBC sternwheeler *Northcote* berthed at Gabriel's ferry landing, the troops looted his store, dismantled his pool table and torched his beautiful two-storey house. Our scouts saw them load the pool table onto the *Northcote* and use it, as well as siding from the stables and barn to reinforce the decks. On the front deck, the American mercenary "Gatling Howard" had installed one of his two Gatling guns, planning to give General Middleton a demonstration of this new war technology in the heat of battle.

On the morning of May 9, 1885, the *Northcote* cast off, heading downriver in the spring run-off. Gabriel and his soldiers watched and waited until the ship turned the last bend before Batoche; they then proceeded to fire, harassing the vessel, pinning down the Canadian troops on board. As the captain manoeuvred the ship towards our shore, Gabriel lowered the ferry cable, catching the stacks and disabling the vessel. Careening downstream, it was unable to stop and drifted out of sight. Its war ended before it began.

With the *Northcote* taken care of, our mighty war leader rode up the riverbank, galloped through Batoche and made his way to the rifle pits in the bush behind the church of St. Antoine de Padoue. From here he could travel unseen throughout our series of interconnected defences. Taking a position up front, with seventy-five men completely concealed in the bush, Gabriel watched as the entire Canadian Field Force, some eight hundred strong, came marching down the road towards Batoche. At their head were two artillery pieces, followed by the general himself, his staff and the different regiments. Fortunately, they were approaching from exactly the direction Gabriel had anticipated.

Advancing, they stopped some five hundred metres down the trail. Presently, we saw a puff of smoke belch forth from one of the guns, followed by another puff of smoke from the other. The first shell ploughed into the empty ground between the church and the rectory where the priests were congregated. The second shot registered a near-miss on the other side of the church. Then mounted Canadian scouts spread out in a line. Followed by troops on foot, they began to advance at a steady pace. Passing the church, the mounted troops moved ever closer to the edge of the bush.

Everyone waited for Gabriel's orders: "When I fire, the rest of you do the same," he ordered. With the scouts advancing unopposed, the troops picked up the pace. When they closed in, Gabriel fired, followed by his sharpshooters. With a number of men hit, the scouts recoiled, retreating to the south side of the church. Then a bugle called, and two companies of soldiers, in bright scarlet and blue and gold uniforms, began advancing on the cemetery. Without breaking step, they passed through it and came on towards our woods. Once again, Gabriel held fire until they drew near. Aiming at their leader, he let him have it. Then his men opened fire. The Canadians, mostly young recruits, were caught and did not know what hit them, or from where. Falling to the ground they shot wildly at an enemy they could not see. Although outnumbered, we were able to keep them pinned down.

Our concern was not so much with these green troops as what lay behind them. I could see they were advancing a pair of artillery guns up a slight rise. Unlimbering, they began to sight in to bombard the village. Moving up in the bush, Gabriel had his men direct their fire towards the gunners. With his gunners under fire and a number of shells harmlessly hitting the outskirts of our little town, Middleton ordered his guns and his infantry to retire. It was but a feint, as he had troops moving towards the gully situated behind the cemetery. What they did not know is that we had them covered in a crossfire from our rifle pits on the riverbank and in the bluffs. When they attempted to advance on us, we again fired on them. Trapped, they could not advance without taking numerous casualties. By noon, we had the Canadians completely blocked, unable to move ahead. We held them in a stalemate, and so passed the remainder of the day. Come evening, Middleton retired with his force to a ploughed field southeast of the church. Through the night we kept the whole camp awake with random shots directed into their camp.

As we were burying our dead Sunday morning in the fully exposed cemetery, a bugle called. We could see Middleton barking out orders as the Canadian troops did a number of manoeuvres, lining up in a parade square, with officers forming up along the front and scouts along the left and right flanks. There was a lot of regimental bluster, and we expected them to march on us and attack. But there was no attack. Instead, falling out, they occupied themselves digging trenches. They were on the defensive, preparing against an attack on our part. In the afternoon, one of the batteries went briefly into action, firing a few shots indiscriminately in a line to the right of the church. Another company of scouts rode off north to make a reconnaissance of our defences above the town. There was scattered fire throughout the day, but no attack.

Each night after the soldiers returned to their camp, we would check their earlier positions, as often there were bullets left on the ground. It was during one of these searches that we came across something very serious: exploding balls. We thought it was understood between nations that only mortars could be explosive, as their debris was very destructive. But for a man in combat to be exposed to exploding bullets was to cause a terrible wound and a type of death that was against the basic principles of war. The government troops committed a huge crime against humanity and against the rights of the men of the Métis nation with those balls.

The next day, while the scouts and an artillery piece made a feint to the north of the village, the Canadian infantry managed to regain the positions they had occupied initially on Saturday. During the process much rifle fire was exchanged. We were definitely running short on ammunition. That evening, when the Canadians retired to their camp, Gabriel gave orders that they were not to be pursued. Our ammunition would last but one more day.

By May 12, we knew the end was near. In the morning, the Canadians appeared to be mounting an attack along the same lines as the previous day. While I watched, the main body of the army drew itself up before our rifle pits guarding the village's southern approaches, and the mounted men, with two pieces of artillery, swung out once again on the northeast plain. The foot soldiers made no move to advance, but the artillery and machine guns, under Middleton's personal direction, opened heavy fire on the houses at Batoche. Gabriel asked me to help the women and children leave the village to protect them from the artillery.

During those first three days, the Canadians could not move their lines of defence. They sat but did not move. However, around two o'clock in the afternoon, on definite information furnished by the priests who betrayed us by telling the Canadians that we had no more ammunition, government troops advanced in large numbers, raining bullets on our rifle pits. Our Métis troops were pinned down as the Canadians charged. With no hope, most of our men came out of their trenches to retreat. Charging into the rifle pits, the Canadians killed José Vandal, who had both arms broken first and then was finished off with a bayonet; Donald Ross, seventy-five years of age, was first fatally wounded then speared with a bayonet. As well, they killed Isidore Boyer, also a very old man; Michel Trottier, another old man, and André Batoche, Calixte Tourond, Elzéar Tourond, John Swan and Damase Carrière, who first had his leg broken and was then dragged with a rope around his neck tied to the tail of a horse. There were also two Sioux who were brutally killed.

Gabriel told me how, when the Canadian troops entered Batoche, our men fell back five hundred metres. Staying on the high ground with six of his brave fellows, Gabriel held up the enemy advance for an hour. He said that what kept him at his post was the courage of our dear friend Joseph Ouellette, ninety-three years of age. Several times Gabriel told him that they must retreat, but the old fellow replied, "Wait a minute! I want to kill another Englishman." When Ouellette was hit and dying, Gabriel thanked him for his courage. He then made his way down to the riverbank where he met seven or eight men in flight. He asked them to come to the ridge and lie in wait for the enemy. When they refused, he threatened to shoot the first one who tried to escape. They held the Canadians in check for half an hour, then came over to a large wood where I was sheltering my family and numerous other women and children.

He told me to take the people deeper in the woods, that he was going back up to the ruins of Batoche to look for some blankets. I told him he was exposing himself too much. He replied that the enemy could not kill him. He was afraid of nothing. Making his way back up into the village and spotting a policeman in the doorway to the nearest house, he killed him, knocking him off his feet; another came to see the body, and he killed him too. Grabbing two blankets and two quilts he carried them to his wife Madeleine and instructed her to give these coverings to Madame Riel for herself and her children during the night. With so many with nothing, we took the two blankets and gave the quilts to others. Then Gabriel went back to Batoche to look for some dried meat and flour. This time, no one saw him and he salvaged some food for the women who had children. Then looking to return once more to steal a horse, he said to Madeleine, "If the enemy captures you and blames you for my actions, you tell them that since the government couldn't manage me, it wasn't easy for you to do so either."

I did not see Gabriel again. I was told that he wanted me to come with him to escape across the line to the United States, but I could not do that. I spent three days in the woods. Upon receiving a note that General Middleton had given one of our men the promise of his personal protection if I gave myself up, I knew I must accept his offer in the hopes of sparing our poor scared and hungry people hiding in the woods. I surrendered to two of his scouts and was taken to General Middleton's compound where I was held in his tent. There is little else I can say. We were attacked by the Canadian Field Force, under the command of a seasoned British officer, and Gabriel and his 250 men fought back bravely.

When he heard that I had given myself up, he and several others crossed the prairies to the United States where he gave himself over to the American authorities. President Grover Cleveland declared Gabriel and his fellows political exiles, after which Gabriel went to Fort Benton where Madeleine joined him. It is rumoured that he sought the means to free me from Regina with horses stashed across the southern prairie, but the police presence was such as to dissuade him. As a celebrity in the United States, he took work with Buffalo Bill's Wild West Show along with my old friend Sitting Bull. I thank my dear colleague. God bless Gabriel Dumont.

COMMISSIONER: Mr. Riel, this Inquiry will now ask you to complete your testimony.

RIEL: Thank you. Now it is time for me to truly answer the question: did Louis Riel rebel in Saskatchewan in 1885? What the world needs to know is that unlike in Manitoba, where there was no legal government to which we owed allegiance, we organized our own government and negotiated with the Canadian government. Our resistance on the Saskatchewan was a genuine revolution against Canadian civil and religious authority. The Provisional Government of the Saskatchewan repudiated the civil authority of the Canadian government, and the Exovidat repudiated the spiritual authority of the Roman Catholic Church. Honing our civic demands into the Revolutionary Bill of Rights, we called on the Canadian government to respect the rights of the population, whether they be Indian, Métis, half-breeds or settlers. We called on Canada not to ignore us, not to oppress us, or make war upon us. We called for the recognition of equality before the law, as guaranteed under the Magna Carta. We sought the same rights as other

Canadians against arbitrary interference by the state. We wanted what Prime Minister Macdonald promised all Canadians: "absolute equality, having equal rights of every kind — of language, religion, and property and of person."

I have provided evidence regarding my ever-deteriorating relationship with the Roman Catholic Church and its priests, bishops and archbishops. Seeking Divine intervention in the affairs of this world, I have been a thorn in their sides, and they have betrayed me time and again. I have paid a heavy price for my resistance. Initially, it was forces within the Roman Catholic Church that called me "insane." Who but they were those "others" who controlled my lawyers declaring me "insane" at my trial? When in the early days I spoke to Bishop Taché, rebuking him for coveting the lands of a poor widow in St. Boniface, he did not repent but saw me held a prisoner for two years in the animal asylums of Quebec. When I asked Père André for assistance on the Saskatchewan, he rebuked me and used his authority in the service of my enemies. In our time of need, the Oblate fathers refused my people their sacraments, and then informed the Canadian troops when we had nearly run out of ammunition.

Throughout my testimony, I have spoken little of the role of these religious officials in the lives of our Métis nation. But I can tell you that after years of religious oppression, with the priests forever meddling in the people's personal lives and affairs, the Métis listened with hope as I declared a new religion, a new Catholic faith based on the universal principles of Jesus Christ and not the corrupt Pope in Rome. In our own small way, with peril all around us, and our sons, fathers and *grandspères* once again fighting for our very existence, for a brief moment in time, we overthrew the authority of the Canadian state and the Vatican. My people rejoiced and my eternal soul found its home in the valley of the Little Sister at Batoche.

Let us take a moment to examine my mystical experience in Washington D.C. "I suddenly felt in my heart a joy which took such possession of me. . . . I was immediately struck by an immense sadness of spirit. . . . Are the joys and pains of man short on this earth?" It is easy to see that joy and sadness are symbolic of my life. I have known joy, extreme joy. As a child I knew the joy of a loving family, a loving community. As a man, I have known the joy of starting a family of my own, of following in the steps of my father, in leading our people towards the light. Against powerful and persistent opposition, I won provincial status for the people of Manitoba, gaining free institutions and securing 1.4 million acres of land for our children and descendants. All of this I did as a result of a direct challenge to the actions and efforts of the Canadians in both the North-West and in Ottawa.

I have also known extreme sadness and pain, including the untimely death of my father whom I last saw as a boy on the trail on my way to Montreal. The rape of Red River and the lost opportunity to create a truly democratic North-West was devastating. By the time of my Washington experiences, I had already lived in this pain for six full years. Instead of living a life with my family, in a peaceful community, I lived in exile, homeless, penniless and hunted by my enemies. Most unbearably, I knew the pain that my poor oppressed people suffered without me. As I mentioned earlier, our first lieutenant-governor, Archibald, put it succinctly, "many of them . . . actually have been so beaten and outraged that they feel as if they were living in a state of slavery."

In this New World, I envision many different peoples making their lives here on the prairie, living in harmony with their Indigenous neighbours. I am also convinced that I am a prophet of this New World. I was called upon to rebel both politically and in the realm of religion. Throughout my life I have attempted to overthrow the pernicious influences of European colonialism and create a New World — free of the sins of the Old World. Religious in my orientation, I took my mission to be the creation of a living apostolic and vital Catholicism in the New World.

I also wish to speak about the subjugation of the Indigenous races in the New World. What happened to us in the North-West is not unique. It is a continuation of the policies of the Church and the European authorities since the time of the Crusades. The Spanish priest Las Casas tells us of the crimes of the lost mariner Columbus, and those who followed, slaughtering millions in the southern hemisphere. Here on Turtle Island, North America, the Europeans declared the land empty, and through their Doctrine of Discovery, claimed sovereignty, subjugating the people and pushing them off their hereditary lands. The Royal Proclamation of 1763, calling on the British and their descendants to treaty with the Indigenous races, has been trampled in the dust. In the United States the expansionist Americans continue to oppress and brutally steal the lands and resources of the Indigenous nations. In Canada, John A. Macdonald's notorious Indian Act overrides all Indigenous rights. This is not right; reconciliation is in order.

Our revolutionary government in Saskatchewan asked that Canada respect us and send commissioners to treaty with us, at which point we would disband our government. Yet no commissioners ever arrived, nor was there any communication beyond a call for our immediate and unconditional surrender. In the end, as history has recorded, we were attacked, and after a heroic defence, we were defeated. I did not run away. I could have escaped, but instead I surrendered to General Middleton with dignity. Charged with the crime of high treason, I have been tried in a territorial court and sentenced to death. Although I am speaking in my own defence, many others also faced this same colonial court, including Poundmaker, Big Bear, One Arrow and William Henry Jackson.

My intention throughout this Inquiry has been to bring forth the evidence I was not allowed to divulge at my trial in front of a colonial court. With the judge, the prosecution and my own lawyers all working to destroy my career and the very future of my Métis people, I was not allowed to defend myself or the cause of the peoples of the North-West until proceedings were wrapping up. In my final address to the court, I explained how I had been caught up in a fifteen-year war with John A. Macdonald and Canadian colonialism. I told the court that I had lived a life in the service of my nation and that I was extremely proud of the part I played in the development of the Manitoba Act. As framed, the Manitoba Act involved two nations, one big, one small, bargaining as equals, joining as one. But at the same time, the invasion of peaceful Manitoba remains John A. Macdonald's eternal shame. In bad faith, he sent Garnet Wolseley's troops to destroy our government and rob and pillage Métis homes and families. I blame him for the murder of Elzéar

Goulet and the others. Métis rights were trampled and our citizens were raped and murdered in the streets of Winnipeg. Fifteen years later, Macdonald sent Major General Middleton to do the same at Batoche.

In my humble opinion, although Canada has condemned me, I have always fought for Canada, not against her. In fact, if I had allowed the Americans to "liberate" Manitoba and the North-West, as they did with Texas and California, there would be no Canada. Today's Canada would have been swallowed up and become but a northern appendage of the American giant.

In the interests of British capital and the Empire, John A. Macdonald recklessly seized and took control of the lands of the Great North-West, our Indigenous homeland. As I explained to those assembled in that courthouse, God cannot create a tribe without locating it. The North-West belongs to the Indigenous nations: those who have lived upon it and raised their families, generation upon generation. As I have said before, we are not birds. We have to walk on the ground. Nevertheless, we will share equitably upon recognition of our title to our lands. When I finished speaking to the people in that courthouse, Judge Richardson banged his gavel, turned to me and sentenced me to be taken to the place appointed for my execution to "be hanged by the neck."

Having been found guilty of the heinous crime of high treason, I now must ask your indulgence as I need to speak to one other persistent accusation that has been levelled against me: that I am an "imposter or deceiver." If I am to be executed, it will not be as an "imposter or deceiver," but as a sane individual. I am more convinced every day that without a single exception I did right. And I have always believed that, as I have acted honestly, the time will come when the people of Canada will see and acknowledge it.

Respectfully, I request this Inquiry to review my evidence and my career and decide if I was guilty of the crime of high treason. I seek reconciliation through exoneration and recognition of my role as Canada's Indigenous (Métis) Father of Confederation. My sincere thanks go out to this Inquiry and I anxiously await your findings. God bless this Inquiry, and all those who have believed in my mission of love.

In God's name,

Louis "David" Riel.

Report of the Commissioner into the Career of Louis Riel

COMMISSIONER: In light of the failure of successive Canadian governments to grant Louis Riel's request for a special tribunal or commission to review his career or hold a retrial on his conviction of high treason, this Inquiry has reviewed Mr. Riel's evidence and draws the following conclusions about the six most critical questions he asked to be answered.

1 Did Louis Riel rebel against legitimate Canadian authority in Manitoba?

Underlying the question of rebellion by Louis Riel and Le Comité national des Métis de la rivière Rouge is the legitimacy of the 1869 sale of Rupert's Land to the Government of Canada by the new owners of the Hudson's Bay Company, the International Finance Society, and the attempted imposition of Canadian jurisdiction prior to the actual date of transfer. This Inquiry finds that as Mr. Riel's Provisional Government declared its allegiance to the British Sovereign, Queen Victoria, and as it did not owe obedience to the Canadian government, no Métis rebellion took place. One can accurately say, however, that Louis Riel led the Red River in its opposition to Canadian colonialism. It is the further finding of this Inquiry that it was the representative of the Canadian government of John A. Macdonald, the Hon. William McDougall M.P., and a group of Canadian settlers known collectively as the "Canadian Party," who rebelled against the de facto Provisional Government of Assiniboia (Red River). It should, therefore, be recognized that it was the Canadians, under John A. Macdonald, who rebelled against the legitimate Red River government. This Inquiry finds Louis Riel not guilty of rebelling in Manitoba in 1869–70.

2 Did Louis Riel murder Thomas Scott when he was executed in Red River?

Although charges were laid, Louis Riel was never tried on the charge of murdering Thomas Scott. This Inquiry finds that as secretary of the Provisional Government, conversant in French and English, Mr. Riel acted as the translator at Mr. Scott's court martial, but did not vote on Scott's sentence or take part in the execution.

It is the finding of this Inquiry that the Provisional Government of Assiniboia, as established by the Convention of Forty, and recognized by Prime Minister Macdonald's Special Commissioner, Mr. Donald Smith, as well as the other Canadian commissioners, had established the right of jurisprudence and protection of the community against armed insurgents. That being the case, the Scott court martial and his execution, although regrettable, were performed by a legitimate entity, the Provisional Government of Assiniboia. It is the position of this Inquiry that no individual, or number of individuals, duly deputized to participate in the authorized court martial and execution, "murdered" Thomas Scott. This Inquiry finds that Louis Riel did not murder Thomas Scott.

3 Did Louis Riel accept or solicit bribes or corruption money?

Various sources have intimated that the money Louis Riel and Ambroise Lépine received from Archbishop Taché to vacate themselves to the United States during the federal election of 1872 was "corruption money." As the commission has learned during this Inquiry, Archbishop Taché told Louis Riel and Ambroise Lépine that the "authorities in Lower Canada," Conservative Prime Minister John A. Macdonald and George-Étienne Cartier, wanted them on the other side of the U.S. border during the 1872 general election. The reason was that they did not want the opposition Liberals to use the issue of Riel and the "murder of Thomas Scott" against them during the election. Cartier had further suggested that the voluntary withdrawal of Riel and Lépine would make it easier for the government to gain "a larger support in the elections, and . . . thus be better able to procure the amnesty." Although Mr. Riel was uncomfortable leaving his people at a time of crisis, and found accepting money from those who had done him wrong distasteful, he also believed that Cartier was the one person who could successfully promote the Métis cause. Moreover, he recognized that the money advanced could equally be payment for his work in bringing Manitoba into the Canadian Confederation — money that was legally owed to him and that had never been paid.

This Inquiry finds that there was no corruption or bribery involved. Louis Riel did not solicit the money. Nor did he use it for any nefarious or corrupt purpose in the election but to support himself and his family while living across the border.

4 Did Louis Riel commit pillage when he seized Fort Garry?

Libelled as a thief, Louis Riel requested this Inquiry to review his and his councillors' actions in the occupation of Fort Garry. Our investigation shows that this defensive action was taken after the Canadian Lieutenant-Governor designate, William McDougall, entered the territory and proceeded towards Fort Garry with the intent to seize the seat of government by force of arms. It is the position of this Inquiry that in order to prevent the seizure of the seat of power by the foreign Government of Canada, Louis Riel, as the nominal head of the Provisional Government, was fully justified in occupying Fort Garry. Furthermore, at this time, the former Hudson's Bay Company government showed a complete unwillingness to hold the seat of power and a total inability to continue to govern. This Inquiry notes that the subsequent use of Fort Garry and Hudson's Bay Company money and provisions by Louis Riel and the Métis National Committee was orderly and used to effect the safe governing of the country. Moreover, a full accounting was given of everything taken. This was not pillage — as it was when Colonel Wolseley and his Canadian troops arrived soon thereafter.

5 Was Louis Riel a fugitive of justice when he was expelled from the House of Commons?

Historically, this Inquiry recognizes that although Louis Riel never campaigned and was in hiding for fear of assassination or arrest, he was three times elected to the Canadian Parliament as the Member for the federal district of Provencher. In the spring of 1874, Louis Riel travelled to Ottawa (under an assumed name) and went to the House of Commons where he signed the Members Register. Thereafter, he was unable to assume his seat in Parliament as there was an outstanding warrant for his arrest and a $5,000 reward offered by the Blake Liberal government of Ontario. It is the finding of this Inquiry that the reward, as well as the indictments against Louis Riel, laid in both Manitoba and Ontario, were invalid, because the Government of Ontario had no jurisdiction over affairs that occurred in the Red River Settlement, nor did Manitoba have jurisdiction over acts prior to Manitoba being formed as a Canadian province.

Moreover, the Inquiry finds that when the Select Committee of the House of Commons appointed to inquire into the causes of the insurrection of 1869–70 pronounced that Riel had "fled from justice," this finding was the result of blind racial animosity and self-interest. The Inquiry agrees with the statement by Wilfrid Laurier, when he said that Riel's "whole crime and the crime of his friends was that they wanted to be treated like British subjects and not bartered away like common cattle. If that be an act of rebellion, where is the one amongst us who if he had happened to have been with them would not have been rebels as they were?" This Inquiry declares that Louis Riel was maliciously denied his seat and that he was not a fugitive of justice, but a fugitive of injustice.

6 Was Louis Riel guilty of high treason in 1885?

As was revealed earlier, the Métis and settlers of the Saskatchewan River Valleys had for many years been sending unsuccessful petitions to Ottawa in order to address their grievances. In 1884, the French-speaking Métis and their English-speaking brethren invited Mr. Riel, who had been successful in gaining rights for the Métis and other citizens in Manitoba in 1869–70, to the Saskatchewan to help with their unproductive petitions. After again petitioning unsuccessfully, and being informed by Hudson's Bay Company chief factor, Lawrence Clarke, that the North-West Mounted Police were on their way to arrest Mr. Riel, the move was made to form a Provisional Government and create a Bill of Rights, which was based upon the grand petition, representing all sectors of the Saskatchewan population, sent to Ottawa in December 1884.

It has been noted that after the creation of the Provisional Government, with Louis Riel as president, Mr. Riel announced that no hostile movement would be made unless word were received from Ottawa refusing to grant the demands in the Bill of Rights. The request was for the Canadian government to appoint a commission to deal with the Métis claims and to pledge itself to deal with the questions affecting white settlers and Indians. In that case, the Provisional Government, on obtaining reasonable guarantees that this would be done, would disband. Bloodshed was to be avoided, unless the provocation amounted to life and death for the settlers. In that case, the authority of the Dominion would in effect be repudiated.

It is the finding of this Inquiry that Louis Riel, bringing his wife and children, came to the Saskatchewan with peaceful intentions. We accept his position: "I did not think of war. I crossed the line without arms and without ammunition. I came to petition for my people and for myself, in the hope of obtaining something, if not complete satisfaction." Our investigation concludes that Louis Riel was an honourable politician. His goal was democracy in the Canadian North-West and beyond. On the Saskatchewan, seeking to bring about responsible government, Mr. Riel petitioned and agitated for changes in the electoral and constitutional process, but so irresponsible was the Canadian government that they hardly even bothered to reply. Instead of dealing with the just claims of the people they obfuscated and then sent more police.

This Inquiry further accepts Mr. Riel's claim that when Prime Minister Macdonald sent in the police and then General Middleton with his armed forces, the Métis had no choice but to defend themselves. We accept that Mr. Riel's establishment of the Provisional Government of the Saskatchewan, his resistance, was a direct result of aggression by the Canadian government.

* * *

COMMISSIONER: Having now concluded our investigation into the career of Mr. Riel, it is the finding of this Inquiry that, for justice to be done, it is incumbent upon the prime minister of Canada to have Parliament revoke all criminal charges against Mr. Riel, and that he be fully exonerated and recognized as Canada's Indigenous (Métis) Father of Confederation.

ABOUT THE AUTHOR

David Doyle, a retired teacher, principal and administrator of First Nations schools in British Columbia and the Yukon, has dedicated his career to decolonizing Indigenous education in Canada. He began his inquiry into the career of Louis Riel on the centenary of the North-West Resistance in 1985. For more than thirty years, Doyle has been an advocate for Louis Riel's exoneration and has uncovered and collected important evidence that has surfaced since Riel's controversial trial in Regina in 1885. Discovering Riel's 1885 Saskatchewan Bill of Rights after it had been lost for some one hundred years, Doyle re-opened the historical record on Louis Riel, his career, and the development of the Canadian North-West. A Research Fellow with the Canadian Plains Research Centre and secretary of the Friends of Louis Riel Society, Doyle has assisted in the collection of the oral history of the Plains Cree and has established the Louis Riel Library and Archive (www.librarything.com) in preparation for Riel's recognition as Canada's Indigenous Father of Confederation. Internationally, David Doyle has spoken on Riel in Iceland, England and Cuba, first introducing Louis Riel to Cuba at the Havana International Book Fair in 2012. He has been invited back to speak at Canadian Studies seminars at the University of Havana, UNEAC, the Cuban Writers and Artists Union, as well as two UNESCO conferences dedicated to Riel's near-contemporary, the Cuban "Apostle of Independence," José Martí. Tending their gardens and a small first-growth coastal forest with his wife Maureen Mason, Doyle lives in Powell River, British Columbia, on the traditional territory of the Tla'amin First Nation. Doyle continues working towards justice and reconciliation between Canada and the Indigenous nations and peoples.